# Songs as *Locus* for a Lay Theology

# Songs as *Locus* for a Lay Theology

Moshe Walsalam Sastriyar and
Sadhu Kochukunju Upadeshi

Philip K. Mathai

Foreword by Mark Bangert

☙PICKWICK *Publications* • Eugene, Oregon

SONGS AS LOCUS FOR A LAY THEOLOGY
Moshe Walsalam Sastriyar and Sadhu Kochukunju Upadeshi

Copyright © 2019 Philip K. Mathai. All rights reserved. Except for brief quotations in critical publications or reviews, no part of this book may be reproduced in any manner without prior written permission from the publisher. Write: Permissions, Wipf and Stock Publishers, 199 W. 8th Ave., Suite 3, Eugene, OR 97401.

Pickwick Publications
An Imprint of Wipf and Stock Publishers
199 W. 8th Ave., Suite 3
Eugene, OR 97401

www.wipfandstock.com

PAPERBACK ISBN: 978-1-62564-550-0
HARDCOVER ISBN: 978-1-4982-8718-0
EBOOK ISBN: 978-1-5326-4578-5

*Cataloguing-in-Publication data:*

Names: Mathai, Philip K., author. | Bangert, Mark Paul, foreword.

Title: Songs as locus for a lay theology : Moshe Walsalam Sastriyar and Sadhu Kochukunju Upadeshi / Philip K. Mathai ; foreword by Mark Bangert.

Description: Eugene, OR : Pickwick Publications, 2019 | Includes bibliographical references and index.

Identifiers: ISBN 978-1-62564-550-0 (paperback) | ISBN 978-1-4982-8718-0 (hardcover) | ISBN 978-1-5326-4578-5 (ebook)

Subjects: LCSH: Music. | Theology. | Philosophy, Religion and Theology. | Communication and the Arts. | India. | Indian Christian Expressions of Bhakti. | Kochukunju Upadeshi, Sadhu. | Lay Theology. | Lay Theology and Faith. | Lex Orandi Lex Credendi. | Malayalam Hymns/Songs. | Songs. | Walsalam Sastriyar, Moshe.

Classification: BR50 .M37 2019 (print) | BR50 .M37 (ebook)

Manufactured in the U.S.A.

To my grandparents and parents

# Contents

*Foreword by Mark Bangert* | *ix*
*Acknowledgments* | *xiii*

Introduction | 1

1. Socio-cultural and Religious Contexts of Travancore during the Late Nineteenth and Early Twentieth Centuries | 10
2. Doxology and Theology—Bhakti, the Indian Doxological Tradition of Songs | 51
3. Moshe Walsalam (1847–1916) | 83
4. Sadhu Kochukunju Upadeshi (1883–1945) | 121

Conclusion | 158

*Appendixes* | 171
*Bibliography* | 177
*Index* | 185

# Foreword

THIS BOOK HAS MUCH to offer, some of which is obvious and transparent, some of which is subtly momentous.

The story of a relatively unknown body of songs unfolds before us clearly and its significance is easily apparent. At all times and in all places, it seems, theologians and historians have wondered about the dynamics between belief and ritual. Sides have been taken over which comes first, or over an imagined hierarchy, or over the ranking of diverse systems devised by Christians, for example, to negotiate inherent tensions. Right in the midst of that continuing lively conversation author Philip Mathai proposes that a significant body of East Indian Christian song represents and mediates for its constituents an operating theology, thereby rendering it as a theological locus serving as creed, catechism, purveyor of Scripture and a kind of moral compass.

In order to fully track the trajectory of this proposal the reader receives preparation through a carefully crafted contextualization process (especially useful to the Western reader) that includes an introduction to the region of Travancore, located in the southwest corner of India and home to the major players in this study, and a review of the political, religious and cultural currents that shaped the lives of the region's people over several millennia. Vivid insights into the caste system provide markers along the way while the complexities of global religious influences offer a counterpoint to the local ebb and flow of Christian groups. Of particular interest is the author's clear rendering of the origins of the St. Thomas Christians and how they both were affected by and responded to the ever-evolving religious scene. Mathai compactly presents an amazing amount of detailed background, enabling his readers to grasp fully the significance of what is to follow.

# Foreword

The core of his study are two hymnists, Moshe Walsalam Sastriyar (1847–1916) and Sadhu Kochukunju Upadeshi (1883–1945). Roughly contemporary, the two individually authored what can be taken jointly as a sizable body of hymnody that is theologically coherent, still widely popular, and prophetically contextual, that is, the songs constitute Christian faith in an "Indian Cup" (p. 192)[x-ref]. Indicative of their pioneering efforts is the matrix of the *Bhakti* tradition of spirituality from which these two poets took both formal and idealistic direction. The results provide the careful reader with more than a casual look at Christian missions in a foreign country with multiple languages and gurus. Here one comes face to face with a faith going through the productive business of taking root in a culture with an august and profound history. In conspicuous ways, then, the author has expanded perspectives on Indian Christian theology and preserved for posterity documentation of an influential corpus of Indian Christian song.

The not so obvious significance of this study, and that which renders it momentous, lies in the author's methodology, that is, in his wise choice to tell his story in the assembly of the church at large as it passionately encounters pressing questions regarding worship, identity and place. This manifests itself in two ways.

First, the flurry of interest in ethnic church music—or global hymnody, however you wish to name it—beginning in the late 1970s led both to a kind of church musical tourism and to the expansion of denominational hymn collections via new worship books, supplements, or sometimes both. The intentions behind these productions were mostly genuine and laudable, and surely yielded widespread enrichment, but were nevertheless not free from that typically Western habit of seeking a new product without regard for producer—a danger that every ethnomusicologist is warned against. Elsewhere I have written that respect for the cultures from which musical gifts come:

> entails a posture of reception that rules out (especially) Western tendencies to plunder other musical cultures for artifacts that titillate or reward a thirst for the exotic ... [Respect] ultimately means allowing the music to lead one to the people whose it is, to their joys and sorrows, their unique insights into God's love for them and for the part of the earth they inhabit.[1]

---

1. Bangert, "The Last Word?," 130.

# Foreword

Even though Mathai has edited a song collection for use by South Asian Christians in diaspora his project here is not to purvey hymns to non-Indian cultures, although many of the texts are endearing and worthy of use by anyone seeking to explore the *Bhakti* tradition of meditation. Rather, this book takes us "to the people," its real gift being the open hearts these texts freely and vulnerably channel.

Second, the Lutheran World Federation sponsored a five-year study on worship and culture (1993–1998) that yielded three volumes of essays on subjects related to the theme together with a series of statements. Of the latter the Nairobi Statement (1996) has attracted the most attention since it proffers a kind of methodological framework through which matters of worship and culture can be addressed. Briefly, it proposes that nearly every factor can be addressed as an element that is either transcultural, contextual, cross-cultural, or countercultural. Much has been written about these categories and their usefulness. Recently, authors from the southern hemisphere have questioned assumptions about what is "transcultural," while others have noted that colonialism has rendered meaningless the notion of what's contextual in a culture, opting instead to think of cultures where Christianity has taken root as mixed, even mongrel.[2]

Mathai knows these things and in fact proposes that we understand these songs and their users as evidence of "hybridity," a word now often used by those trying to find their way through the thickets of postcolonialism. In a sense he is an important voice in the post-Nairobi conversation regarding worship and culture, showing how these songs represent what one might call a transcultural faith that flowers in the *Bhakti* meditative tradition. One can't help but see that there is some trailblazing going on here. And if it should happen that the hymns herein are never again *tuned* into auditory existence—as he implies (what a pity), Mathai's study nevertheless counts as highly important because of his mapping of the tectonic movements of worship and culture.

Mark Bangert
John H. Tietjen Professor of Worship and Church Music, *emeritus*
Lutheran School of Theology at Chicago

---

2. See essays by Gordon Lathrop, Scott Anderson, and Stephen Burns in the volume noted above.

# Acknowledgments

WRITING A DISSERTATION AND further working on it for publication could be a lonely, isolating, and depressing endeavor if it were not for the support, encouragement, and inspiration of mentors, friends, and family. There are many that have been part of this journey and contributed significantly, in various ways, to make this goal a possibility and I am indebted to all who contributed in making this a reality and not remain in the realm of *maya*! In that, this was, in the profoundest sense, an experience of grace!

I remain grateful that the Lutheran School of Theology at Chicago (LSTC) was most sensitive to my financial, theological and academic needs, and provided a conducive space for candid and meaningful theological inquiry, and widen my horizons. I am indebted to my professors at LSTC, Catholic Theological Union, Chicago Theological Seminary and the University of Chicago for their contributions in my academic pursuits.

My journey in the academics also took me to new horizons of vocation and I am grateful for all the patience and support of members of St. Paul's Lutheran Church, Yorktown, Illinois; Faith Lutheran Church, Chicago, Illinois; and Trinity Lutheran Church Lanark, Illinois, while a student. I could not have accomplished this without these homes away from home. I am also indebted to the Purnajiwan South Asian Church, Chicago, for making it possible for me to reflect on the nuances of the role of music and songs in the expression of faith by a community. My sincere gratitude to the Northern Illinois Synod of the ELCA, and the ELCA Churchwide Offices for all the support during my program.

I deeply owe my doctoral committee, Professors Jose David Rodriguez, Mark Bangert, Mark Swanson, and Mark Thomson, for sharpening my skills, polishing my output, and widening my horizons, their comments and suggestions were very astute and fitting.

## Acknowledgments

I deem it a privilege to have had Professor Vitor Westhelle as my mentor to guide me through the journey of writing my dissertation. He was more than an advisor but a friend, always readily available and, though a man of few words, his critiques and comments were always extremely perceptive, appropriate, and insightful.

I wish to thank the many friends and family, especially Dr. George Zachariah Kidangalil, who stoked in me the passion to explore the role of songs and music in the sustenance and formation of the faith and beliefs of a community, it was their encouragement and support that gave me the drive to persevere. I would like to specially mention my maternal grandparents and my own parents who introduced me to the songs of my root community, especially that of Sadhu Kochukunju, my maternal grandmother's father.

The folks at Mt. Zion Lutheran Church, Waterloo, Ontario, have been especially supportive as I worked on the manuscript for publication. Very special thanks to Ms. Pauline Finch who painstakingly went through the manuscript and skillfully transformed it, as she herself says, "from a dissertation to a book that anyone could read!"

None of this would have been possible without the love and patience of my family. Our daughter Cheryl, and our son Cherub, lived most of their lives through the ranting and frustrations and also the joys and celebrations of this journey. They were wonderful in cheering me on and mature beyond their years in perceiving the travails of having both parents doing the doctoral program at the same time and adjusting to that. If not for Joy (Dr. Mary Philip), my wife, companion, and friend, this would never have materialized. Through this journey, she was ever at my side, through all the highs and lows, egging me on. No words can express my gratitude and love.

# Introduction

WHILE AT DREW UNIVERSITY, I attended a camp for South Asian theological students studying in eastern Pennsylvania and New Jersey. One evening, as we sat around the bonfire, I found myself alongside a friend from the Pentecostal Church. Another student was getting ready to lead the singing. As I was new to the group, my Pentecostal friend filled me in on the various people in the circle, including the young man about to lead the music. "(*Name*) takes a very radical stand in public," he said, "but wait till he starts singing; that will show what he truly believes."

My friend's words struck a deep chord, for although my initial academic interest was in the area of theology of religions and the context of religious plurality in theologizing,[1] the songs of Sadhu Kochukunju[2] I'd learned within the church of my roots captured my attention long before I started PhD studies. While at LSTC (Lutheran School of Theology Chicago), I compiled a hymnal called *Jeevan Sangeeth* for South Asian mission congregations of the ELCA (Evangelical Lutheran Church in America), published in 2003 by the ELCA's Association of Asians and Pacific Islanders. While deliberating with the team as we selected and assembled these songs, what struck me was how richly they reflected the theology of those who sang these songs regularly in corporate and family worship; they were truly music from the heart. That hymnal experience, along with conversations among friends with whom I shared my interest, led me to focus on Moshe Walsalam[3] and Sadhu Kochukunju; I wanted to explore how their songs and writings impacted the church in Central and South Travancore (India), and how they reflected (and still reflect) the faith and spirituality of people in the pews. Instead of moving from

---

1. My MTh Thesis at UTC (Bangalore) was in this area, as were my qualifying exams at LSTC.
2. A lay hymn writer and composer from Southwest India
3. Another lay hymn writer and composer from Southwest India

theoretical to practical applications, as most research tends to do, my work in this context begins with the use of these musical resources and examines the theoretical aspects of *why* we use them.

## Thesis

Hymns and songs used by a given community have been seen as the most frequent and characteristic expression of that community's beliefs. As C. Daniel Crews says of Moravians' beliefs in his article, *Zinzendorf: Theology in Song*, "our doctrine tends to be sung [rather] than spoken."[4] In Lutheranism, hymnody may not be on the same plane as creeds, confessions, and catechisms, but for faithful believers, it is hymns that remain in their hearts and on their lips as a primary expression of praise, worship, and the means of articulating their perception of the Divine.

This is especially true of the churches in India that do not depend as much on codified statements of faith and doctrine, as compared to the confessions, catechisms, and *Book of Concord*. Besides the creeds, liturgy and traditions of the church, the most observable expression of the beliefs and faith of congregational communities are their hymnodies, especially in non-liturgical contexts. Studying the hymnodies of South India in particular reveals that the authors of these local and regional hymns[5] were mostly lay evangelists, musicians, or of other professions. Many had little or no formal theological or even musical training, yet their songs gained wide popular usage and found their way into more formal compilations. So one could justly affirm that these hymns express the lay theology of the Indian church.

This book focuses primarily on the texts of Moshe Walsalam Sastriyar and Sadhu Kochukunju Upadeshi, whose hymns had a significant influence on their respective churches. Their songs will be used as the *locus theologicus*, or source of lay theology, hence the title: *Songs as Locus for a Lay Theology: Moshe Walsalam Sastriyar and Sadhu Kochukunju Upadeshi*. Other writings, where available, are also used to throw additional light on aspects of their thoughts and beliefs.

---

4. Crews, "Zinzendorf."

5. I use the term *hymns* non-technically to identify all forms of sacred song as well as those known in the West. Unlike the Marthoma hymnal, the Anglican-influenced Church of South India hymnal makes the distinction between hymns and lyrics, where hymns are translations of Western hymns and lyrics are songs written in the Indian context.

Introduction

# The Socio-cultural and Religious Context of Travancore during the Late Nineteenth and Early Twentieth Centuries

Historical developments from the dawn of the Common Era (CE) and the Sangam Period (covering the first 500 years of the Common Era) are traced. This period gave birth to Malayalam culture and language around the eighth century CE. The late nineteenth and early twentieth centuries were very significant in the history of Travancore/Kerala and of Christianity in particular; this was primarily due to the work of the London Missionary Society (LMS) in South Travancore and the Church Missionary Society (CMS) in Central Travancore, both of which impacted society as a whole.

The caste system still held sway and the practice of *ayitham* or *theendal*[6] was rampant; it denied those of lower castes the use of public roads, access to education, and for women, even the right to cover their upper bodies. In Travancore, caste was a major factor in determining social relations. The principle of ritual purity achieved its most extreme expression in the elaboration of "distance pollution." Lower caste people were permitted to approach those of higher castes only to a certain distance; the greater the ritual distance, the greater the spatial distance. It is said that the caste system was more rigidly observed in Travancore than in other parts of India.

At the top of the caste hierarchy were the *brahmins*, who combined their economic wealth as land owners with spiritual authority as temple priests. The earliest Brahmin settlements in present-day Malayalam-speaking areas originated during the seventh century CE. The establishment of *brahmin* settlements paved the way for *brahmin* ritual and socioeconomic dominance through a complex system of hierarchical service and marital relationships, based on relative ritual purity between and among castes.

Next were the *nairs*, a warrior and ruling class that dominated political, economic and military realms, including the temporal affairs of the *brahmins*. From around the eighth century CE, St. Thomas Christians enjoyed privileges and honorific titles that they shared with the high-caste *nairs*. Among the lower castes and untouchables, major groups included the *shanars* and *ezhavas*, as well as the slave castes,[7] *pulayas* and *parayas*. *Nadars* were a distinct sub-section within the *shanar* community.

---

6. *Ayitham* and *theendal* refer to the practice of untouchability based on pollution and purity.

7. As referred to in earlier documents.

## Songs as *Locus* for a Lay Theology

The popular *bhakti*[8] folk movement, with its emphasis on devotion to a personal deity, traced its beginnings to South India and the *alwars*[9] who created a body of devotional poetry expressing ecstasy and yearning for the divine; their presence and influence in Travancore were considerable. A main characteristic of this group was the expression of faith through *bhajans*, or sacred songs.

Although Christianity existed in Travancore from very early times, it remained confined to the St. Thomas community until the arrival of Roman Catholic and Protestant missionaries during the early nineteenth century. At the beginning of this period there were two major groups within the St. Thomas community; Syro Malabar Roman Catholics and the Jacobite Orthodox.

LMS missionaries began their work in South Travancore in 1806 and CMS missionaries followed in Central Travancore from 1816. The first Malayalam Bible was published by CMS missionaries in 1849, leading to a reformation movement among the Jacobite Orthodox group and resulting in the separation of the Marthoma Church. The presence of Western missionaries, combined with the influence of local British residents, hastened the abolition of slavery among *pulaya* and *paraya* castes in Travancore through major government proclamations in 1812 and 1855. In 1812, the combined influence of LMS missionaries and rising social awareness among the *shanar/nadar* people led to the overturning of an ancient tradition that forbade lower-caste women to cover their breasts. But the order was rescinded when riots broke out among the opposing upper castes. The *shanar/nadars* rebelled in turn, but it took until 1859 to achieve a new proclamation by the queen of Travancore permitting *shanar/nadar* women to cover their upper bodies.

Under Protestant missionaries the spread of education to all, regardless of caste, was another significant change during the late nineteenth and early twentieth centuries; this led to opportunities for lower castes to access schooling and in turn become socially aware and assertive.

---

8. A way of devotion to a personal deity as opposed to the path of knowledge.

9. *Alwars*; Vaishnavite saints, a group within traditional Hinduism owing allegiance to the deity Vishnu.

Introduction

# Doxology and Theology: Bhakti, the Indian Doxological Tradition of Song

The question of the place held by doxological traditions in theological reflection is an emerging field of inquiry. In *Theology in Hymns*, Teresa Berger points out differences of emphasis among Roman Catholic, Protestant and Orthodox traditions in drawing relationships between doxology and theology.

> Roman Catholic liturgiology debates the relationship of the *lex orandi* to the *lex credendi* while Protestant systematic theology takes as its theme the question of linguistic differences between doxological and theological speech. On the other hand, the Orthodox tradition accepts as a foregone conclusion the theological character of liturgical language and the doxological roots and orientation of theology.[10]

An overview of the history of hymnology will illustrate its parallel development with liturgy, which led to their becoming closely intertwined.

Craig Atwood mentions Moravian doctrine which (as noted above) tends to be sung rather than spoken; this observation is especially true in the Indian context. Indian author K. M. George, quoting A. Cherian in reference to Sadhu Kochukunju's songs, points out how they are "the matured fruit of deep spiritual experience. Hence it touches the heart, awakens noble thoughts. To the weak and sorrowing they bring comfort."[11] Sacred songs could thus be seen as a spontaneous overflow of powerful spiritual experiences. Mark Bangert, in discussing Bach's cantatas for example, sees them as "musical microcosms of the process of the faith experience."[12]

This in turn makes the study of the doxological tradition of hymns and songs crucial to a study and articulation of the theology of the faithful, especially in contexts where (unlike Western Christianity) confessions or catechisms are not guiding factors. R. R. Sundara Rao points out that in the absence of other theological treatises, it is song that "is indeed the main theological handbook of laymen and clergy alike"[13] in the Indian context.

---

10. Berger, *Theology in Hymns*, 55.
11. George, *Sadhu Kochukunju*, 121.
12. Bangert, "A Brook Runs Through It," 19.
13. Sundara Rao, *Bhakti Theology*, 12.

As an encounter of praise with God, doxology is also a consequence of the encounter with truth. This being so, the doxological tradition of hymns and songs could be seen in itself as a *locus theologicus* or a source of theology. James Cone in *Spirituals and the Blues* uses spirituals to articulate the theology of black slaves, an historical context that also calls for using a sociological paradigm to explore songs as *locus theologicus*.

In the Indian context, *bhakti* tradition employs the doxological content of hymns as the *locus theologicus*, in that they use the medium of song to communicate collective experiences, as well as to articulate and express their faith. While the *bhakti* tradition can be traced to pre-Christian times, it was the *nayanars* and *alwars* of southern India that popularized *bhajans*, devotional songs in the *bhakti* tradition, as a medium to convey spiritual messages. An important feature of this movement was the use of local vernacular languages rather than traditional Sanskrit. A key reason for this change was that many poet-singers of this tradition were illiterate in Sanskrit, a language whose learning was reserved for the upper castes.

*Bhakti* is generally understood as having faith in a personal God, love for God as for a human being, dedicating everything to God's service, being in God's presence, loving God, serving God, and enjoying God. The *bhakti* movement found expression initially in *alwar* songs of the ninth and tenth centuries, according to Ramanuja's twelfth century CE theistic exposition of Hinduism, which includes a constructive and elaborative formulation of *bhakti* doctrine.

In *The Theology of Hindu Bhakti*, A. J. Appasamy highlights Ramanuja's characteristics of *bhakti* as follows:

1. Meditation: a continuous recollection of God, declared as being like a vision wherein the object becomes present to the eyes. It is meditation of God infused by a deep love for God.

2. Needing moral preparation: elaborated as purity of body, detachment from desires, frequent practice of the meditation which is begun, doing righteous actions, being truthful, straightforward, merciful, generous, and not covetous.

3. Bliss: the individual soul's realization of its mutual relationship with the Supreme Soul leads to extreme love and joy. The *bhakta*[14] considers his favorite Lord as a friend in whom one can place trust and loyalty.

---

14. Devotee.

Introduction

4. Exclusive: there should be no ulterior object except that of worship, which is directed to God alone.

The *bhakti* tradition, as with the *alwars*, was quite influential in the Travancore kingdom. Along with different theological aspects, various technical characteristics of Hindu Carnatic musical tradition are also reflected in the songs of Walsalam and Kochukunju.

In the second chapter a discussion of the *Lex Orandi* and *Lex Credendi* is presented, as well as a brief overview of the history of hymnody.

## Moshe Walsalam Sastriyar and Sadhu Kochukunju Upadeshi: Songs and Writings as *Locus Theologicus*

Moshe Walsalam belonged to the lower-caste *nadar* community, while Sadhu Kochukunju belonged to the St. Thomas tradition, which some Indian Christians refer to as "the Brahmins among Christians," in reference to their higher status in the social structure that they were part of.

Walsalam was born in 1847 in southern Travancore Kingdom[15] where the London Missionary Society (LMS) was prominent. His father, a schoolteacher, joined the Protestant church from the Roman Catholic tradition. Walsalam received some theological training at the LMS seminary in Nagercoil where he studied Greek, Latin and Hebrew. He taught briefly in the Orthodox Seminary at Kottayam, then went on to teach at the LMS School in Neyyattinkara, near Trivandrum. While a teacher he took training in music, became a good violinist, and also studied poetry in various genres. He was also known for his gospel-preaching tours in Travancore.

Sadhu Kochukunju, born 1883, was from central Travancore and grew up in the St. Thomas Christian community. He was from a farming family and studied until the age of 14 at an English school close to his home. The following year, he took on the responsibility of running his family's farm. But during his free time from farm work Kochukunju read voluminously and taught himself, so much so that he later qualified to become a teacher. He was also active in his church, and in 1905 dedicated himself to becoming an evangelist.

Both Walsalam and Kochukunju wrote extensively. While Walsalam penned all of his works in the form of poetry, Kochukunju wrote not

15. Travancore comprised the southern half of present-day Kerala State and the southernmost district of Tamil Nadu, Kanyakumari.

only poems and songs, but also articles in journals, tracts and booklets. His prose works reveal his position concerning various issues, both theological and ethical, that don't necessarily emerge in his songs. Both men addressed contemporary theological and social issues that affected the people of their day. The concept of gospel transforming culture can be traced in both their writings.

*Bhakti*, with its emphasis on warmth, love, personal devotion, experience of grace, and utter self-abandonment (mystic experience) to the love and power of God, is reflected in their songs and writings, which well up from the depths of personal life experiences.

Various theological themes stand out in their writings, which speak in very distinct voices against rampant social evils, notably the exploitation and injustice rooted in the caste system, including punitive demands of marriage dowries, business dishonesty, usurious rates on loans and mortgages, and so on. The central focus of this book is to study songs of Walsalam and Kochukunju that are still current in Christian communities, through these and other windows that may open in the course of my explorations. Major theological themes that stand out in their compositions will also be explored.

In the context of Indian Christian literature, where hymnody and theology were dominated by nineteenth-century missionaries from the West, these songs and writings from the fringes went on to be owned by the faith communities that inspired them, and so became in that sense an expression of those communities.

My intent is to articulate the theology latent in these songs and other writings. Being closer to lay-consciousness than official church teachings, I believe this would serve to place this movement meaningfully within the broader historical, social and religious context. The focus is primarily on songs still in circulation through their official inclusion in hymnodies of the Church of South India, South Kerala Diocese, the area that was home to Walsalam, and that of the Marthoma Church to which Kochukunju belonged. I also consult *aashwaasagiithangal*, a songbook by Kochukunju that is still on the market.

A question that naturally arises here is the rationale behind choosing these two particular song writers when there are other notable Malayalam artists whose songs are also extensively used, such as Yusthus Joseph, T.J. Varkey, T.J. Andrews, K.V. Simon, T. Koshy, T.D. George, and M.E. Cherian. Walsalam, however, was by far the most prolific hymn writer in Malayalam.

## Introduction

As for Kochukunju, who was primarily a preacher rather than musician, he had a significant influence on a number of Christian leaders of his time, and for that reason some of his songs are among the most heard and loved in the language. Kochukunju also comes from the tradition of my roots, being one of the most prolific hymn writers of the Marthoma Church. As noted earlier, both men came from very different settings, the *nadar* and St. Thomas communities, which were caste-determined social structures. The choice of these two individuals covers a broad spectrum of the Christian community, encompassing traditions of both the Mission Church and the reformed Orthodox tradition, as well as the two aforementioned caste groups.

My conclusion includes comments on whether these documents could be postcolonial in nature. As Sugirtharajah points out, the postcolonial enterprise begins "whenever a native put quill pen to paper to contest the production of knowledge by the invading power."[16] Could this be seen as an emergence, at the liminal edge, of something new; a hybrid that mimics the dominant influences of Hindu and Western thought?

## Methodology

Primary resources for this study comprised all available works by the writers under consideration. A textual study of their songs and other writings was the core methodology used, in order to identify and highlight the theological themes they dwell upon. The study and analysis of my reading into and outside the chosen texts, including exploration of the *bhakti* tradition, provided groundwork for this research and the conclusions derived from it. Secondary sources about the writers and their work, though few, were helpful. These included recorded interviews with close associates and family members of both Walsalam and Kochukunju. My research also extended to pertinent previous work in the areas of sacred music, hymns, songs and theology. All translations from Malayalam are mine.

When Malayalam was phonetically transcribed into the Latin alphabet of the English-speaking world, upper and lower case characters were not used as Malayalam does not have upper and lower cases.

I have followed that practice in citing Malayalam words, caste names, phrases, and hymn stanzas and italicizing them throughout this book, in order to give readers an authentic feel for the character of the native language used by Moshe Walsalam Sastriyar and Sadhu Kochukunju Upadeshi.

16. Sugirtharajah, "A Brief Memorandum," 3.

*Chapter 1*

## Socio-cultural and Religious Contexts of Travancore during the Late Nineteenth and Early Twentieth Centuries

BEFORE THE ARRIVAL OF European colonists, the presence of Christianity in India was contained within Malabar, a strip of land on the southwestern tip of the Indian peninsula. Its coastline is shared by the Arabian Sea and Indian Ocean, while the Western Ghat Mountains form a natural inland boundary. The belief that St. Thomas (popularly known as "doubting Thomas") introduced Christianity in this region is prevalent, not only among the local St. Thomas Christians who historically identify with him, but also among scholars from other faiths. As A. Sreedhara Menon points out, "... it must be stated that there is nothing intrinsically improbable in the St. Thomas Tradition."[1] Similarly, Padmanabha Menon asserts that this is a tradition "not to be scoffed at."[2] However, details of Christianity's beginnings here and the conversion of the Namboodiri people (believed to have formed the earliest Christian community) have been challenged in the light of more recent scholarship.[3] One accepted certainty is that believers were present in Malabar from the earliest beginnings of Christianity itself.

Four principal royal houses ruled over Malabar at the beginning of the colonial period: Travancore, Cochin, Zamorin and Colastri.[4] The largest of these was the kingdom of Travancore, occupying the southern coastal

---

1. Menon, *Survey of Kerala History*, 99.

2. Menon, *History of Kerala*, 479.

3. Later in the study it is shown why the argument that *namboodhiris*, who were *brahmins*, were the first converts is improbable, as *brahmins* did not migrate to Malabar until close to the seventh century CE.

4. Menon, *History of Kerala*, 1.

regions which today comprise the southern districts[5] of Kerala State and Kanyakumari, the southernmost district of Tamil Nadu State.

The southwestern coast of India had been a prominent foreign trade center from very early times and international contacts were a major influence on the socio-economic and cultural lives of the populace. The ancient ports of Muziris, Barace and Tyndis traded spices and agricultural products with countries to the West, including Europe. Pliny (first century CE) and Ptolemy (second century CE) refer in their writings to a long trading tradition that originated hundreds of years before the arrival of Christianity.[6] Archaeological evidence, as well as the writings of Tamil poets from the Sangam Age, point to the prosperity of the region.[7]

## The Sangam Age

Dravidians, who were natives of the Indian subcontinent, gradually moved to the South, as Aryan peoples migrated to northern areas.[8] Scholars agree that the ancient Indus Valley Civilization is Dravidian and actually predates the Aryan migration, but the development of Sanskritic[9] culture in the region is attributed to Aryan influence. One could trace Dravidian culture in southern India as a parallel to Sanskritic developments in the north. The first major period was the Sangam Age, spanning the opening five centuries of the Common Era (CE). Malayalam-speaking areas,[10] comprising present-day Kerala, had not yet evolved into a separate cultural or political entity. They were still part of Tamilakam, which would geographically include Kerala and Tamilnadu;[11] thus the Tamil heritage (as the dominant language, literature and culture) was common to the entire region.

During the early Sangam Age, covering the first to third centuries CE, the region was ruled by three dynasties: the Ays in the south, the Ezhimalas in the North, and the Cheras in the region between them.

---

5. Districts are subdivisions of states in India.
6. Menon, *Social and Cultural History*, 45.
7. The Sangam Age covers the first five centuries of the Common Era.
8. This is contested by Hindu nationalists who would argue that Sankristic or Brahminic Hinduism was also native to the region, not an alien religion or culture.
9. This refers to both the religion and culture of Vedic Hinduism and its developments.
10. The native region of Moshe Walsalam and Sadhu Kochukunju (see Introduction).
11. Menon, *Survey of Kerala History*, 64. (See Appendix i for a map of the region.)

## Songs as *Locus* for a Lay Theology

The early Sangam Age—a period of well-organized social systems and governance—was a high point in the social, cultural and literary history of the region. A notable feature was that society was not stratified according to the caste system (which became part of the landscape later); in fact, the Sangam Age is described by historians as being free of caste distinctions.[12] Unlike the restrictions of the caste system, individual freedom and equality were integral to the Sangam Age social ethos. The dignity of an individual's labor was recognized and no one was denigrated or regarded as socially inferior because of what they did for a living. There is evidence for example, of *panas, kuravas, parayas,* and *vetas*[13] all being held in high social esteem. And before the caste system became entrenched, *panas* were even regarded as superior to *brahmins* in their intellectual and cultural accomplishments. The protection of these communities was considered a duty of the Chera[14] king, confirming that conventions of untouchability and unapproachability were unknown to the Sangam Age.[15]

Another significant feature of this era was the equal status of women and men. Kilimanoor Vishvambharan points out: "The most noticeable social good of the time was the equality of women and men. Along with men, women also had the privilege to get an education and to work in the public arena."[16] Unlike later Sangam Age society, women in this early period had complete freedom of movement and social life, could work at occupations of their choice, and had the right to full education; in fact, the poetess Auvvaiyar was among the outstanding writers of the era. Widows were allowed to remarry and child marriage was considered unacceptable.

Art forms such as music, poetry, and dance were widely cultivated throughout the land. *Tholkappiyam*, the most ancient of Tamil literature, explains the foundations of the language. Some major early Sangam works include: *ettuthokkai, pathupattu,* and *pathinen keezhkanakku*. Another work of the same period, *silappadhikaram*, describes and embodies the cult

---

12. Chendharassery, *Kerala Charitradhara*, 110–14.

13. These groups do not fall within the caste system of Sanskritic Hinduism and would be considered among the *dalit* communities, regarded as Untouchables by caste Hindus.

14. One of the four kingdoms in Tamilakam during the Sangam Age, the others being Cholas, Pandyas and Ay. Of them Cheras and Ay were from the later Malayalam speaking areas. These three dynasties were Dravidian and natives of the land.

15. Menon, *Survey of Kerala History*, 80–81.

16. Vishvambharan, *Kerala Samskara Darshanam*, 48; translation mine.

of a chaste wife; but it is also a faithful portrayal of the life, culture, and society of early Tamilakam, which included present-day Kerala.[17]

Governance at the village level was carried out by bodies called *manram*, who represented the local populace. Each village had a *manram* that made decisions about its affairs. *Manrams* would meet under a central banyan tree, where the *moopan* (village head) presided. It was the *moopan's* responsibility to settle disputes and other contentious issues. Through the *manrams*, local governance at the village level evolved into a sophisticated and effective system.[18]

Dravidian religious life was not as organized as it became during the later Sangam period (third to fifth centuries CE) under Aryan dominance. While the populace generally followed Dravidian traditions, there was no particular religion common to all. Scholars have observed that Dravidian worship practices were influenced by their fear of natural forces and could thus be categorized as nature worship, focused on the relationship between humans and the natural world. It is said that the worship of snakes, for example, is as ancient a practice as Kerala culture itself.[19] As the primary deity, the goddess *Kottavai* was propitiated with elaborate offerings of meat and toddy.[20] It should be noted that Buddhism and Jainism[21] had spread to the region by this time and co-existed alongside Dravidian traditions.

During this period, the region experienced a high level of economic prosperity and social well-being. Herodotus (484-413 BCE), Dioscorides (40-90 CE) and Pliny (23-79 CE) all refer in their writings to extensive trade with foreign countries in pepper, spices, ivory, precious stones, and pearls, dating from pre-Sangam and early Sangam times. This east-west mercantile tradition is further evidenced by archeological discoveries of Chinese artifacts in Malabar dating from the first century BCE.[22]

---

17. Menon, *Social and Cultural History*, 45–46; Vishvambharan, *Kerala Samskara Darshanam*, 41–42.

18. Menon, *Social and Cultural History*, 50.

19. Vishvambharan, *Kerala Samskara Darshanam*, 57–59.

20. *Toddy* is the sap from young buds of coconut palms which is fermented into an alcoholic local brew. Menon, *Kerala History*, 84.

21. Two reform movements in Hinduism which began around 500 BCE.

22. Menon, *Survey of Kerala History*, 55–57.

## Aryan Influence

The migration of Aryans to southern India had far-reaching consequences. Brahmins are thought to have reached the Dravidian society of Kerala during the third century CE, along with Jain and Buddhist monks, who originated from the north.[23] Some early Sangam literature makes reference to sacrifices by *brahmin* priests according to sacred scriptures, and also to the fact that Chera kings gave gifts to *brahmins* as a gesture of honor. Though there is no consensus as to whether Aryan migration occurred before the Common Era, most scholars agree that the Aryans were on the move by the fourth century CE and that their pace of migration rapidly increased during the sixth, seventh, and eighth centuries CE, the time of the Chalukyas, Pallavas and Rashtrakutas.[24] Research suggests that later migrations of Aryan Brahmins served to strengthen and consolidate the small population already in the region. The beginnings of Sanskritic Aryan religion can be traced back to these migrations. The growing influence of the Aryan religion also coincided with the weakening of Buddhism and Jainism; eventually their presence in the region disappeared altogether.

Another consequence of the growing Aryan influence was the reorganization of what had been an equitable Sangam Age society into the caste system. Swami Vivekananda,[25] on observing the caste practice in Kerala, described it as a madhouse. The egalitarian Dravidian society had been transformed backward into one rigidly divided along caste and color divisions, as in the *varnashramadharma* of Sanskritic Hinduism.

As a late twentieth-century Human Rights Watch publication stated: "India's caste system is perhaps the world's longest surviving social hierarchy."[26] Caste, which is a defining feature in Hinduism, "encompasses a complex ordering of social groups on the basis of ritual purity."[27] One is born into a caste and remains in it until death. The different caste groups are accorded varying degrees of respectability and circles, or levels, of permitted social intercourse. Caste is still the most generally practiced form of

---

23. Menon, *Social and Cultural History of Kerala*, 47.

24. Ruling dynasties in the south at that time.

25. Vivekananda is considered the patron saint of India, who stirred up national consciousness during the late nineteenth and early twentieth centuries. He shot to prominence in 1893 as an eloquent spokesman for Hinduism at the Chicago Parliament of Religions.

26. Human Rights Watch, *Broken People*, 24.

27. Ibid.

social organization in India and is very different from the prevailing social strata of Europe or the Americas. It is a unique feature of Indian society and has persistently eluded attempts to abolish it. Some scholars refuse any attempt to define caste, arguing that it is a far more complex phenomenon than many make it out to be.[28]

Caste is most often defined as a ranked social division in which membership is determined by birth, with each group being associated with a particular occupation and common customs.[29] The concept of *varna*,[30] determined the caste into which one was born and fixed an individual's lifelong position within the system; thus innate endowment was seen only in the context of the caste. A *brahmin* was a *brahmin* due not only to intellectual capacity, aptitude for studies, or ritual purity, but simply by virtue of being born one.

In theory there are four castes:

1. *brahmins*, the intellectual élite, were assigned ritual and religious duties as priests, as well as studies and religious teaching.

2. *kshatriyas* were the ruling nobility (kings, etc.), warriors and aristocrats.

3. *vaisyas* were engaged in the production and distribution of wealth and included traders, merchants, and those engaged in other financial professions.

4. *sudras* were farmers, servants, manual laborers, etc.

---

28. Ghurye, *Caste and Class in India*, 1. Ghurye does not attempt to define Caste because of its complexity. Instead, he dwells on the underlying features of the caste system in the first chapter, identifying six features of Hindu society governed by the social philosophy of caste and which are unaffected by modernity or the influence of rights and duties. These are: 1. Segmental division of society—wherein caste groups had a well-developed life of their own, where membership was not by selection, but by birth. 2. Hierarchy—There is a definite scheme of social precedence among the caste, with *brahmins* at the top and outcasts at the bottom. 3. Restrictions on feeding and social intercourse—Rules regarding diet and from whom food can be accepted, etc. 4. Civil and religious disabilities and privileges—this is reflected in segregated housing, where one may go, what one may wear, etc. 5. Choice of occupation—each group had its own hereditary occupations, but if one chose to do something different this would be mainly the prerogative of higher castes. 6. Restrictions on marriage—marriage only to someone within the same caste or sub-caste. On occasion, a man could marry a lower-caste woman, but not vice-versa. Ghurye describes India's caste system very well.

29. Gupta, *Caste Hierarchy*, 27.

30. The natural endowment.

Within these four principal castes, there are thousands of sub-castes, depending on region, language and other social factors. There is also a fifth category for those traditionally called Untouchables. Today they are known as *dalits*[31] and are often described as *varna-sankara*, meaning outside the system. They were typically assigned tasks too ritually polluting to be included within the traditional castes and were regarded as being so inferior that other caste members refrain from touching them for fear of ritual pollution. Ancient Hindu laws go so far as to forbid all social contact with Untouchables, who were categorized as sub-human; consequently, they were prohibited from entering temples and other places of worship. They could not participate in feasts and sacrifices, and were kept in ignorance of the higher religious values of Hinduism and its sacred scriptures. In some places, if they even heard the scripture being read, molten lead was poured into their ears; and if they recited scriptures, their tongue was cut off.[32]

The texts of the ancient *Rig Veda*[33] deal with two clearly different groups of people, the *aryas* and *dasyus*; notable instances occur in Hymn 51 of Mandala 1 and Hymn 34 of Mandala 3.[34] *Arya* in the Vedas is the normal designation for the three upper castes—*brahmin*, *kshatriya* and *vaisya*. At the opposite end in status are the indigenous *dasyus* and *sudras*; both are referred to in the *Rig Veda* as dark-skinned people who fled and scattered, leaving behind their possessions.[35] Other Hindu scriptures, such as the *Mahabaratha* (circa fifth century BCE) and *Ramayana* (composed between 600 and 500 BCE), provide some insight in understanding the plight of the *sudras* and other outcasts.

The caste system, which Hindus believe to be of divine origin, was codified by *Manu*[36] and is traditionally revered as the highest authority on their customs and practices. Because the four instituted castes or orders were held as divine and immutable, it was believed that no one could challenge them.[37] In theory, each caste comprised a self-sufficient soci-

---

31. Means "broken ones."

32. Devasahayam, "Pollution, Poverty and Powerlessness," 9.

33. *Rig Vedas* are the most ancient literary sources of Indian history; the text is addressed to *Indra*, one of the deities in the Hindu pantheon.

34. *Mandala* refers to the section.

35. *Rig Veda* 7.5.3.

36. Manusmriti; the discourse by Hindu sage Manu on the law of social classes, dated between 1,500 to 200 BCE.

37. O'Malley, *Indian Caste Customs*, 12. See also, De Bary et al., *Sources of Indian Tradition*, 222–26.

ety, with distinct roles allotted to its members. But Untouchables were considered beyond and outside the castes; the very sight of them was abhorred as polluting.

By the end of the Sangam Age, the growing influence of the *brahmins* further consolidated casteism in Kerala. Those who had once occupied high positions were now relegated to the lower castes. Along with women, their members were denied access to education; moreover, the dignity of their physical labor was no longer recognized as a mark of social status. It has been suggested that the *brahmins*, in order to firmly entrench casteism, were responsible for designating the indigenous *vaisyas* and the *sudras* as two of the lower castes. The *nayars*, another indigenous people who were traditionally warriors, were no longer considered higher-order *kshatriyas* but demoted to the lower *sudra* caste. Tradition has it that *kshatriyas* were brought in from outside the area to oversee temple properties and the governance of temple affairs.

Dravidian practices and religion were also accommodated within Brahminic Hinduism. The Goddess *Kottavai*, their primary deity, took the forms of *Durga, Kali,* and *Bhagavati* in Hinduism. Due to a gradual process of assimilation and cultural blending, Hinduism in Kerala became a synthesis of both Dravidian and Aryan practices. Having successfully assimilated local religions and cultures, as well as ordering society through the caste system, Sanskritic or Brahminic Hinduism had fully established its hegemony by the end of the Sangam Age.

A significant consequence of this was the development of Malayalam, a new language that developed from a fusion of Sanskrit and the local language of Tamilakam.[38] This development was in turn reflected in local literature and arts.

## Kulashekaras

The "dark" end of the Sangam Age—some three centuries during which other kingdoms of Tamilakam overran Kerala—ended with the reestablishment of the Chera kingdom in 800 CE. The new dynasty that emerged as the dominant power came to be known as Kulashekaras, named after their founder, Kulashekara Varman. Under the Kulashekaras, Kerala attained its distinct political and cultural identity.

---

38. Vishvambharan, *Kerala Samskara Darshanam*, 99.

## Songs as *Locus* for a Lay Theology

Kulashekara Varnan also figures in the history of the *alwar* movement of southern India under the name of Kulashekara Alwar, who authored one of the most celebrated devotional works in Tamil, *perumal thirumozhi*, as well as other writings in Sanskrit.[39] Kulashekara Varman was succeeded by Rajashekara Varman, who appears in the *nayanar* movement as the Saivite saint, Cheraman Perumal Nayanar. The Malayalam or the Kollam Era began in 825 CE during the time of Rajashekara Varman.[40]

Sankara, the great Advaitic philosopher, was a contemporary of both Kulashekara and Rajashekara Varman. Sankara's monistic philosophy of *Advaita Vedanta* had its roots in the *Upanishads*, grounded in the understanding that only Brahman was real, that human souls were just sparks of Brahman, and that everything material was just an illusion, or *maya*. Sankara established *mutts*[41] in four corners of India—Badrinath in the north, Puri in the east, Dwaraka in the west and Sringeri in the south—all of which continue to exist as centers of Hindu higher learning.

Sankara's work in establishing and reforming Hinduism to be India's dominant faith, includes borrowings from some popular features of Buddhism, particularly the aforementioned major monasteries. He also established four local *mutts* in Kerala with their heads chosen from among his chief disciples, as well as teams of *sanyasins*, or missionaries, to further spread the Hindu faith. To this day it is Sankara's teachings that provide the core intellectual framework for Hinduism; similarly, the *mutts* he founded still influence Hinduism's organizational framework. By weaving the best elements of Hinduism and Buddhism into his philosophical system of Advaita, Sankara can be credited with laying the foundation of a renewed Hindu religion that encouraged synthesis.[42]

## Early Bhakti Movements

While the Sanskrit teachings of Sankara and his school appealed to the intelligentsia and literati, the Advaita philosophy remained largely beyond the grasp of common people. During the Sangam Age, Buddhism, Jainism, and local Dravidian traditions were the popular faiths of the land. However,

---

39. Menon, *Survey of Kerala History*, 123–24.

40. Though the Gregorian calendar is followed generally, for all religious and cultural purposes the Kollam era is still followed in Malayalam-speaking areas.

41. Monasteries.

42. Menon, *Survey of Kerala History*, 146–47.

## Socio-cultural and Religious Contexts

the *bhakti* movement, led by the Saivite and Vaishnavite saints, and characterized by its "intense emotional surrender to a personal God in the form of Vishnu or Siva,"[43] established Hinduism as the region's dominant faith by the end of the Sangam Age. An integral feature of this movement was its tradition of worship through songs.[44]

The chief means of propagating the new *bhakti* movement was through its devotees, who roamed the countryside singing *bhajans*,[45] songs they composed out of their own religious experiences. A pre-existing genre of devotional songs called *carya gitas*, composed by Sahaja Buddhist saints, may have influenced the emergence of *bhajans* in the *bhakti* movement.[46] A unique feature of *bhajans* was that they were conceived and sung in the local vernacular of Tamil, not Sanskrit; thus they touched the innermost feelings of ordinary people.[47] It was these hymns that awakened popular interest in Hinduism by giving its deities a "colorful personality of their own."[48] The Hinduism rejuvenated by the teachings of Sankara now established its roots among everyday believers. During this period, temples were constructed in nearly every village and educational institutions called *salais* played a primary role in promoting learning. The Kulashekara and other rulers supported these institutions and acted as their patrons. In addition to primary schooling, the *salais* also offered more advanced courses in philosophy, grammar, theology, law and other disciplines. The temples also operated their own traditional centers of learning in the *gurukula*[49] style, where students and teachers lived under the same roof.

The tradition of singing *bhajans* to express and communicate one's faith can be traced to the *nayanars* and *alwars* of Tamilakam. Two of the 12 *alwar* saints, as well as two of the 63 *nayanar* saints, came from the region now called Kerala. Kulashekara Alwar (also known as Kulashekara Varnan), founder of the Second Chera Empire, was among South India's greatest Hindu religious leaders. He was a renowned scholar in both Sanskrit and Tamil and his *perumal thirumozhi* is a sublime expression of Bhakti

---

43. Ibid., 147.
44. Vishvambharan, *Kerala Samskara Darshanam*, 131.
45. *Bhajans* refers to a genre of traditional Indian devotional songs.
46. Sundara Rao, *Bhakti Theology*, 3.
47. Gladstone, *Protestant Christianity*, 49.
48. Menon, *Survey of Kerala History*, 148.
49. The practice of the *sishyas*, or disciples, living with their *guru* (teacher) and being trained.

literary tradition. His writings and songs were major influences on Vaishnavism in Kerala.

Cheraman Perumal, Kulashekara Alwar's successor, was a *nayanar* saint, known otherwise as Rajashekara Varman. He is mentioned in the Tamil Bhakti composition, *periyapuranam*, and his own work, *ponvannattandadi*, is acclaimed for its musicianship and beauty.

After a period of peace under Kulashekara rule during the ninth and tenth centuries CE, conflict arose between the Kulashekaras and the Cholas,[50] resulting in the erosion of Kulashekara centralized power. The land was divided into areas or principalities called *nadus*, governed by *naduvazhis*.[51] With the weakening of the ruler's central authority, the *naduvazhis* asserted their own independence, with the result that the later Kulashekara period saw the rise of a number of smaller principalities and chiefdoms throughout the empire.

The decline of the Kulashekaras coincided with an enormous increase in the power and influence of the Namboodhiri Brahmins in all areas of society. The rise of a feudal or *janmi* system in Kerala was also a direct consequence of the Kulashekara-Chola wars. The Namboodhiri Brahmins had been trustees of temple lands, but with the weakening of Kulashekara central power, they assumed ownership of the lands and appropriated their revenue. Moreover, many landowners transferred their property to the Namboodhiri Brahmins as it would then be seen as temple land and not only escape devastation by enemies, but also be exempt from state taxes. In this way, the Namboodhiri Brahmins became wealthy and influential *janmis*.

Yet another consequence was the disappearance of Buddhism and Jainism from the religious landscape and the establishment of a very rigid Hindu society based on castes and sub-castes.[52] The tradition of singing *bhajans* continued in the *alwar*, *nayanar* and other movements.

## Venad

The twelfth century CE saw the rise to prominence of Venad, a small principality just north of the Ay region. In the conflict between the Cheras and the Cholas, Venad was sacked by the latter. The Chera forces under Rama Varma Kulashekara later defeated the Cholas from Tamil-speaking areas.

---

50. Another ruling family of *Tamilakam*.
51. Could be translated as place or region; the *naduvazi* would reign over the *nadu*.
52. Menon, Survey of *Kerala History*, 156–58.

Rama Varma moved his capital to the Venad city of Quilon and this heralded the beginning of Venad's history as an independent kingdom.

A significant event during Rama Varma's reign was the giving of land to the Rameshwarathukoil temple in Quilon, as atonement for having offended the Namboodhiri *janmis*. This is the first recorded instance of a ruler acting on *brahmin* directions, reflecting the immense social and political power they had attained.[53] By the early fifteenth century, the Venad kingdom had split into two, with one branch moving further south. The southern Venad family would later become rulers of Travancore.

## European Colonialism

### The Portuguese

In 1498 CE the seafaring explorer Vasco da Gama (1460-1524) was sent eastward by King Manuel of Portugal to find a shipping route to India and thereby expand the country's trade in spices. Da Gama landed at Calicut (or Kozhicode) in May that year, marking the beginning of a new epoch in the history of Kerala and the entire Indian sub-continent. Calicut was north of Venad, and its hereditary kings or rulers were called *zamorin*. While the *zamorin* of Calicut refused to cede a monopoly of the pepper trade to the Portuguese, the rulers of Cochin, Canannore and Quilon welcomed the Europeans and even offered them help in loading their ships. As a result of conflicts between competing small kingdoms in the area, the Portuguese established supremacy here with little difficulty. Between Vasco da Gama's second voyage and subsequent Portuguese trips to the region, Cochin was brought completely under Portugal's control.

Spice trading was now possible only with the Portuguese, leading to protracted conflict between Cochin and the Zamorin of Calicut. But in 1513, despite protest from the Cochin ruler, the Portuguese ratified a new treaty with the *zamorin*, cutting out Cochin and Canannore, their former allies. By then the Portuguese had also established a presence in Goa to the north of Kerala and moved their headquarters there. In 1518, after making an unsuccessful attempt on the life of the ruler, the Portuguese again entered into an alliance with Cochin and Venad. It is from this point that the era of dominant Portuguese presence in the Venad region can be traced; their hegemony in the Kerala region would continue for another 150 years.

---

53. Ibid., 160–61.

However, it would not be a period of prolonged stability. Political disunity and divisions between the various kingdoms and principalities reached their peak during the Portuguese era.[54]

Besides exerting social and economic influence, the Portuguese presence was felt in their attitude of "narrow religious intolerance and bigotry,"[55] beginning with an aggressive campaign to convert the peoples of Kerala to Catholicism. Hindus, Muslim and others who resisted them risked severe persecution, as a number of Hindu authors have recorded.[56] During their early colonial years, the Portuguese had avoided harassing Hindus so as not to offend local Hindu rulers who were initially useful for economic and political reasons; but before long, they turned on the Hindus as well and plundered many temples. The Jewish community also suffered under Portuguese aggression, and the synagogue in Cochin was partially destroyed. The once-independent St. Thomas Christians were brought under the Roman Catholic umbrella at the Synod of Diamper in 1599, a career triumph for Dom Alexis de Menezes (1559–1617), the Roman Catholic Bishop of Goa.[57] From then on, the Syriac liturgy followed by the St. Thomas Christians of Kerala was replaced by the Roman Catholic Latin rite.

Under the Portuguese, seminaries and colleges were opened in various parts of Kerala, notably at Cochin, Cranganore, Angamaly, and Vaipicotta. With them came the introduction of European-style printing presses, and printeries were established in Cochin and Vaipicotta. Roman Catholic mission work among the Hindus was concentrated mainly along the coast of South Kerala and carried out by prominent historical figures such as St. Francis Xavier. It was during this period that Western scholars began showing interest in Indological studies and research.[58]

This period also saw a renaissance among Hindus with the revival of the *bhakti* movement in Kerala. As Sreedhara Menon points out: "The peculiar political, social and economic conditions of the age created a mental and religious stir among the Hindus and led to the widespread popularity of the doctrine of bhakti."[59] As well, the accompanying context of violence,

---

54. Vishvambharan, *Kerala Samskara Darshanam*, 175.

55. Menon, *Survey of Kerala History*, 227.

56. Vishvambharam, *Kerala Samskara Darshanam*, 180; Menon, *Survey of Kerala History*, 228.

57. A brief history of the St. Thomas Christians is given later in the chapter.

58. Menon, *Survey of Kerala History*, 227.

59. Ibid., 231.

social degeneration and economic hardship motivated people to seek solace in faith. With a renewed inclination toward the religious life, there was also a renewal of attraction to *bhakti*,[60] as evidenced by literary works of the period.

> A number of literary works were produced with *Bhakti* as the all-embracing theme. Vishnu, in the form of Krishna and Rama, came to be glorified in the writers of the age. The most outstanding exponent of the *Bhakti* cult was Tunchat Ezhuthachan, the 'Father of Malayalam Language'. He wrote such devotional works as *Adhyatma Ramayanam, Mahabharatam, Harinamakirthanam* etc. in which he preached to the common people the doctrine of selfless devotion and surrender to God in the form of Vishnu. Ezhuthachan's *Ramayanam* became the most popular poem in the Malayalam language and it won for him the same place in Malayalam as is held by Kambar in Tamil and Tulasidas in Hindi.[61]

Other contributors to *bhakti* literature of the time were Melpattur Narayana Bhattathiri and Puntanam Namboodhiri. Puntanam's works in Malayalam—*gnanappana, srikrishnakarnamritam* and *santanagopalam*—were long considered the supreme literary expressions of the *bhakti* cult. Manaveda's *krishna giti* devotional verses, also written during this period, evoke great musical charm.

## The Dutch

Dutch presence in the Kerala region originated in 1604, when a treaty was signed with the reigning Zamorin of Calicut, forming a mutual alliance against the Portuguese and giving them facilities to trade and to station merchants in Calicut. In 1619 the Dutch entered into an agreement with Britain to further curb the activities of the Portuguese, thus marking the early seventeenth century as the onset of their decline in influence. In 1658 the Dutch captured the Portuguese fortress in Quilon and entered into a treaty with the local queen. Although the Portuguese briefly recaptured the fort, they were repelled for the final time in 1661. Thanks to an existing defense and trade treaty with the reigning queen, the Dutch enjoyed exclusive rights to the region's pepper trade.

---

60. Vishvambharan, *Kerala Samskara Darshanam*, 185.
61. Menon, *Survey of Kerala History*, 232.

## Songs as *Locus* for a Lay Theology

When the Dutch succeeded in fully capturing the Cochin kingdom from the Portuguese in 1663, that event marked the beginning of their colonial dominance in Kerala. A new treaty with Cochin in 1663 gave the Dutch sole rights not only for the lucrative pepper trade, but cinnamon as well. By adding treaties with the smaller kingdoms of Kayamkulam, Purakkad and Martha, the Dutch consolidated their dominance in Kerala. Besides multiplying the spice industry, the Dutch also contributed to the commercial development of other local products,[62] notably the scientific cultivation of coconut and the development of the coir fibre industry derived from it.

The eventual decline of Dutch colonial presence in Kerala can be traced to the rise of the native kingdom of Travancore. Working closely with the British, Travancore ruler Marthanda Varma inflicted a severe defeat on Dutch forces at Kolachal in 1741; as a result, a number of smaller kingdoms on the northern border that were previously aligned with the Dutch were all absorbed into Travancore. Matters became worse still for the Dutch with the growing power of northern Muslim ruler Haider Ali and his son Tippu Sulthan, who went on to conquer Calicut and areas around Cochin. The Dutch were finally decimated in October 1795 by the British army conquest of Cochin. In 1814, the convention of Paris caused Thangasherry, a small territory in Quilon, to be ceded to the British.

With the coming of the Dutch one can also trace the beginnings of Reformed Protestant Christianity in the region, although it did not have any long-term impact on the existing Christian community in Kerala, which was tolerant and liberal in its relations with the Reformed faith and other local religions. Although Indian Christians in the regions of Dutch influence were placed under colonial protection, Jesuits and Catholic priests were expelled. Many of their churches were demolished or turned into undignified purposes, such as ammunition dumps. It is also recorded that the Dutch razed the magnificent Jesuit library in Cochin and destroyed the collection of volumes in it.

By the late 1600s, however, the Dutch had a change of heart and reversed their intolerance toward Roman Catholicism and its various holy orders. Jesuits, Carmelites and others were allowed to return and resume their work. In 1682 the Catholics built a theological school at Verapoly, which has since been raised to the status of a Pontifical Seminary.

---

62. Vishvambharan, *Kerala Samskara Darshanam*, 189.

## Socio-cultural and Religious Contexts

This heralded a period of calm for the non-Catholic St. Thomas Christians. The Dutch even helped them recruit new bishops and retain their independence from Rome. Jews and Hindus who had been the targets of Portuguese oppression now enjoyed the patronage of the Dutch, whose military policy was to avoid destroying temples and other places of worship during conflict.

Otherwise, Dutch contributions to the fields of religion, education, and culture in Kerala were minor against the bigger picture of history; they showed no inclination to establish religious centers or schools, for example. Their one notable contribution, however, was the unique document *Hortus Malabaricus* (The Garden of Malabar). Conceived by Dutch Malabar governor and amateur naturalist Hendrik van Rheede (1636–1691), this mid-seventeenth-century Latin treatise on the native healing practice of *ayurveda* extended to 12 massive volumes, describing the medicinal properties of more than 700 local plants.[63]

### *The Rise of Travancore*[64]

During the reigns of Marthanda Varma (1729–1758) and Karthika Thirunal Rama Varma, also known as Dharma Raja (1758–1798), Travancore became a prominent and powerful military state. While Marthanda Varma was instrumental in expanding the boundaries of Travancore, his successor consolidated the kingdom's influence over its newly conquered territories and preserved its integrity in the face of attacks from Mysore.

Marthanda Varma entered into an alliance with the British East India Company and the Nayaks of Madurai[65] and with their help subdued the power of feudal barons within the kingdom, which resulted in a strong and centralized monarchy in Travancore. His most noticeable military achievement was the defeat of the Dutch at Kolachal in 1741—one of the few successes native rulers achieved over European colonial powers.

Among many political and social reforms of the time, the feudal system of *janmis* was replaced with a new administrative structure where the village represented the lowest unit of civic power. During this period the practice of framing annual budgets was initiated in Travancore. On

---

63. Ibid., 191; Menon, *Survey of Kerala History*, 259.
64. See appendix ii for a map of this region.
65. The kingdom of Madurai was to the East and North of Travancore.

January 3, 1750 Sri Padmanabha of Trivandrum[66] dedicated the kingdom to his deity Padmanabha. From then on, all the rulers of Travancore became *padmanabhadasas*[67] and the kingdom's rule was considered a sacred trust. Temples in surrounding regions were repaired and renovated and the management of temple lands became a government responsibility.[68]

This period also saw significant progress in literature and the arts. Ramapurathu Warrier, and Kunjan Nambiar were two prominent poets of the time. The temple arts of *kuthu*, *thullal*, and *kathakali* were encouraged and mural painting also became very popular.

Dharma Raja, Marthanda Varma's successor, was himself a renowned scholar, poet and composer of *kathakali* poems. He periodically held intellectual gatherings called *panditha sadas*[69] to encourage and reward scholars and writers, and also patronized followers of other religions. During his reign the capital of Travancore was moved from Padmanabhapuram to Trivandrum.

### Travancore Kingdom and the British

The British arrived in the region by the early seventeenth century and pursued alliances that served their interests in both trade and manufacturing. The first organized revolt against their colonial policies in Kerala can be traced back to the 1721 Attingal Outbreak, when a British contingent of 140 men proceeding to the palace of the *rani*[70] of Attingal were killed by local insurgents.[71] The rebels went on to lay siege to the British fort at Anchuthengil, an attack that lasted for six months until reinforcements arrived.[72] The British later consolidated their position by ratifying treaties with Travancore and its smaller neighboring principalities.

When Haider Ali and his son Tippu Sultan advanced from Mysore in the north, the British actively entered the war in 1789 to aid local rulers in driving the Muslim forces out of Travancore.

---

66. Refers to the place where a temple to the deity is situated.
67. Servants of Padmanabha. Menon, *History of Travancore*, 171.
68. Nayar, *Venadinte Parinamam*, 340.
69. Learned ones' council or gathering.
70. Queen.
71. Menon, *Survey of Kerala History*, 308.
72. This is dealt with in more detail in the section about Political, Social and Religious Movements for Change.

## Socio-cultural and Religious Contexts

The regions to the North of Cochin, referred to as Malabar,[73] came under British control just a few years later in 1792, through the treaty of Srirangapatnam, made with the same Tippu Sultan they'd helped to defeat. An interim arrangement for the administration of the region was negotiated by Britain with the local rulers. A notable event at the time was the prohibition of slave trading in the region. In 1800, Malabar came under the direct rule of the Madras Presidency.

Although the Cochin kingdom became a vassal of the British East India Company, Travancore developed a different colonial relationship. After a number of treaties that culminated in an agreement of 1805, it became a subsidiary ally and protectorate of the British. Velu Thampi, the *dewan*[74] (equivalent to prime minister) of Travancore from 1800, played a crucial role in establishing British influence there.[75] In 1810, Gouri Lakshmi Bai, aged just 20, was crowned queen of the kingdom. In 1811, she invited the designated British Resident, Col. Munro, to take on the office of *dewan*. He accepted, and with this event, the administration of Travancore fell completely into the hands of the British. There was now nothing local rulers could do about the British hegemony if they wanted to retain their independent existence. Under his administration, Col. Munro focused on reforming the St. Thomas Christians and supporting the work of Protestant missions in the kingdom. In a letter to the secretary of the Church Mission Society (CMS) he wrote:

> Regarding as I do, the diffusion of genuine Christianity in India, as a measure equally important to the interests of humanity and to the stability of our power, I view, with the most sincere pleasure, the commencement of a systematic plan for the attainment of that object . . . Indeed from the situation of the Portuguese in India, strong arguments may be adduced for the diffusion of the English language, as a means of supporting the British Power, as well as of extending the protestant religion ...[76]

Gouri Lakshmi Bai was succeeded as queen of Travancore by Gouri Parvati Bai, who reigned from 1815 to 1829, a period that was significant

---

73. The northern half of Kerala is referred to as the Malabar region.

74. *Dewan* refers to the Prime Minister of the Kingdom. In some resources he is referred to as the *dalawa*.

75. Shobanan, *Dewan Velu Tampi*, 109. Though he initially helped the British to impose the subsidiary treaty on the Raja of Travancore against his will, he later changed position and rose against the British.

76. Munro's letter to the Secretary of CMS, cited in Gladstone, *Protestant Christianity*, 55.

in the kingdom's social and religious context for the number of reforms that advanced the causes of freedom and civic equality. Non-*brahmin* Hindus of the higher castes were permitted to wear gold and silver jewelry without paying customary fees to do so, and people of all castes were now allowed to have tiled roofs on their homes. Christian missions were helped through free land and wood given for building churches. As S. Menon notes: "The London Missionary Society at Nagercoil established itself on a firm footing in 1816 under the Rani's patronage. The Church Mission Society was given all help to carry on its activities at Alleppy and Kottayam."[77] But R.N. Yesudas, in his book *British Policy in Travancore: 1805 to 1859*, gives a contrary view, pointing out that during the last year of her rule, the proclamations issued by Gouri Parvati Bai actually restricted the freedom of work and movement for missionaries in Travancore.[78]

Swati Tirunal Rama Varma (1813–1846), a son of Gouri Lakshmi Bai, succeeded Parvati Bai as ruler of Travancore at age 16 in 1829 and ruled until his death. Praised from early childhood for skills in mastering multiple languages, scholarly subjects, arts and music, he made major contributions to reforming and reorganizing the kingdom's educational system. The beginning of English education in Travancore is credited to his reign, along with the establishment of schools of higher and specialized learning.

Utram Tirunal Marthanda Varma (1814–1860) succeeded to the throne in 1847 and also ruled until his death. Notable social changes under his reign included the abolition of slavery in Travancore (1855), and rescinding old laws that had forbidden *shanar* women of South Travancore from covering their upper bodies (1859). He also established schools for the equal education of girls. Ayilam Tirunal Rama Varma (1832–1880), ascended the throne of Travancore in 1860 and continued his precursors' progress in expanding educational facilities throughout the kingdom and advancing the status of women.

In fact, as early as 1922, Travancore women had the right to vote in elections for members of the kingdom's Legislative Council, although only a small percentage of the female population exercised their votes.[79] In another historically significant step, the temple entry proclamation of 1936

---

77. Menon, *Survey of Kerala History*, 329. The London Missionary Society and the Church Mission Society are often simply referred to as LMS and CMS respectively.

78. Yesudas, *British Policy in Travancore*, 24.

79. Menon, *Survey of Kerala History*, 334. It was only those that paid a tax of Rs. 5 per year that enjoyed the privilege.

extended the privilege of worshipping in government-controlled temples to the lower castes. By signing this document into law, the Travancore government removed at a single stroke all state-sanctioned recognition of untouchability.[80]

## The Practice of Caste

Aryanization of India's previously casteless society was complete by the eighth century CE. As the most powerful social group, *brahmins* asserted their primacy in civic and religious matters where they oversaw both the ruling-class *shatriyas* and the *nairs*, who although they were *sudras*, were the dominant warrior class. Ranking below these groups were the *ezhavas*, *shanars*, *kammalas*, and *mukkuvas*.[81] Existing completely outside the caste structure, as noted previously, were the Untouchable *pulayas* and *parayas*. Dick Kooiman, in his book *Conversion and Social Equality in India*, refers to the latter groups as slave castes, since many of the upper castes "bought and sold (them) like cattle."[82]

The caste system, with its rigors of exclusivity and ostracism, manifested itself in a number of demeaning and restrictive practices, including "untouchability," "unapproachability," and "unseeability," which were observed by all levels of society.[83] The concept of "distance pollution" evolved to prescribing by measurement the minimum proximity within which a lower-caste person could approach someone of higher caste. Even the sight of a *pulaya* (at any distance) was enough to make a *namboodhiri* feel polluted. If the prescribed distance was violated, the higher caste individual had to undergo a cleansing ritual.

If a higher caste *savarna* used a public road, a warning was continuously shouted so that any low caste *avarna* using the same road could move away out of range to the prescribed distance until the *savarna* had passed.[84] Some *avarna* castes were not allowed to use public roads at all before their

---

80. Desai, *Epic of Travancore*, 40.

81. The *ezhavas* and *shanars*, also referred to as *nadars*, were toddy-tappers by profession; the *kammalas* were artisans, and the *mukkuvas* were fishers.

82. Kooiman, *Conversion and Social Equality in India*, 18.

83. Menon, *Social and Cultural History*, 66.

84. *Savarna* refers to high caste Hindus and *avarna* refers to low caste Hindus; the term itself refers to skin color or complexion.

emancipation. And in places where *avarnas* were forbidden to spit in public, they had to go about with spittoons tied around their necks.

For easy recognition and avoidance by *savarnas*, *avarna* women were not allowed to cover their upper bodies. Also, for castes just below the *brahmins*, though women were permitted to cover their breasts, they were obliged to expose their upper bodies fully in the presence of someone from a higher caste. As strange as this seems in current Western society, showing the bare breast was seen as a sign of respect to one's superiors and was considered the proper salutation of women to those of higher caste.[85]

Slavery, as noted earlier, was another prevalent practice. Members of the *pulaya* and *paraya* castes suffered the humiliation of toiling for their entire lives in the fields of higher caste masters. Domestic slavery was not practiced, however, due to the aforementioned protocols around inter-caste proximity pollution. Thus slaves were not allowed to enter their masters' dwellings and were condemned to toiling day and night in cultivating and nurturing the land.[86] While working on the fields, they were obliged to hang green leaves on the boundaries, so that higher caste people would know that slaves were present and keep their distance. Slave castes were thus forced to live on the fields where they worked or on the banks of canals. When there was no work, they were left to starve or scavenge for food.[87] If slaves belonging to different owners had children, the offspring became the property of their mother's owner.[88] Though slavery was abolished in 1855, many higher caste members continued the practice secretively, using *parayas* and *pulayas* as bonded laborers for life. Whether called slaves or workers, they provided cheap and reliable labor. Perhaps the most preposterous practice is that some wealthy *avarnas* even owned slaves from their own castes!

The practice of *pulappedi* and *mannappedi* was another dreadful custom that prevailed in this caste-conscious society. Women who had a relationship with someone from a lower caste were treated as outcasts and sold as slaves to Christians, Muslims, or foreigners. And during a certain time of year, *pulaya* and *mannan* men were allowed to molest women of the *nayar* caste. Women who were touched by them had to declare the act, leave their homes and families, and seek shelter in an *avarna* home, so as to avoid polluting their families. If they did not declare their contact with men

---

85. Mateer, *Native Life*, 291.
86. Menon, *History of Kerala*, 272.
87. Kooiman, *Conversion and Social Equality*, 18.
88. Mateer, *Native Life*, 58–59.

## Socio-cultural and Religious Contexts

and were found out, they were sold as slaves to lower castes, or foreigners, or even subjected to "honor" killing.[89]

Similarly, higher and lower castes, such as *savarna* and *avarna* could not eat at the same table. All higher caste homes had separate vessels in which to make and serve food for lower castes; if any higher caste food vessels were polluted, they were destroyed. As mentioned earlier, slave castes were not allowed to enter higher caste homes. When food was served to lower caste slaves or bonded workers, a precise anti-pollution method was used: a bowl-shaped depression was made in the ground at a prescribed distance from the owner's home, a banana leaf placed in it, and the food was placed on top of it.

The rigid practice of distance pollution made it impossible for *avarnas* to have the same opportunities as *savarnas* in worship, education, access to public facilities (such as roads and businesses), and so on. *Avarna* worshipers had to leave sacrifices to the deities at a prescribed distance from the temple and after they retreated, the priests collected them. *Brahmins* were the only caste that could interpret the law and they determined the severity of punishment for offenses, which depended on how low one was in the caste structure. If *avarna* merchants wanted to sell their products, they had to leave them displayed at the roadside and retreat while buyers inspected the goods, took what they needed, and left the money.

Samuel Mateer mentions another consequence of distance pollution, which created unique difficulties for Christian missions wanting to build churches where all would be welcome, regardless of caste. These churches had to be constructed at a distance from public roads, or in lonely areas not frequented by the higher castes.

For *avarnas*, conversion to Christianity was not only a religious event, but a social movement for liberation as well. It promised freedom from the shackles of a 3,500-year-old tradition of discrimination and deprivation that had become solidly entrenched in the life and psyche of the people. Unfortunately, casteism remained a reality in the Church and prejudice from neighboring Hindus continued unabated.[90] Yet low-caste Christian

---

89. Menon, *Social and Cultural History*, 67–68.

90. The Madhya Kerala Diocese of the Church of South India, comprising both St. Thomas Christians and lower-caste converts, has appointed only one bishop from among its lower castes members since the formation of the diocese in 1947. Another example is the MM Church of Nadar Christians and Christ Church of the St. Thomas Christians, both near neighbors in Thiruvanandapuram. In the Marthoma Church converts from the lower castes had their own *sabhas* (interestingly *sabha* is translated as "church" in

converts still enjoyed privileges that their Hindu kinfolk did not. For example, they were no longer bound by traditional occupations or social stigma; opportunities for education empowered them to move up the economic ladder and become increasingly conscious of their rights and privileges. A number of social movements in Travancore could be traced to the proactive involvement of missionaries on behalf of *avarna* human rights and they became faithful allies in their struggle for emancipation.

## St. Thomas Christians and Reformation in the Church

There are differing opinions about St. Thomas's apostolate in India,[91] the earliest being the live tradition in Kerala. It is believed that the Apostle Thomas, from whom this faith community took its name, arrived at Kerala in 52 CE and proceeded to found seven churches. Some claim that the earliest written record of St. Thomas living and preaching in India is found in the apocryphal *Acts of St. Thomas*, written in Syriac between the later second and early third centuries CE. Third- and fourth-century Christian writings also refer to St. Thomas communities in India.

According to the Kerala tradition, St. Thomas came by sea and landed at Cranganore around 52 CE. He preached to the local population, performed miracles, and converted some high caste Hindu *namboodhiris*, who were *brahmin* priests.[92] In addition to establishing seven churches (whose locations he marked with crosses), Thomas ordained new priests from among his high-caste converts.

The next significant event in the Kerala tradition involved another Thomas, not a saint, but a merchant traveler. Sometime between the fourth and ninth centuries CE, Thomas of Cana arrived in India from Syria, accompanied by some 400 men, women and children. Although there are differences of scholarly opinion on the exact date of this migration, there is no doubt about the event itself.[93] The Knanaya churches within the St.

---

Malayalam), while the St. Thomas Christians had their *edavakas* congregations. It is only recently that *sabhas* were given the same privileges as *edavakas* in the Marthoma Church. To date, there have still been no bishops or priests in any major leadership role from the lower castes.

91. Mundadan, *Traditions of St. Thomas Christians*, 3.

92. As was pointed out earlier, this tradition is now contested in the light of later findings and studies of Kerala history.

93. Kuruvilla, *History of the Marthoma Church*, 1.

Thomas tradition trace their origins to the Thomas of Cana group. To this day, they have separate dioceses with their own bishops, in both the Roman Catholic and Jacobite (or Syrian Orthodox) churches.

The St. Thomas Christians who traced their roots to the apostle of that name were ecclesiastically affiliated with the Nestorian Church in Assyria, until Roman Catholicism arrived with Portuguese merchants and colonists during the late fifteenth century CE. Efforts to bring the Kerala Christians within the Roman Catholic fold culminated with the arrival from Portugal of Archbishop Aleixo de Menezes, who convened the Synod of Diamper in June, 1599. A small group resisted at that time and chose to retain ties with the Nestorian tradition. But in 1653 most of the St. Thomas Christians (with the exception of 400 dissenting families), broke away from the Roman Catholic Church with the Coonen (or "bent cross") Oath[94] at Mattancherry, Cochin. The breakaway group aligned itself with the Jacobite Church and that same year, the Bishop of Jerusalem consecrated Parambil Thoma Cattanar, or Mar Thoma I (circa 1615–1680), as the first native metropolitan bishop.[95] That historic relationship continues to this day.

## The Church Missionary Society

By the early nineteenth century, the British were the dominant political and economic influence in Travancore, and the Church of England took an active interest in the spiritual welfare of the local non-Roman Catholic St. Thomas Christians. Colonel John Munro, the East India Company's official British Resident in Travancore from 1810 to 1819, who was an avid scholar, linguist and cultural historian, took the initiative in 1813 to establish a theological seminary in Kottayam to train ordinands for the Syrian Orthodox Church.[96] He created an endowment for this purpose and requested further support from the Church Missionary Society of London. The CMS responded by sending Thomas Norton in 1816 as its first missionary to Travancore.

---

94. *Coonen* means bent; they tied a rope to a cross and all assembled there, held to the rope, and took an oath severing their connection with the Roman Catholic Church, resulting in the cross leaning or bending.

95. Kuruvilla, *History of the Marthoma Church*, 11–12; see also Ayyar, *Anthropology of the Syrian Christians*, 37–38.

96. Earlier the candidates were trained under *Malpans* (religious teachers) on an individual basis, closer to the Indian *Guru-Sishya* (teacher-student) relationship.

## Songs as *Locus* for a Lay Theology

The presence of the CMS had a profound impact on the Church in Kerala. Benjamin Baily, who joined Norton by the end of 1816, translated the New Testament into Malayalam from Syriac and also established the first press to print in the Malayalam language. By 1841 the entire Bible had been translated and published in Malayalam at the Kerala press. The CMS maintained that it did not want to create a new Christian denomination, but rather to help the local church regularize its training, administration, and finances. Despite this assertion, suspicion and conflict emerged, and at the Synod of Mavelikara in 1836, the Church decided to reject all reforms suggested by the British missionaries and reaffirm its allegiance to the Syrian Orthodox Patriarch. In a subsequent arbitration, the seminary remained with the Marthoma Church.[97]

In picturing the ancient church Alexander Marthoma observes;

> The pre-reformation Church was satisfied with the observance of certain rites and ceremonies. It was believed that by praying to the Saints and by celebrating special festivals connected with them, benefits could be derived and evil could be avoided. This is very much like the festivals observed by the non-Christian community around them. They just formed another social group observing Christian ceremonies, but having no special message for the world.[98]

Even after parting ways with the Church Mission Society, the desire for reformation continued within the Orthodox Church. In 1836, twelve clergy led by Abraham Malpan and GeeVarghese Malpan,[99] submitted a memorandum to the British Resident, Col. Fraser (successor to John Munro), suggesting changes to incorrect teachings and various abuses. Their memorandum listed 23 areas in which the reform group felt that the church had deviated from scripture and its early traditions. Juhanon Marthoma, the former Metropolitan of the Marthoma Church, affirmed that the reform group was going back to pre-Jacobite and pre-Roman Catholic doctrines and practices.[100] Alexander Marthoma, his successor, refers to the 1836 reform movement as "a return to the purity of the life and practice of the early church."[101]

---

97. Marthoma, *Marthoma Church*, 10-13.
98. Ibid., 14.
99. Religious teachers.
100. Mar Thoma, *Christianity in India*, 31.
101. Marthoma, *Marthoma Church*, 18.

## Socio-cultural and Religious Contexts

Abraham Malpan revised the liturgy and translated it into Malayalam, the local vernacular. This revised liturgy was used in his parish at Maramon, and at Kozhencherry and Ayroor.[102] Among the major changes to worship was a renewed emphasis on preaching the Word, along with exposition of the Bible during services. Revised wording now described Holy Communion as the "bloodless sacrifice of grace, peace and praise," rather than a repetition of the sacrifice of Christ. In the epiclesis, or invocation of the Holy Spirit, the prayer was changed to read: "May the Holy Spirit sanctify this bread/wine to be the body/blood of our Lord Jesus Christ." The words "transform" and "descend on" were no longer used; moreover, all monophysite references to the Person of Christ were removed from the liturgy. Monophysitism asserted that the person of Jesus Christ comprised only one divine nature, rather than separate divine and human natures, as asserted at the Council of Chalcedon in 451 CE.) Another notable change was in the understanding of the mediatorial priesthood; now it was affirmed that Christ alone is the Mediator. Thus, where priests offered prayers on behalf of the people, wording of the petitions was changed to first- or second-person plural, emphasizing the priesthood of the laity. The practice of giving money to obtain favor or blessings from saints was also done away with, along with praying to saints and the dead to spiritually mediate on one's behalf.[103]

Throughout these reforms, the Malpan group continued to uphold both the liturgical and ecclesial traditions of the Oriental Churches and to retain the tradition of historical episcopacy. The intent was not to break with their mother church, but to reform it proactively from within; hence, they did not leave to join those few who formed the Anglican Diocese in Kerala.

Following this desire to reform the church from within, Abraham Malpan sent his own nephew to Mardin, where the Patriarch of Antioch resided; there, he was ordained a priest and metropolitan by the Patriarch, taking the name Mathews Mar Athanasius. On his return, a struggle developed between Mathews Mar Athanasius and Chepat Mar Dionysius, the sitting Bishop of the Orthodox Church, resulting in lawsuits from both sides vying for recognition as the rightful head of the church. In 1889, the Royal Court of Trivandrum declared Joseph Mar Dionysius (successor to Chepat Mar Dionysius) as rightful head of the church. Thomas Mar Athanasius (successor to Mathews Mar Athanasius) lost his case and had to leave with the rest of the reform group.

---

102. Brown, *Indian Christians of St. Thomas*, 140–41.
103. Marthoma, *Marthoma Church*, 15–17.

These developments defined the parting of ways between the Orthodox faction that continued ties with the Jacobite Patriarch at Antioch, and the Marthoma Church that remained autonomous and continued to claim its origins in the apostolate of St. Thomas. The reform group retained possession of only three churches. Two of them (Maramon and Kozhencherry) were acquired through a court decision, and the third (Kottarakara) was ceded without legal contest. Though he was not a member of either the Maramon or Kozhencherry congregations, Sadhu Kochukunju was raised and lived in Edayaranmula, only 10 miles from both churches.[104]

Later on, some in the Orthodox group had issues with the authority of the Jacobite Patriarch, resulting in the establishment of the Catholicate of the East at Kottayam in 1912, which declared autonomy from Antioch in temporal matters, while continuing to recognize the Patriarch as spiritual head of the church. This was followed by intermittent periods of peace and conflict between the two groups. A final separation came about after the Supreme Court of India verdict of 1995 which affirmed the autonomous nature of the Catholicate of the East, while also affirming the spiritual authority of the Patriarch of Antioch over the Orthodox Church in India.

---

104. Maramon and Kozhencherry could be considered twin towns or villages, as they were located on either side of the river Pamba with a bridge connecting them.

# Socio-cultural and Religious Contexts

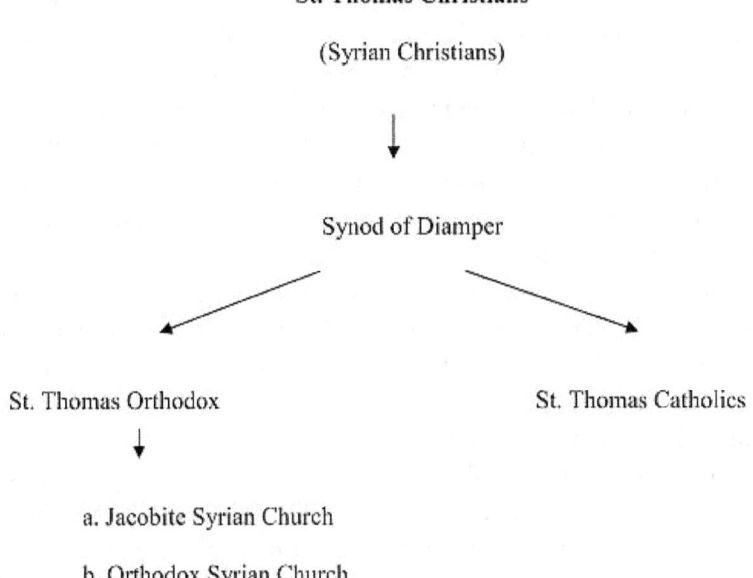

a. Jacobite Syrian Church

b. Orthodox Syrian Church

c. **Marthoma Church**

d. Church of South India (one diocese of the CSI)

e. St. Thomas Evangelical Church

Those churches whose traditions trace their origins to St. Thomas were confined to the southwestern part of the Indian peninsula. With the advent of European colonization and growth of missionary movements, Christianity in India spread far beyond the geographical areas in which the St. Thomas Christians originally took root.

## *St. Thomas Christians and the Caste System*

Over nearly two millennia, the St. Thomas Christians had come to enjoy a privileged position within the existing traditions of Indian society and were not considered a threat to it. This process of inculturation gave the church there its present form and is reflected in both social and ecclesial dimensions.

## Songs as *Locus* for a Lay Theology

In many anthropological studies, the St. Thomas Christians were in fact seen as part of the Hindu caste system. Throughout history, the community traditionally saw itself in both mission and identity as a *jathi*, or sub-caste. The autonomous Syro Malabar Tradition refers to St. Thomas Catholics of Malabar who continued within the Syrian Rite, while converts to Catholicism from other faiths were (and still are) referred to as Latin Rite Catholics. The Orthodox Church's mission does not involve proselytism; the missionizing Marthoma Church, on the other hand, maintained separate churches for its converts until the mid-1980s. This aberration was corrected by the late Metropolitan Alexander Marthoma so that converts would share the same privileges. In practice, however, social and marital alliances between them are still uncommon. Even now, its status as a particular *jathi* or sub-caste gives St. Thomas Christians their particular identity within the prevailing social fabric.

One of the caste-related tasks of the St. Thomas Christians[105] was to neutralize distance pollution, which was practiced in Kerala as well the rest of India. If an *avarna* came within a certain distance of *savarna* food, it was considered polluted. But for the *brahmins* and *nairs*,[106] the touch of a St. Thomas Christian purified food that was otherwise polluted,[107] a reflection of the respect accorded their position in the caste hierarchy. The tradition of shouting *poyin, poyin*,[108] in some places during processions after the Easter service could be traced to the practice of warning the lower castes to stay away from the Christians' path.

In fact, local rulers granted privileges to St. Thomas Christians from very early times. Two sets of ancient copper plates, dated 774 and 824 CE[109]

---

105. The caste hierarchy was primarily based on the division of labor.

106. *Nairs* are the *kshatriyas*, the warrior caste, who are just below the *brahmins*.

107. Visvanathan, *Christians of Kerala*, 3; Varghese, "Marthoma Christhyanigal" (an article for which I have few publication details, except that it was in the *Sabhataraka*, the official journal of the Marthoma Church. The theological implications of such a practice and the role of the Christian community there, in terms of the mission of the Church, would also form an interesting study!)

108. *Poyin* means "go away."

109. There are differences of opinion about the dates of these plates. Kuruvilla, Ayyar, Pothen and others date them as above; but Mundadan, Brown and others would date both to around 880 CE. Kuriakose in his compilations of Indian Christian Historical Source materials dates the plates to 849 and 1225 CE. See Kuruvilla, *History of the Marthoma Church*, 2; Ayyar, *Anthropology of the Syrian Christians*, 50–51; Pothen, *The Syrian Christians of Kerala*, 35; Brown, *Indian Christians of St. Thomas*, 74–75; Mundadan, *History of Christianity in India*, 166–67; Kuriakose, *History of Christianity in India*, 10; 14. The St. Thomas

respectively, bear inscriptions granting the Christians special rights. Because of this patronage and protection, they soon came to be numbered among the "noble races of Malabar."[110] They were preferred over the warrior *nairs*,[111] and enjoyed all caste privileges of the *kshatriyas*. Even *nairs* themselves regarded the Christians as equals[112] and their bishops "were respected and feared like kings."[113] Like *brahmins*, the St. Thomas Christians were permitted to build enclosures in front of their houses.

## Political, Social and Religious Movements for Change

British political hegemony and the internal oppression caused by the caste system did not go unchallenged in Travancore. As early as the eighteenth century, one could trace movements against the colonizing presence of the British.

The previously-mentioned revolt of 1721 in Attingal is considered the first such uprising in the region.[114] The British had enticed the queen of Attingal to allow a factory and fort to be built at Anchuthengil, an act resented by the local populace. Through a Mr. Gifford, their leader in Attingal, the British maintained the queen's favor by regularly giving her gifts. *Pillamars*, the local leaders, were incensed by this practice and demanded that the British give gifts to the queen only through them. The British refused and continued to give her gifts, causing the local people to lose patience and attack the 140 member British group by surrounding the Anchuthengil fort. The siege lasted for six months until reinforcements could arrive from Tellicherry to free the fort.

Kerala Varma Pazhassi Rajah of the Kottayam royal family led the next significant revolt against the British. The Rajah objected to the way they collected revenue in his domain, so he openly challenged the British by stopping the collection in Kottayam. In April 1795, British forces attacked the palace intending to seize the Rajah, but he had already fled to

---

Christians are also referred to as Syrian Christians because of their Syrian connections.

110. Ayyar, *Anthropology of the Syrian Christians*, 54. Malabar also refers to the Kerala coastal region.

111. Ibid.

112. Ibid., 55.

113. Ibid.

114. In Kerala history this is referred to as *Attingal kalapam*, where *kalapam* means revolt.

the mountains of Wyanad and led a guerila war from there. As a result, the British were forced to stop all traffic on the road through the mountain passes. They eventually signed a truce after which the Rajah returned to Kottayam. But fresh conflicts in 1797 again pushed the Rajah and his allies into the mountains. Initially they forced the British to withdraw and later that year another battle resulted in heavy British casualties. The British were compelled to agree to a truce and the Rajah "accepted a pension of Rs. 8,000 per annum and agreed to live in peace with the Company."[115]

But this truce also did not last long. When Pazhassi Rajah protested the annexation of Wyanad in 1800, fresh conflicts broke out. He again withdrew to the hills and gathered his forces. The British responded much more firmly this time, building a network of new roads and forts that made them better able to counter the Rajah's guerila tactics. The long drawn out rebellion was finally crushed and the Rajah died in battle in November, 1805. Kilimanoor Vishvambharan writes: "Though they did not get the final victory in their great revolt to push out the British conquerors from their motherland the Pazhassi revolt did great damage to the British."[116]

In 1808 on the heels of the Pazhassi upheaval, Velu Thampi and Paliath Achan, *dalawas* (equivalent to prime ministers) of the kingdoms of Travancore and Cochin respectively, led yet another uprising against the British. Initially Velu Thampi had maintained friendly relations with them, but interference in the administration of the kingdom by designated British Resident, Col. Macaulay, as well as British demands to pay tribute arrears during difficult economic times, pushed them to revolt. Their initial assault on Cochin on December 18 forced Col. Macaulay to flee by ship, but the combined local forces were beaten back a month later and suffered heavy losses at the hands of the British. Velu Thampi continued urging local people to rise against the foreigners and they responded to his call. But the colonial powers proved too strong. Dalawa Thampi committed suicide early in 1809, before he could be captured by the Rajah, who wanted to appease the British. Paliath Achan defected from the anti-British alliance after being defeated in February 1809. That marked the end of the uprising. The native army of Travancore was soon disbanded and Travancore and Cochin were completely subjugated under the British[117] who took over their policing and security.

115. Menon, *Survey of Kerala History*, 319.
116. Vishvambharan, *Kerala Samskara Darshanam*, 229.
117. Kumar, *Political Evolution in Kerala*, 17.

## Socio-cultural and Religious Contexts

In rising up against the British and exhorting his people to join him in the cause, Velu Thampi became one of India's first freedom fighters against colonialism. As Sreedhara Menon notes; "He was the first statesman and leader of modern India who made effective use of his hold on the people to organize a mass revolt against foreign domination."[118] Though Velu Thampi failed in his goal of ousting the British, he left a major impact.

Political developments soon changed the social and religious fabric of Travancore and other Malayalam-speaking areas. From the early nineteenth century, a trend by rulers to centralize land administration, as well as invasion by the sultans of Mysore, loosened the stranglehold of feudalism over society. Additionally, the influx of European colonizers and the spread of an effective school system raised the education levels of ordinary people throughout the region, who in turn became newly conscious of their rights and identity. Protestant missions were particularly significant, with missionaries becoming involved in emancipation movements for change among the marginalized. Mission support, especially through universal schooling, went a long way toward making social justice movements effective. Christian missions also impacted the majority Hindu religion; many reform initiatives in Hinduism could be traced to their influence, not only in Travancore, but throughout India.

Among the major movements for social change at the time was that led by Chattambi Swamigal (1854–1924) of the *nair* caste. From the late nineteenth through the early twentieth centuries, *nairs* fought for the right to play a legitimate role in society. Chattambi Swamigal attempted to return society to the egalitarian pre-Sangam period, where no group was considered superior to another.[119] In his book *vedhadhikaara niroopanam*, he argued that all have the privilege of learning scripture, not only *brahmins*. In support of his opposition to *brahmin* dominance, he drew upon Sankara's monistic teaching that each human being is a *brahmin* in their own right "who is without duality." He also advocated the doctrine of *ahimsa*[120] and encouraged substituting vegetables and grain for the practice of animal sacrifices. Chattambi Swamigal also led the struggle for local employment rights because the minority Tamil *brahmins* in the kingdom had usurped all the most prestigious jobs. His slogan was "Travancore for Travancoreans."

---

118. Menon, *Survey of Kerala History*, 324.

119. Gladstone, *Protestant Christianity*, 221.

120. *Ahimsa* is the doctrine of non-violence made famous by Gandhi during the struggle for India's freedom.

## Songs as *Locus* for a Lay Theology

Sri Narayana Guru (1856–1928), a near contemporary of Swamigal, was another notable contributor to social and religious reforms in Travancore. Narayana Guru belonged to the *ezhava* caste and also revolted against *brahmin* dominance over society, as well as fighting for the removal of caste barriers. Narayana Guru came to public prominence by appropriating for himself the right to consecrate the *Shiva Linga*[121] in Aruvippuram temples in defiance of Brahmin protocols. He also appointed *ezhava* priests to serve in the temple and opened its doors to lower castes and even those completely outside the caste system. In response to vehement *brahmin* objections that only their caste could consecrate a temple, Narayana Guru declared that this was "not a Brahmin Shiva, but an Ezhava Shiva."[122]

Narayana Guru went on to consecrate a number of other temples and priests for the *ezhava* community. In two places, instead of consecrating the temple god or goddess, he installed mirrors, so that worshipers saw reflections of themselves in place of the deity.[123] His motto, "one caste, one religion and one god . . ." showed him to be a true universalist who worked to abolish all boundaries of caste and creed. He encouraged his fellow *ezhavas* to learn Sanskrit, which the *brahmins* had maintained as their exclusive language; this was the only effective means by which the *brahmin* monopoly over classical learning could be overcome. He opened a school of Sanskrit at his Advaita Ashram in Alwaye for this purpose; his own ashram and headquarters were at Varkala.

Among Narayana Guru's major social reforms was his campaign against the practice of *thalikettu kalyanam*, the ritual marriage of infant girls (followed by marriage rites as young adults). He soon succeeded in eliminating this tradition among the *ezhavas*.[124] Another practice he opposed was *thirandukuli*, the celebration and ritual observed when a girl attained maturity. The traditional occupation of ezhavas was "toddy tapping,"[125] but he successfully urged them to give up making, providing and drinking this traditional alcoholic beverage, because of its destructive influence. Those who continued to deal in toddy were ostracized from their community.[126] Narayana Guru's stand against toddy-tapping marked a radical breakaway from a caste-enforced occupation. On January 7, 1903 the Sri Narayana

---

121. *Shiva Linga* refers to the representation of Shiva in the Hindu pantheon.
122. Menon, Survey of *Kerala History*, 382.
123. Gladstone, *Protestant Christianity*, 238.
124. Ibid. 239.
125. Alcoholic brew made of sap tapped from coconut and palm trees.
126. Gladstone, *Protestant Christianity*, 241.

Dharma Paripalana Yogam (SNDP) organization was formed to address and advocate for all issues and needs of the *ezhava* community.

In the forefront of the struggle against untouchability during this period was Ayyan Kali[127] (1866–1941), who belonged to the *pulaya* slave caste. His first act of defiance was to buy a pair of bullocks and cart, a right allowed only to higher castes. In 1904 he organized the *pulayas* to claim their right to use public roads.[128] In 1908 he established a school at Vengánoor[129] and agitated for the right of all *pulaya* children to receive an education; he even forcibly entered schools in the face of violence and threats from higher castes. In direct contrast to Chattambi Swamigal, Ayyan Kali urged fellow *pulayas* to counter violence from higher castes with violence in return.[130] As many historians have pointed out, this was a turning point in the political and social history of Travancore. One protest tactic by the *pulayas* was refusing to work in the fields until their children were given the opportunity to attend school along with the higher caste children.[131]

In 1907 Ayyan Kali founded the Sadhu Jana Paripalana Yogam (SJP), similar to the SNDP Yogam organization of the *ezhavas*, to work for the advancement of the *pulaya* community. For his contributions to the welfare of his people, Ayyan Kali was nominated in 1911 to the Mulam Praja Sabha, the legislative body of Travancore. As a member of that body, he was instrumental in convincing the government to declare that the lowest castes were academically and socially deprived and thus should be granted education scholarships. As a result, schools in the kingdom finally began admitting *pulaya* children.[132]

The official abolition of slavery in 1855 was a significant historical event in Travancore, but with caste being as entrenched as it was in the religious and social psyche of the privileged, it took time for various depraved and unjust practices to be rooted out so that the *dalits* and lower castes could benefit. Important among early social movements was the Upper Cloth Revolt[133] by the *shanar/nadar* community.

127. Also spelled as one name, Ayyankali.

128. Jose dated the gaining of this right as 1901 (*Ayyankali*, 121); Gladstone dates it 1904 (*Protestant Christianity*, 267).

129. Jose, *Ayyankali*, 136.

130. Ibid., 139–40.

131. Gladstone, *Protestant Christianity*, 269. See also; Jose, *Ayyankali*, 147–52.

132. Jose, *Ayyankali*, 152.

133. Some refer to this as the Upper Cloth Controversy, or Upper Cloth Revolt; Yesudas refers to it as The People's Revolt.

## Songs as *Locus* for a Lay Theology

One of the most abhorrent practices inflicted upon non-*brahmin* women was the mandatory uncovering of their upper bodies when in the presence of higher castes. The "upper cloth" was a light piece of fabric worn across the breasts by *nadar*[134] women, with one end thrown over the shoulder. Even before the Christian influence, *nadars* and *ezhavas* had demanded that women of their castes be permitted to cover their upper bodies, but this right was forbidden by the higher castes. The arrival of the London Missionary Society in Southern Travancore brought welcome support to the lower castes' struggle for freedom and dignity. Thanks to the influence of LMS missionaries, the official British Resident, Col. Munro, issued an order in 1812 allowing " . . . women converted to Christianity to cover their bosoms as obtains among Christians in other countries . . . "[135] Another proclamation in 1814 further regulated the dress code for women of the *nadar* and *ezhava* castes, allowing them to wear a loose blouse like that of St. Thomas Christians and Muslims. Unfortunately, stiff opposition from the higher castes resulted in this regulation being suppressed.

During certain times of the year *nadar* men from Travancore migrated to the British province of Tinnevelly for employment and often married local women there. Unlike their counterparts in Travancore, women of Tinnevelly were not restricted in how they dressed and had the freedom to cover their upper bodies. When these women accompanied their new husbands back to Travancore, they were expected to bare their breasts, but refused.[136]

The movement for change was encouraged by the missionaries but faced recurrent challenges and opposition. In 1822 it came to the attention of LMS missionary Charles Mead that *nadar* Christian women in the Kalkulam and Erenial areas who wore upper cloths were being ill-treated. Mead filed a local complaint, which was ignored. He then complained to the British Resident, who ordered an inquiry and demanded that the court act on the case.[137] In 1828, *nadar* Christians were attacked by *nairs* and their women stripped of their upper cloths. The Christians were also accused of not fulfilling their caste responsibilities of *ooliyam* work, which included free labor to the government, and of evading taxes. When the violence spread, the *dewan* (prime minister) gave assurance that there would

---

134. From this point I use the caste name *nadar* instead of *shanar*, which was used in earlier literature.

135. Cited in Yesudas, *People's Revolt in Travancore*, 115.

136. Ibid., 114.

137. Gladstone, *Protestant Christianity*, 83.

be a decision on the issue. In February 1829 the Travancore government issued the following proclamation:

> As it is not reasonable on the part of the Shanar women to wear clothes over their breasts, such custom being prohibited, they are required to abstain in future from covering the upper part of their body. An order had been issued on the 7th Edavam 989 to all places prohibiting the Shanar women of the families of such Shanars as may have embraced Christianity from wearing clothes over their breasts and requiring them to substitute for these the kuppayam.[138]

The proclamation also decreed that *nadar* Christians were to do their obligatory *ooliyam* work like all others, but were excused on Sundays. In a move to prevent foreign missionaries from interfering in the local administration, it was also declared that Christians would not have any other tribunal for their complaints. Higher castes continued to object to the Christians' privilege of wearing the *kuppayam*, and *nadar* women continued to defy the proclamation. The high castes now considered Protestant Christianity as a threat to the social fabric of India.

The next phase of agitation for social change occurred in 1858–59, with the marked difference that Christian *nadars* were now joined by Hindu *nadars*. As more and more women defied the breast-baring custom, widespread violence from higher castes ensued, with Christian churches and schools being destroyed; this spurred the *nadars* to retaliate in kind.

On becoming aware of such disturbing developments in Travancore, the British Chief Secretary, Sir Thomas Pycroft (1807–1892; served 1855–1862), ordered the local British representative, Gen. Cullen, not to be seen as condoning the practice. Pycroft asked that the king of Travancore be persuaded that allowing the caste conflict to continue was not becoming of a monarch of the time.[139] With constant pressure from the missionaries as well, the matter was referred to Lord Stanley, the first Secretary of State for India (served 1858–1859) and its highest political authority at the time. This and subsequent protests forced British authorities to intervene on behalf of the lower castes. The king of Travancore was finally convinced that the proclamations of 1814 and 1829 were unbecoming and contrary to human dignity and justice. Consequently, the king issued another proclamation on

---

138. Translation of the proclamation as quoted in Yesudas, *People's Revolt in Travancore*, 126. *Kuppayam* is a short loose blouse worn by St. Thomas Christian women.

139. Yesudas, *People's Revolt in Travancore*, 150–51.

July 26, 1859 asserting the right of both Christian and Hindu *nadar* women to cover their upper bodies. The new proclamation read in part:

> There is no objection to other *shanar* women wearing the kuppayam like Christian *shanar* women, or all *shanar* women irrespective of their religion could dress in coarse cloth and tie it around themselves like woman of the fisher folk, or could cover their breasts in any manner except like the high caste women.[140]

But the more liberal proclamation still did not fully satisfy everyone. The upper castes were unhappy that some of the age-old privileges they exclusively enjoyed were now being extended to their inferiors; they could see that the rigid caste practices were breaking down and there would be no turning back. It was a severe blow to the assumed power that higher castes had always exercised over lower ones. And while the lower castes were experiencing unprecedented emancipation toward new levels of dignity, there was discontent as this privilege was enjoyed only by nadar women.

The *nadar* women, having won a small concession to their dignity of dress, now wanted all the privileges and rights that their sisters in Tinnevelly and the rest of British India enjoyed. The missionaries continued to protest and complained about "the weakness of this proclamation."[141] In response, British authorities pressured Travancore to extend freedom of dress to all lower-caste women, which it did through another proclamation in 1865.

The Upper Cloth Revolt was a watershed event in the struggles of the lower castes against the systemic denial of their rights and dignity. It was the first major uprising of the lower castes demanding equality before the law, as well as equal protection by the law. This spurred radical changes in the socio-political climate and a number of subsequent activist movements of the later nineteenth and early twentieth centuries could be traced to the impetus gained from the Upper Cloth Revolt.

## The London Missionary Society in Travancore

The beginning of the London Missionary Society (LMS) presence in Travancore can be credited to the arrival of William Tobias Ringeltaube in 1806. A

---

140. Translation of the proclamation from Malayalam in Raimon, *Thiranjedutha Rajakeeya Vilambarangal*, 302.

141. Gladstone, *Protestant Christianity*, 92.

## Socio-cultural and Religious Contexts

Prussian by birth, a Lutheran by affiliation, he was one of the first three LMS missionaries posted to India.[142] Ringeltaube studied Tamil in Tranquebar and was associated with the work of the SPCK (Society for Promoting Christian Knowledge) in Tanjore. While there, he was approached by Vedamanickam, a Hindu convert from Travancore who embraced Christianity after encountering Christian relatives during a pilgrimage to Hindu shrines in Tanjore. Vedamanickam attended a church service with his relatives and was immediately attracted to a faith that was so different from his native religious tradition. For him, the experience was "like a sudden shining of a star to one wandering in thick darkness."[143] He was instructed in his new faith by J.C. Kohlhoff, an SPCK missionary at Tanjore, and subsequently baptized.

Vedamanickam returned to his native village of Mayiladi to work as an evangelist among his Hindu relatives and neighbors. As a result, about 30 came to publicly profess Christianity,[144] but opposition from the higher castes prevented them from building a church. Vedamanickam considered moving with the other new Christians of Mayiladi to the relative safety and protection of Tanjore, which was outside Travancore and under direct rule by the British. But on hearing that the LMS missionary Ringeltaube was at Tranquebar preparing to work in Tamil-speaking areas, Vedamanickam invited him to work in his own village.

Ringeltaube agreed and in April 1806 moved to Mayiladi. His first impressions of the place were disappointing, but he took the people under his care and appointed Vedamanickam as their catechist. Initial requests for permission to build a church were rebuffed by the *dewan* (prime minister) Velu Thampi. But he later relented and they received permission to erect Travancore's first Protestant church in Mayiladi in 1809.[145] Within just a year, churches were built in nine neighboring towns as well. In 1814 Ringeltaube was also able to convince Velu Thampi and the British Resident Col. Munro, to persuade the local *rani* (queen) to grant two paddy fields to the mission, thus providing employment to a number of *nadar* Christians and enabling the mission to partially support itself and not depend wholly on home mission funding.[146]

---

142. Hacker, *Hundred Years in Travancore*, 20.
143. Cited in ibid., 21.
144. Gladstone, *Protestant Christianity*, 59.
145. Hacker, *Hundred Years in Travancore*, 24.
146. Kooiman, *Conversion and Social Equality in India*, 54.

Ringeltaube left the Mayiladi mission in 1816 and Charles Mead took over in 1817. Between the two, Vedamanickam acted as interim leader. During the first year of Charles Mead's posting in Travancore, it was recorded that "as many as three thousand" *nadars* joined the Christian community and the number of churches grew to 15.[147] In 1819 a seminary was opened in Nagercoil and Mrs. Mead[148] founded a school for girls. A Christian settlement soon grew up around the mission at Nagercoil. By 1821, the mission's active territory stretched from Nagercoil to Quilon, covering the southern third of Travancore.

With the growth of the mission, other staff members were added to those already present. John Roberts joined in 1831 and is credited with starting government-sanctioned higher education in Travancore. The school established in Trivandrum grew to become the Maharajah's College, one of the city's premier institutions.

The practice of *ooliyam*, which obliged lower castes to provide free labor to the government and also to give supplies to government-supervised temples, was a huge economic burden for them. Thanks to pressure from the missionaries, Christians were exempted from these tasks on Sundays. The unfair practice of *ooliyam* was finally abolished in 1865 and it was thereafter deemed a criminal offence.[149]

As this chapter has illustrated, Christian missionaries were involved from the beginning in the emancipation struggles of the lower and untouchable castes. The event that propelled the movement to ban slavery in Travancore was the signing of a petition to the British Resident by missionaries in 1847, on behalf of local slaves. Under persistent pressure from the British, Travancore finally abolished slavery in 1855. The success of the movement for the right of lower-caste women to wear clothing on their upper bodies (the Upper Cloth Revolt) can also be attributed to the intervention of Christian missionaries on behalf of the deprived lower castes. But the higher castes persisted in accusing them of "helping the people to break the traditions and customs."[150]

In his book, *Protestant Christianity and People's Movements*, Gladstone points out that one could detect prejudice in the attitude of missionaries toward the natives, in spite of the proactive positions they took on

---

147. Hacker, *Hundred Years in Travancore*, 34–35.
148. The first wife of Charles Mead.
149. Kooiman, *Conversion and Social Equality in India*, 120.
150. Gladstone, *Protestant Christianity*, 168.

various social justice issues. When Charles Mead married a local woman from the *paraya* caste after the death of his British wife, other missionaries complained about him to the home board in England, describing his marriage as being "to the daughter of a Catechist and of the Pariah caste, which in this part of Travancore is the slave caste." Fellow missionary C. Mault wrote: "The marriage of Mr. Mead to a young native woman, of the Pariah caste, has filled us with surprise, disappointment and sorrow."[151] As was the case in most mission endeavors, and in spite of valuable contributions to the emancipation struggles of the downtrodden, local mission workers and others were treated by the Europeans and British more as "subordinate servants than fellow workers."[152]

In 1866 the first four native Indian ministers were ordained. At the same time, the Order of Evangelists was established; the Evangelists were in charge of the various congregations of a parish.[153]

The work of missionaries' wives among the *nadar* women helped raise support for Christian missions. Travancore Lace, made by the women as a cottage industry, was very popular, both locally and in Europe. As Goodall points out: "The supreme value of these cottage industries lay in their influence, educative and cultural, upon thousands of women drawn from the poorest classes in the community."[154] The contributions of the mission to the social, intellectual, medical, and economic well-being of the lower castes were immense. By 1920, the membership of LMS churches in Travancore had grown to 100,000.[155]

Although the earliest movements to embrace Christianity came from the *nadar* community, from 1860 onward mass movements from the *pulaya* and *paraya* communities also flowed into the church.[156] However, *paraya* leadership was not acceptable to the higher caste *nadars*, so the Nagercoil church refused to accept Vedamanickam's grandson, Masillamani (ordained in 1866), as their pastor. In 1886, Masillamani left Travancore for Madras to work for another organization and it is said that with him "the last prominent agent from the paraya community left the LMS."[157]

---

151. Both references as quoted in Gladstone, *Protestant Christianity*, 192.
152. Kooiman, *Conversion and Social Equality in India*, 66.
153. Hacker, *Hundred Years in Travancore*, 54.
154. Goodall, *History of the London Missionary Society*, 49.
155. Ibid., 43.
156. Ibid., 48.
157. Kooiman, *Conversion and Social Equality in India*, 178.

## SONGS AS *LOCUS* FOR A LAY THEOLOGY

Continuing complaints from *pulayas* and *parayas* about being sidelined from higher positions in the mission organization went unheeded. Mateer wrote to the home board in 1889 that since Rev. Masillamani left, there had been no *pulaya* or *paraya* minister or evangelist at the mission.[158] This vacuum in representative leadership and lack of recognition pushed the *pulayas* and *parayas* to leave the mission. Most joined the Salvation Army.

The ordination of four native ministers in 1866 could be seen as a first step in the promotion of local leadership. This was followed by the formation of the Travancore Church Council in 1874. Membership in the Council included foreign missionaries, all Indian ministers, and some elected lay native representatives. The Council continued to lobby for local representation in higher church administrative bodies, but was consistently turned down by the Travancore District Committee, where the real power was vested. The continued appeals were seen as being indicative of the "absence of religious and spiritual condition."[159]

The next development was a restructuring of the church administration in a system consisting of Church Committees, Circle Councils, District Councils, and Church Council. A native person was appointed Chair of one of the District Councils, but this did not satisfy the desire of other native members to have a greater role. Influenced by the growth of Indian nationalism, the mission authorities eventually changed their strategies and moved toward handing over more responsibility to local leaders. But it still took until 1934 for more local leaders to be appointed as District Chairmen. While Indians were given management of village day-schools and of local congregations, control of the parent institutions remained with the missionaries.[160]

The gradual acceptance of local people into administrative posts began the slow but steady transition from Travancore being a mission to a self-governing native Indian church. Subsidies from the mission home board in England were cut and financial support was now raised locally. The movement culminated in the formation of the Church of South India in 1948 and the creation of its two dioceses: the South Kerala Diocese and the Kanyakumari Diocese.

---

158. Ibid.
159. Gladstone, *Protestant Christianity*, 328.
160. Ibid., 336–37.

# Chapter 2

## Doxology and Theology—Bhakti, the Indian Doxological Tradition of Songs

A COMMON PERCEPTION IS to understand music as belonging to the realm of aesthetics and more personally, as an expression of one's inner self. To regard music and its vocal expression in song as a source of theology, however, might seem initially surprising.

In setting the context for his book *Doxology: The Praise of God in Worship, Doctrine and Life*, Geoffrey Wainwright notes that while theology is an intellectual activity, the sources and resources with which it is realized are greater than intellect alone, for it is a rational and logical reflection on all of God's "dealings" and relationships with humankind.[1] He writes:

> Worship is the place in which that vision comes to a sharp focus, a concentrated expression, and it is here that the vision has often been found to be at its most appealing. The theologian's thinking therefore properly draws on the worship of the Christian community and is in duty bound to contribute to it.[2]

Verbal theology is only one among many modes of revelation. Luther, in a letter to Georg Spalatin, points out that in song the word of God continues among the people.[3] And as revelation in worship comes through various modes, one is invited to respond in totality. Thus believers are invited to bring all of themselves—intellect, emotion, and their entire existence—so that it may be gathered up in praise. *Doxology* is a term describing praise

---

1. Wainwright, *Doxology*, 1.
2. Ibid., 3.
3. Luther, *Luther's Works*, 49:68.

that is specifically directed to God. Berger describes doxological speech as "the explicit and implicit speech of praise, confession of faith, prayer, and thanksgiving, as directed to God for God's glorification."[4] She goes on to point out how doxological speech is found in "prayers, hymnic confessions, and songs." A broader definition of doxology would also include prayers of thanksgiving, praise, petitions and liturgies.

In defining doxological speech for the purpose of this work, however, I have approached it in the narrower sense of its expression in hymnic confessions and songs.

## Doxological Traditions in Theological Reflection

It has not been long since the question of the place that doxological tradition holds in theological reflection emerged. In *Theology in Hymns*, Berger points out differences in emphasis among Roman Catholic, Protestant and Orthodox traditions in how they relate doxology and theology.

> Roman Catholic liturgiology debates the relationship of the *lex orandi* to the *lex credendi* while Protestant systematic theology takes as its theme the question of linguistic differences between doxological and theological speech. On the other hand, the Orthodox tradition accepts as a foregone conclusion the theological character of liturgical language and the doxological roots and orientation of theology.[5]

An overview of the history of hymnology demonstrates that it developed in parallel with liturgy and that the two streams are closely intertwined.

The Latin usage of *lex orandi, lex credendi* is usually taken to mean the rule of prayer or worship is the rule of belief; that is, what you pray or worship is what you believe. The usage of the *lex orandi* principle is traced to a lay monk, Prosper of Aquitaine, a disciple of Augustine,[6] between 435 and 442 CE. In a letter to Pope Celestine, Prosper wrote, "*ut legem credendi lex statuat supplicandi*," which could be translated, "that the law of supplication might establish the law of believing."[7] Here, it is the supplication, the

---

4. Berger, *Theology in Hymns?*, 17.
5. Ibid., 55.
6. Ibid., 32.
7. Church, "The Law of Begging", 442–53.

bending down, that shapes believing; it is the act of bending as the act of worship, which creates belief.

It could be argued from historical and exegetical perspectives that from the early years of the church until beyond the fourth century CE, practice moved from worship to doctrine, from *lex orandi* to *lex credendi*. Piet J. Naude points out in an article that most early Christian communities were liturgical in nature and as they evolved the link between baptismal and creedal formulas was very evident. Quoting Paul Meyendorf, Naude emphasizes that as people worship, so they believe. During its early period, for example, the liturgical assembly itself was the church's source of theology, especially when growth increased dramatically following the political support of the emperor Constantine (272–337 CE).[8]

Wainwright points out that Jesus was the center of the early church's worship, the content of its preaching, and the presence in its sacraments, the primary locus where Christ was recognized as Lord and Savior.

> There is no doubt that worship constituted the primary locus of Christ's recognition as Lord by Christian believers. He was confessed as Lord at baptism: . . . He was invoked as Lord in the Christian assembly: . . . He was already worshipped as Lord by Christians, in anticipation of the day when every knee should bow: . . . The ethical acknowledgement of Christ's sovereignty in everyday living is secondary to the religiously primary acknowledgement of Christ as Lord in the context of worship.[9]

He goes on to argue that, besides recognizing the divinity of Christ, the early church evolved its doctrine of Trinity based on the threefold pattern of baptism, as well as other dogmas resulting from the worship of the community; worship always preceded dogma or doctrine. Magisterial authority was "brought to bear on the liturgy for the sake of establishing a developing or developed doctrine …"[10] Arianism was pitted against "liturgical devices" which was also useful in establishing Nicene orthodoxy in the face of emerging heresies. The text of the Nicene Creed itself was a product of the "liturgical life" of the community. Hence, if theology is to reflect the entire faith of the church, it is in the context of worship and liturgy that one could expect to find the fulfillment of this goal.

---

8. Naude, "Regaining Our Ritual Coherence."
9. Wainwright, *Doxology*, 47–48.
10. Ibid., 250.

Another question raised in this context is whether developed doctrines would be affected, or perhaps disappear entirely, if worship and public devotion within a community were to wane. Wainwright points out that besides decreased public devotion, another reason for decline could be "a differently advised or constituted magisterium," or even changing "cultural circumstances." But the place of liturgy and worship in sustaining a faith community is nevertheless irrefutable and supported by history.

## *Lex Orandi, Lex Credendi* in Church Traditions

The principle of *lex orandi, lex credendi* has been used and emphasized differently by mainstream Christian traditions. It can mean that what you pray is what you believe; it can also mean that what is believed by the community governs or determines what you pray. Is prayer the determinant of doctrine, or doctrine the determinant of prayer? Referring to Maurice Wiles, James Kay in his article "Lex Orandi in Recent Protestant Theology" discusses how appeals to worship could settle theological controversies or establish Christian doctrine. He emphasizes that the practice of prayer not only has had its effect on doctrine, but that it *should* effect doctrine.[11] Wainwright also raises the issue around the emergence of Trinitarian doctrine in the fourth century CE, asking whether it was "a necessary or legitimate development from the baptismal practice." He also explores the interplay of doctrine and worship on both sides of the Reformation divide.

Even before Prosper, his mentor St. Augustine had used the argument of liturgy in support of doctrine. On the issue of whether children are born with original sin, Augustine refers to the practice of pre-baptismal exorcism, and infants receiving communion for eternal life, asking "Why have recourse to the remedy if the ailment is absent?"[12] Augustine also used liturgical examples or illustrations in his sermons. Both Augustine and Prosper affirmed that what gave worship its doctrinal authority was the indwelling and leading of the Holy Spirit in the life of the church. St. Ambrose of Milan also uses liturgy to elucidate the doctrine of the Trinity.

> So you went down (into the water). Remember what you answered: that you believe in the Father, you believe in the Son, you believe in the Holy Spirit. It is not a case of: I believe in a greater, a lesser, and a least. But by the pledge of your own word you are bound to

11. Kay, "Lex Orandi," 12.
12. Wainwright, *Doxology*, 227.

believe in the Son in the same way as you believe in the Father, and to believe in the Spirit in the same way as you believe in the Son.[13]

For Ambrose, liturgy served as evidence to establish a doctrinal position rather than to correct or change it. Wainwright traces the use of the *lex orandi, lex credendi* principle in the early church through Basil, Cyprian, Tertullian, Irenaeus and others. Both Tertullian and Irenaeus rely on the Eucharist and sacraments to establish their argument on the resurrection of the body.

It has been pointed out that the neglect of the principle of *lex orandi, lex credendi* by Protestant theologians could be due to its use in Roman Catholicism. The latter typically prioritized liturgy as a norm for doctrine while the former prioritized doctrine as the norm for worship. "Catholics have appealed to past and present liturgical practice in order to justify doctrinal positions and developments which Protestants have considered unacceptable."[14] The focus here was on the language of the liturgy and not on personal or individual devotion.

On the role that worship played in "preserving the deposit of faith," early twentieth-century modernist George Tyrrell wrote:

> The 'deposit' of faith is not merely a symbol or creed, but is a concrete religion left by Christ to his Church; it is perhaps in some sense more directly a *lex orandi* than a *lex credendi*; the creed is involved in the prayer and has to be disentangled from it; and formularies are ever to be tested and explained by the concrete religion which they formulate . . . But theology is not always wise and temperate; and has often to be brought to the *lex orandi* test . . . (W)hen it begins to contradict the facts of that spiritual life, it loses its authority; and needs itself to be corrected by the *lex orandi*.[15]

The critique against such a position was that this would allow one to understand Christianity in a reduced or symbolic sense. Although the Roman Catholic magisterium of Prosper's time was skeptical about the principle, the church used the argument later to assert its dogma. The dogmatic emphasis on Mary's Immaculate Conception in liturgical texts and rites was made in a pronouncement by Pius IX in 1854.[16] The Catholic

---

13. Ibid., 229.
14. Ibid., 219.
15. Tyrrell, Through Scylla and Charybdis, cited in ibid., 221.
16. Berger, *Theology in Hymns?*, 33.

Church's interest in the principle again traced back to Latin liturgiologists of the seventeenth and eighteenth centuries in the process of collecting the texts of Eastern rites for publication in the West. In *Liturgiarum orientalium collectio*, E. Reanudot argues that "Eastern liturgies, not being simply the words of the one great doctor to whom they might be attributed, but having apostolic roots and having received the unanimous and uninterrupted approval of entire churches, possessed a value equal to the Latin and second only to the scriptures as witness to the tradition."[17]

The 1947 encyclical, *Mediator Dei* XII points out how "sacred liturgy" has close connections with church doctrine and therefore must be in conformity with pronouncements of the faith.[18] The encyclical understands *lex orandi, lex credendi* to mean that "the law of our prayer is the law of our belief." Use of liturgy in defense of (or support for) theological arguments was a traditional pattern in Roman Catholicism. While the church has fallen back on *orandi* to support *credendi*, the reverse also could be argued from the parallel position that liturgy was subject to church teachings.

Among late twentieth-century Roman Catholic theologians, Aidan Kavanagh brings back the notion of liturgy's "intrinsic value" in relationship to theology, arguing for its prior place ahead of theology. He notes that " . . . theology is to be formulated from the liturgical action that makes possible, determines, and forms it."[19] Kavanagh also points out that liturgy "is not an *authority* or a *locus theologicus*; it is the ontological condition of theology."[20] To him, the community at prayer and worship is the "starting point and center of all theology."

The Reformation brought about a shift in focus among its constituent churches. The primary task of the movement was to correct erroneous traditions and teachings, with the main emphasis being on correct doctrine; here we see the primacy of doctrine over liturgy. The Reformation itself began amid confrontation with existing liturgical practices and church doctrine: Catholicism believed dogma and liturgy were infallible, Protestants did not. As Berger points out, for Protestants " . . . the relationship between theology and doxology is not primarily a liturgical concern, but rather a theological one."[21] She draws a distinction in the

---

17. Wainwright, *Doxology*, 220.
18. Issued by Pope Pius XII.
19. Berger, *Theology in Hymns?*, 39.
20. Kavanagh, *On Liturgical Theology*, 75.
21. Berger, *Theology in Hymns?*, 41.

shifting emphasis from a "language of liturgy" to a "language of devotion." Consequently, the Protestants did not hesitate to change practices and ceremonies that they considered to be flawed in nature. The Anglican *Book of Common Prayer* notes:

> Of such ceremonies as be used in the Church, and have had their beginning by the institution of men, some at the first were of godly intent and purpose devised, and yet at length turned to vanity and superstition; some entered into the church by undiscreet devotion, and such a zeal as was without knowledge; and for because they were winked at in the beginning, they grew daily to more and more abuses, which not only for their unprofitableness, but also because they have much blinded the people, and obscured the glory of God, are worthy to be cut away, and clean rejected: other there be, which although they have been devised by man, yet it is though good to reserve them still, as well for a decent order in the Church (for the which they were first devised), as because they pertain to edification, whereunto all things done in the Church (as the Apostle teacheth) ought to be referred.[22]

It was the doctrinal positions of the constituent churches that determined the role and practice of liturgy in the Protestant tradition. Differences in the elevation of the consecrated elements between the Church of England and the Lutheran traditions could be traced to this diversity. While a number of more recent Protestant theologians, including Ebeling, have dealt with the topic of doxology and theology, it was Geoffrey Wainwright's book, *Doxology: The Praise of God in Worship, Doctrine, and Life*, that most effectively unpacked systematic theology from a doxological or liturgical perspective. This, he has pointed out, was a pioneering effort to link worship and doctrine as he "attempted to meld the traditionally Protestant genre of systematic theology with the Orthodox, Roman, and Anglo-Catholic traditions of theological reflections on the liturgy."[23] Wainwright acknowledges the complexity of using the *lex orandi*. As he points out; "It is hard to see how absolute certainty could attach to any doctrinal conclusion drawn from the worship of the Church. Such conclusions will possess varying degrees of probability and must remain open to revision.[24]

To answer what it is that gives the church's worship "any authority which it carries in matters of doctrine," Wainwright refers to both Orthodox and

---

22. Wainwright, *Doxology*, 264.
23. Kay, "Lex Orandi," 11.
24. Wainwright, *Doxology*, 230

Lutheran traditions. To the Orthodox, worship is primarily the presence and act of the triune God and not of human initiative, while in Lutheranism worship is primarily "God's service to us before it can be our service to God."[25]

Berger refers to German Lutheran theologian Gerhard Sauter's article, "*Reden von Gott im Gebet*," in which he emphasizes the need to view theology "not only as speech about God but also as speech directed to God."[26]

Thomas C. Oden and Alistair McGrath are two contemporary Protestant theologians who, among others, claim worship as a source and norm for Christian doctrine. They assert that liturgy and church practice, more than formal church teaching, is the medium of tradition. And one of the most important elements of Christian tradition is the fixed form of worship called liturgy.[27]

As was pointed out earlier in reference to Wainwright, the Orthodox position on liturgy and worship is very different from that of Protestantism, in that it invokes the very presence and acts of the triune God. Worship is "nothing else than heaven on earth,"[28] and liturgy embraces both heavenly and earthly realms; thus what happens in liturgy is a reflection of the heavenly. Alexander Schememann refers to liturgy as the "main source of knowledge and religious life and inspiration in the Orthodox world."[29] He adds that all spiritual culture and theological learning evolved through the church and its cumulative experience of Divine Liturgy.

In his book, *Being as Communion*, John Zizioulas establishes the church's universality through the example of worship and the Eucharist, seen as a collective and catholic (universal) act.[30] The Orthodox tradition, on the other hand, does not have formal dogmatic definitions as does Roman Catholicism or Protestantism. Timothy Ware, later Bishop Kallistos, argues it would be wrong to conclude that what is not dogmatically stated is just opinion and not part of the Orthodox tradition. To the Orthodox, some dogmas not formally stated are held by the church with "inner conviction" and "unruffled unanimity," and are considered to be just as binding as formal decrees. Such inward traditions, "handed down to us in a

---

25. Ibid., 242. Orthodox and Lutheran perspectives will be examined in more detail later.
26. Berger, *Theology in Hymns?*, 43.
27. See Kay, "Lex Orandi," 13–14.
28. Clendenin, *Eastern Orthodox Theology*, 12.
29. Schememann, *Historical Road of Eastern Orthodoxy*, 228.
30. Zizioulas, *Being as Communion*, 145.

mystery," are preserved above all in worship. "*Lex Orandi, lex credendi*: our faith is expressed in our prayer."[31] In fact, all Eastern Orthodox beliefs are contained within the prayers and hymns used at worship. Ware clarifies that it is not just words, but words, gestures, and actions together that express the truths of the faith.

In Lutheran terms, worship is God's service to us before it can be our service to God. "Luther charged the Roman Church with having made the mass a human *sacrificium* directed towards God, whereas the gospel sacrament is a divine *beneficium* directed towards humanity."[32] In this context, our praise and worship are only a response to God's gift. Since worship is the place where God is made known to us in a saving encounter, it is the source of doctrine. Words and acts combined in worship are the *locus* of Lutheran theology as vehicles of God's self-communication to believers.

## A Brief Overview of the History of Hymns

It is said that music is intrinsic to humanity, having been part of daily life from the dawn of our species. Vocal music in particular is intimately linked to routines and rituals of community life and worship. Paul Westermeyer agrees with ethnomusicologist Curt Sachs that music began with singing and later evolved as instrumental forms. Besides being the origin of human music, singing is central to worship and "therefore related to the verbal ones and to the corporate participation of the people through them."[33]

The Christian Church inherited its singing from the Jewish tradition of chanting the psalms, often antiphonally, in worship. Erik Routley highlights New Testament passages that may have "some of the characteristics of hymnody."

> Awake, thou that sleepest, and arise from the dead; and Christ shall give thee light. (Eph 5:14).

> He who was manifest in the flesh, justified in the spirit, seen of angels, preached among the nations, believed on in the world, received up in glory (1 Tim 3:16)

> Great and marvellous are thy works,

---

31. Ware, *The Orthodox Church*, 204.

32. Vajta, *Die Theologie des Gottesdienstes bei Luther*, cited in Wainwright, *Doxology*, 242.

33. Westermeyer, *Te Deum*, 18.

> O Lord God Almighty;
> Righteous and true are thy ways,
> Thou king of the ages.
> Who shall not fear, O Lord, and glorify thy name?
> For thou only art holy;
> For all the nations shall come and worship before thee;
> For thy righteous acts have been made manifest.
> (Rev 15:3–4)[34]

These lines, according to Routley, "say mighty things in homely language and tell a great story in half a dozen words."[35] Such phrases met the need of the early church to express its experience, bind members to one another, and to engage them in a vehicle of worship. Pliny in 110 CE refers to Christians singing in worship. The words they sung summed up their faith; they codified doctrine, unified the church as the body of Christ, and glorified God.

During the Arian controversy, when the Arians were forbidden to hold public worship by Emperor Theodosius (ruled 378–396), they paraded defiantly through the streets singing hymns. John Chrysostom (c. 349–407), Archbishop of Constantinople, is said to have organized rival choral groups who competed for excellence in the expression of faith in song.

St. Ambrose, Bishop of Milan from 340 to 397 CE, is credited with originating the "office hymn." When it was clear that hymn-singing had come to stay as a feature of Christian practice, church leaders felt the need to have hymns appropriate for the various types of worship. It was Ambrose who composed the first hymns specifically for use at various stages, or "offices" of worship and their texts reflect key aspects of early Church faith and teaching.

> Creator of the earth and sky,
> Ruling the firmament on high,
> Clothing the day with robes of light,
> Blessing with gracious sleep the night.
>
> Day sinks; we thank thee for thy gift;
> Night comes; and once again we lift
> Our prayer and vows and hymns that we

---

34. Routley, *Hymns and Human Life*, 17.
35. Ibid.

## Doxology and Theology

Against all ills may shielded be.

Thee let the secret acclaim,
Thee let our rueful voices name,
Round thee our chaste affections cling,
Thee sober reason owns as king.

Pray we the Father and the Son,
And the Holy Ghost: O Three in One,
Blest Trinity, whom all obey,
Guard thou thy sheep by night and day.[36]

Augustine permitted music in the church, but with the restriction that the meaning of the words had to be paramount, not the singing.[37] In *Confessions*, he dwells on hymns and how "these sacred words stir my mind to greater religious fervor and kindle in me a more ardent flame of piety than they would if they were not sung."[38] He refers to the singing of songs in an "appropriate tune" as a moving experience and approves of the practice in church "in order that by indulging the ears weaker spirits may be inspired with feelings of devotion."[39] To Augustine, songs should be a vehicle of truth and he saw their value as a mode of instruction; but when singing lost that focus he regarded it as sinful.

This is an appropriate moment to bring in the hymnographer-theologian St. Ephraim the Syrian (c. 306–373 CE), considered the most influential of the Early Church Fathers of the Eastern and Western Syriac liturgical traditions. He is best known and admired for his theologically-based hymn cycles; from the eighth and ninth centuries onward, his hymns were included in the "vast festal hymnaries designed to cover the whole ecclesial year."[40] As Kathleen McVey notes in her biography of Ephraim, "the literary and hymnic forms that he used, some of which he may have invented, became the standard forms of subsequent Syriac literature and hymnography."[41]

Throughout the Middle Ages, hymn-singing was very much a part of the Mass, which in itself was the "great act of public worship." But in

---

36. Ibid., 21–22.
37. Westermeyer, *Te Deum*, 88.
38. Augustine, *Confessions*, 238.
39. Ibid., 239.
40. Ephraem, *Hymns on Paradise*, 34–35.
41. McVey, *Ephrem the Syrian*, 3.

## Songs as *Locus* for a Lay Theology

both the Mass and daily Offices[42] of the church, singing was performed by members of the monastic orders, rather than by lay congregation members. While monasteries were the basis for public devotion, the role of the laity in public acts of worship during this period was a passive one.

The 93 hymns composed by Peter Abelard (1079–1142 CE), come closest to the form of Christian hymnody as we know it, apart from Office hymns. Abelard wrote both words and music for use by the French abbess Heloise (c. 1100–1163/4 CE) in her convent.[43] A number of other groups and sects of the later Middle Ages also had their own hymns.

The history of hymnody often credits the Protestant Reformers for teaching Christian congregations to sing, but not all Reformers encouraged the use of vocal music. Westermeyer notes that "Luther recovered the congregation's singing, Zwingli denied it and Calvin restricted it."[44] In fact, Luther was very reluctant to discard the ceremony of the Roman Mass; as a musician, composer, and poet in his own right, he could not condone the exclusion of music from worship.[45] Luther himself perceived an affinity between song and theology in his writings. "It is clear," he wrote, "that the Devil, the author of all sad worries and restless confusion, flees from the voice of music in almost the same way as he flees from the Word of theology."[46] When worship and music combined, he believed the human spirit was "stirred more easily and more strongly."

In explaining Luther's position on music, Oskar Soehngen says,

> That music comes from the auricularia, i.e., from the sphere of the miraculous audible things—like the Gospel, that it is a unique gift of God's creation which comes to us in the same way the Word of God does, namely, mediated by the voice, that is a point Luther is lost in wonder again and again.[47]

For Luther, the theological reason for music's existence is that its very being is a gift to us from God. Hymns are music in words, thus music and the word of God are closely related in the act of singing. Luther also seems to regard sacred song as parallel to preaching, referring to singing

---

42. Short services of worship held throughout the day and evening, when scriptures were read, psalms recited and prayers offered.

43. Routley, *Hymns and Human Life*, 30.

44. Westermeyer, *Te Deum*, 141.

45. Routley, *Hymns and Human Life*, 34.

46. Oettinger, *Music as Propaganda*, 43.

47. Soehngen, "Fundamental Considerations," 15–16.

## Doxology and Theology

as the "Gospel preached through the medium of music."[48] Consequently, he encouraged the writing of vernacular hymns (in the language of the congregation, rather than Latin) so that members of the general public could meaningfully participate in worship. He put his own principles into practice by personally composing, translating, or adapting some two-dozen hymns.[49] In Luther's sacred songs we see a combination of "high" and "low" music, since both Gregorian chant and folk tunes influenced his congregational chorales. He was always emphatic, however, that the music used in worship be appropriate.

In the development of Lutheran church orders of service, one could find these hymns being used in place of the fixed parts (or "propers") of the Medieval service, as well as the variable psalmody of the traditional Catholic Mass. Luther himself saw the function of hymns as a means of transmitting Christian doctrine. Hymns were sung before and after the sermon, as well as often being used for sermon texts; in this way the laity was encouraged to reflect on their meaning.[50] Lutheran vernacular hymns become so popular that "there were more than two million hymnals, song sheets, and other hymn-related materials circulating in sixteenth century Germany."[51]

The origins of English hymnody[52] trace back to Benjamin Keach (1640–1704), but his hymns did not immediately find popularity and acceptance. Unlike Germany and much of Europe, there was no other source of vernacular hymns until Isaac Watts (1674–1748) came along a generation later to meet the musical needs of the faithful. As Westermeyer observes; "He did for the English-speaking world what Luther had for the German-speaking world two centuries earlier and what Ambrose had done for the Latin world twelve centuries before that."[53]

Watts, an independent pastor of Nonconformist religious background, is widely referred to as the "Father of English Hymnody." As a teenager, he disliked the metrical psalms sung in church and complained about them to his father, who responded by urging him to write his own sacred songs. The young Watts accepted the challenge and over his lifetime created some 750

---

48. Westermeyer, *Te Deum*, 146.
49. Brown, *Singing the Gospel*, 9.
50. Ibid., 11–12.
51. Ibid., 5.
52. Westermeyer refers to hymns as poetry sung in place of psalms (see *Te Deum*, 201).
53. Westermeyer, *Te Deum*, 201.

English hymns, hundreds of which are still in regular use. His first hymnal was published in 1705, when he was 31.

Watts' theological rationale for rejecting the exclusive singing of metrical psalms in worship was that "(w)hen Christ makes all things new, why must our praises remain in the old covenant?"[54] But while he objected to the lack of Christian gospel references in the Psalms, he still used material from psalmody in his own compositions. Like the rest of the Bible, Watts felt, Psalms were part of God's word to humanity and hymns were our word back to God. Being suitable to the times and experiences of Christians, they expressed the collective "sense and apprehensions" of God's "essential glories," and were offered in obedience to sing and give thanks in Christ's name (see Eph 5:19–20 and Col 3:16–17).[55]

After Watts, the Wesley brothers, John (1703–1791) and Charles (1707–1788), emerged as the prominent hymn composers of the English-speaking world. The Holy Club, organized by the Wesleys and a group of Oxford University friends, was their reaction to the church's sacramental neglect. Members of the Holy Club worshiped according to the Church of England's Book of Common Prayer and centered their lives on methodically following a disciplined routine of "study, sacramental recovery and serving the needy." While Charles Wesley drew his hymn texts primarily from the Bible, his brother John felt that the Book of Common Prayer spoke to him with "solid, scriptural and rational piety."[56] The Wesleys' dislike of formalism in worship gradually drew them away from the Church of England.

Teresa Berger points out that it is "this single book, the Bible, which grounds the Wesleyan (religious) poetical corpus . . . Methodist admirers of the Wesleys have sometimes taken solace in the notion that if one day the Bible should disappear, its text could nearly be completely reconstructed based on the Wesleyan deposit of hymns alone."[57] Those hymns in themselves collectively formed the theological declaration and faith statement of the English Christians who came to be called Methodists.

Isaac Watts' compositions were written for congregational use, while those by the Wesleys were meant not only for private devotions, but also for the huge open-air congregational revival meetings at which both brothers ministered. Routley refers to Watts as the father of liturgical hymns and

54. Routley, *Hymns and Human Life*, 63.
55. Westermeyer, *Te Deum*, 203–4.
56. Ibid., 207.
57. Berger, *Theology in Hymns?*, 100–101.

the Wesleys as fathers of the "enthusiastic" or devotional hymn.[58] After the Wesleys, John Newton (1725-1807) and William Cowper (1731-1800) continued the English tradition of congregational hymns, rather than hymns for personal devotion or mass gatherings. Though hymn-singing was still not officially sanctioned by the Church of England, compositions by Watts, the Wesleys, and others were being used more frequently by the eighteenth and early nineteenth centuries. Finally, in 1820 Archbishop Vernon Harcourt permitted the use of Thomas Cotterill's *Selection of Psalms and Hymns*, in Church of England worship.

The legalizing of hymn-singing for Book of Common Prayer services sparked an explosion of new hymnody composed by both clergy and laity. The first edition of *Hymns Ancient and Modern*, published in 1861, is seen as the apex of this movement. This hymnal was patterned after the sequence of worship familiar from the Book of Common Prayer, while at the same time serving as a resource for hymns appropriate to any saint's day or liturgical office. As Erik Routley notes, *Hymns Ancient and Modern* became "the most famous hymnal in the world, and its first edition, of 273 hymns . . . was the opening of a dynasty which is still in active operation and which made its latest contribution to hymnody as recently as 1980."[59]

## Hymns and Songs as Vehicles of Doctrine: *Locus Theologicus*

Moravian doctrine tends to be sung rather than spoken and this is even more applicable in the context of Indian Christianity. Indian author K.M. George, (citing A. Cherian in reference to Sadhu Kochukunju's songs), points out that these songs are "the matured fruit of deep spiritual experience. Hence it touches the heart, awakens noble thoughts. To the weak and sorrowing they bring comfort."[60] In this light, such sacred songs could be seen as the spontaneous overflow of powerful spiritual experiences, making the study of their doxological tradition crucial in understanding the theological articulation of the faithful, especially in contexts where (unlike Western tradition) confessions or catechisms are not the guiding factors. R.R. Sundara Rao notes that in the absence of any other theological

---

58. Routley, *Hymns and Human Life*, 74.
59. Routley, *Christian Hymns Observed*, 55.
60. George, *Sadhu Kochoonju*, 121.

## Songs as *Locus* for a Lay Theology

treatises it is sacred songs that are "indeed the main theological handbook of laymen and clergy alike" in the Indian context.[61]

Doxology is not only the believer's encounter with God through praise, but also a consequence of the encounter with truth, thus making the doxological tradition of sacred hymns and songs a *locus theologicus*, or source of theology. In *Spirituals and the Blues*, James Cone draws upon spirituals to articulate the theology of black slaves,[62] bringing a sociological paradigm into the exploration of song as *locus theologicus*.

This naturally raises the question of how to define theology itself. Definitions are frequently exclusionary and misleading, but are nevertheless important to attempt, as any study or investigation is impacted by one's pre-existing assumptions. The virtue of the definition process is to aid in revealing and clarifying those assumptions.

Theology has been variously defined, but generally understood as the critical reflection about God and human existence, about the nature of the universe and faith. It involves participation in and reflection on the religious faith that is the subject of study and the attempt to express that faith in the "clearest and most coherent language available."[63]

Both Leith and Macquarrie argue that theology, being "critical reflection," is distinct from prayer and faith. It is rather a reflection on how the church has understood faith in the past and how it experiences faith in the present. Macquarrie deviates from the traditional sources of theology and looks at its "formative factors," listing experience as primary among them. He explains that "theology implies participation in a religious faith, so that some experience of the life of faith precedes theology and may indeed be said to motivate it."[64] In the theological endeavor we try to make sense of our experience and give a clear expression to it.

Inasmuch as prayer and worship remain vital experiences within the church they are valid and legitimate sources of theology.[65] John Leith contrasts "academic theology" with this dependence of "Christian theol-

---

61. Rao, *Bhakti Theology*, 12.

62. Cone, *Spirituals and the Blues*.

63. Macquarrie, *Principles of Christian Theology*, 1. (See also Leith, *Basic Christian Doctrine*, 1.)

64. Macquarrie, *Principles of Christian Theology*, 5.

65. Macquarrie uses the term "formative factors" due to the many "disparate items," on the list. But as prayer and worship are expressions of our faith directed to God, I would contend that they are valid source for theologizing, even while submitting to Macquarrie's position.

ogy upon prayer, or on a community that prays, worships, and hence participates in the very subject matter of theology."[66] In contrast to a theology that rises from corporate worship, academic theology draws much of its vocabulary from non-ecclesial contexts which do not necessarily illuminate "worshipping communities."[67] Leith argues that Christian theology is that which emerges directly from believing communities; thus the expression of such a theology, unlike scholastic language, is "the language and idiom of the worshipping, believing congregation," which in turn is the language of scripture and prayer.[68]

An individual's faith-life experience develops through participating in a "community of faith" which helps its members meet a quest inherent in all human existence, or as Macquarrie puts it, "opening up of the dimension of the holy."[69] This approach keeps theology and theological language from becoming abstract and irrelevant to the given human context. He does warn against exaggerated emphasis on experience, however, because it can "easily become distorted" by particularities and therefore ought to be kept in "closest relation with other formative factors of a more objective kind." [70]

Theology articulated in this way is not merely speculation about God, but becomes part of a living relationship with God. As applied to hymns, it has been pointed out that they are to be concerned with "orthodoxy." This term not only refers to holding a right opinion about God, but also to rightly glorifying and worshiping God. In other words, it affirms that "I think, suppose, hold an opinion" and "I magnify, extol, praise and glorify." As one online source (unfortunately defunct since consultation) aptly put it: "Glorification of God is through our holiness of life, our orthopraxis, right practice, in effect—and that practice is indeed a reflexive practice, informed by theological thought and indeed doctrine, but a doctrine prayed and praised, lamented and celebrated, not just speculated."[71]

The role of hymns here is to bring together the thinking, feeling and willing elements of our response to God, for they are the "primary way that the liturgical year and the theological imagery are appropriated by

66. Kay, "Lex Orandi," 14.
67. Leith, *Christian Doctrine*, 7–8.
68. Kay, "Lex Orandi," 15.
69. Macquarrie, *Principles of Christian Theology*, 5.
70. Ibid., 6.
71. From an internet source (now offline) lacking an identified author: http://www.eamtc.cam.ac.uk/x/residentials/2004-05/sept2004/sept04-theolreflhymn.htm.

the laity."[72] In this context, they can be understood as doxological speech, speech directed to God. Both doxology (as expressed in liturgy and song) and theology (as expressed in doctrines), are statements of faith "that assume faithful response to the saving acts of God."[73] Both are systematic responses by the people of God to the same reality.

Another coming together of hymns and theology occurs where the singing of hymns is "connected to the believer's intention to enter into immediate relationship with God."[74] In worship one reaches out to God, who is immanent and transcendent in the totality of divine selfhood; thus it is music and song, more than secular colloquial speech, that encompass the total spiritual expression of human beings. And that encounter with the Divine is transformed into a *locus* for theological exploration, because it is also an encounter with truth.

In their book, *Sing With Understanding: An Introduction to Christian Hymnology*, Harry Eskew and Hugh T. McElrath, title the first section of chapter 4 "The Hymn—a Bearer of 'Grass-roots' Theology,"[75] reflecting that hymns are indeed the ordinary person's poetry and theology. While the recitation of creeds and confessions are important in corporate worship, it is hymns that consistently stand "as an alternative means of objectifying belief corporately," regardless of whether one belongs to a creedal and confessional tradition or not.

In these lines by Sadhu Kochukunju and Moshe Walsalam, written for Malayalee believers, one can feel the expression of their understanding around the death of Jesus Christ and how it emotionally affects them:

> *krushinmel, krushinmel, kaanunnadharidha,*
> *praana naadhan praana naadhan enperkai chaagunnu.*
>
> *aathmave paapathil kazhcha nii kaanuga,*
> *daivathin puthranii shaapathil aayallo.*
>
> On the cross, who is it that I see,
> the Lord of life dies for me.
> O, my soul in sin, see this sight,
> alas, the Son of God has gotten into this curse.

---

72. Ramshaw, *Words That Sing*, 3.
73. Berger, *Theology in Hymns?*, 171.
74. Soehngen, *Music and Theology*, 8.
75. Eskew and McElrath, *Sing With Understanding*, 59.

*vannen kalvary kurishadhin arige,*
*nookki ninnen en papa bali aayavane.*

*enne pradhi murinja kaalkarangal,*
*ksheenam eere sahicha thiru aruma jadam,*
*thannil thanne vyasanam adakkiyadhum,*
*pranan thaanaayi vitta diyya nilayeyum njan kandu.*

I came near the cross
and I gazed at the one who became the sacrifice for my sin.
I saw the hands and legs wounded for me,
the holy body that was greatly tired,
he kept his sorrow to himself,
and let go of his life by himself.

## Bhakti Tradition: The Use of Sacred Hymns and Songs as Locus Theologicus in the Indian Context

In the Indian context, the *bhakti* tradition references or privileges song as the medium for articulating and expressing the faith experience of the *bhaktas*, thereby making sacred song and hymnody the doxological element of their *locus theologicus*. In India, *bhakti* tradition originated in pre-Christian times, but it was the *nayanars* and *alwars* of the south who popularized the movement's devotional songs to convey their spiritual messages. An important feature of this movement was the frequent use of local vernacular texts rather than the traditional Sanskrit. As noted in the previous chapter, not all the poet-singers who created these songs were learned in Sanskrit, a language typically reserved for the upper castes.

*Bhakti* is generally seen as expressing personal faith in a personal God; loving God as one would love a human being; dedicating everything in one's life to the service of God; being continually in God's presence and enjoying God. The *bhakti* movement that initially found expression in *alwar* songs of the ninth and tenth centuries CE, is referred to in Ramanuja's twelfth-century-CE theistic exposition of Hinduism, a constructive and elaborate formulation of doctrine.

Hinduism, the majority religion of India, is generally agreed to have originated with the ancient Aryans who migrated to that part of the world

## Songs as *Locus* for a Lay Theology

in antiquity,[76] around 3000 BCE. The primary records of Hinduism's development are found in the *Vedas* and *Upanishads*, the holy scriptures of the faith. The *Ramayana* and *Mahabharata* form the latter sections; the *Bhagavad Gita*, the most popular text governing the spirituality of ordinary people, forms the last chapter of the *Mahabharata*. Later clarifications of the *Bhagavad Gita*, called the *Bhagvata puranas*, were written between 400 and 900 CE and are also considered sacred.

The root word of *bhakti* is the Sanskrit[77] *bhaj* which can be translated as meaning to serve, honor, love, share, revere, and adore.[78] Chhaganlal Lala elaborates, noting that "etymologically, the word '*bhakti*' is derived from the Sanskrit root '*bhaj*' with suffix '*ktim*'. It means service, devotion, attachment, loyalty, worship or homage. It includes entire submission to the Lord in word, mind and body."[79] In common usage today, *bhakti* has retained the meaning of loving adoration and devotion to one's personal god, the *ishtadevata*. Sundara Rao points out that no single English word adequately describes *bhakti* because "it is participating in the whole process of sharing with God, His divinity, His bliss and His grace. It expresses an unquestionable trust and a loving relationship to a personal god."[80] G. M. Tripathi further describes *bhakti* as meaning "standing in the presence of God, serving Him, loving Him, hearing Him and in fact enjoying the deity."[81]

In a religious sense it could be used to mean not only loving devotion to a personal God, but also supreme human love directed to God. L.J. Sedgwick describes *bhakti* in an even more encompassing and nuanced fashion, as a "personal faith in a personal God, love for Him as for a human being, the dedication of everything to his service, and attainment of *moksha*, final bliss—by this means rather than by knowledge, or sacrifice or works."[82] His definition gives primacy to *bhakti marga* over *jnana marga* and *karma marga* as means of attaining *moksha*.[83]

---

76. Hindu nationalists would now contest the theory that the ancient Aryans, who comprise the higher castes, were once foreign to the land.

77. Sanskrit is the sacred language of the Hindus, the language in which Hindu scriptures were written.

78. Williams, *Sanskrit-English Dictionary*, 743.

79. Lala, *Bhakti in Religions of the World*, 148.

80. Rao, *Bhakti Theology*, 20.

81. Tripathi, *Classical Poets of Gujarat*, 11.

82. L. J. Sedgwick, "Bhakti," cited in Rao, *Bhakti Theology*, 22.

83. Hindu tradition has three ways to attain *moksha*: *jnana* or knowledge, *karma* or

## Doxology and Theology

*Bhakti marga* is the most popular doctrine among Hindus; unlike *jnana marga* and *karma marga*, *bhakti marga* is primarily about the inner self, rather than outward observation or changes in lifestyle. It allows the believer to lead a normal life and still be absorbed in the bliss of the divine, providing what one "has to do ... to create an *alaukika*, non-worldly, atmosphere wherever he is,"[84] and enjoy the deity. Though the *bhakti* movement emerged with the *alwars* and *nayanars*, whose origins date from the fourth century CE, traces of the *bhakti* concept have been found in earlier scriptures and traditions of southern India.

Appasamy traces the origins of *bhakti* to the Upanishads though the Rig Veda, referring to the love of God in passages such as: "Dyaus is my father," and "Aditi (the boundless) is father, mother and son."[85] Thirugnanasambandham argues that "the concept of *bakthi* is as ancient as the Rig Veda."[86]

Appasamy attributes to the later *Upanishads*, *Katha Upanishad* and *Svetasvatra Upanishad*, references to belief in a personal god who may be worshipped. The *Katha Upanishad* is believed to have been written between 500 and 300 BCE, and the *Svetasvatra Upanishad* between 250 and 200 BCE. The story of Naciketas and Yama in the *Katha Upanishad* indirectly points to the concept in Yama's answer to Naciketas' question; "What happens after death?" In the later-written *Svetasvatra Upanishad* one finds the term *bhakti* being used to refer to "the attitude of devotion and surrender to God."[87]

Although the exact origin of the *bhakti* concept is still widely and diversely debated, most would agree that the concept gained greatest eminence and popularity with the writing of the *Bhagavad Gita*, the last section of the *Mahabharata*. It is presented as a conversation between Krishna, an *avatar*[88] of Vishnu and Arjuna, one of five princes at war with their cousins. When Arjuna indicates he does not want to fight his cousins, Krishna reminds Arjuna (who is his devotee) to stand up for what is right; then Krishna goes on to explain the relationship of a devotée with the Divine and of the Divine with the devotée. The sole motive for one's actions should be to please and benefit the Divine, not oneself. In response, the Divine manifests graciousness in relating with the devotée and adding to the de-

---

works, and *bhakti* or personal devotion.

84. Rao, *Bhakti Theology*, 23.
85. Rig Veda 1.164.33 and 1.89.10, cited in Appasamy, *Theology of Hindu Bhakti*, 17.
86. Thirugnanasambandham, *Concept of Bhakti*, 3.
87. Appasamy, *Theology of Hindu Bhakti*, 21.
88. Translated as "incarnation."

votée's joy and bliss. Here, the Divine is seen as an intimate friend whose presence is real.

Appasamy points out the three important marks of the *bhakti* movement found in the *Bhagavad Gita*. First, the Absolute is identified with Vishnu; second, one who has seen Krishna has seen the Absolute; third, the way of devotion to Krishna is emphasized.[89]

Buddhism and Jainism emerged after the fifth century CE, both as offshoots of Hinduism; many argue that they originated as protest movements within Hinduism against *Brahminic* religious practices and caste structure. Buddhism and Jainism flourished in South India and one of the main reasons for the popular spread of *bhakti* was the abhorrence of these upstart religions, both their political and religious hegemony. R.C. Zaehner also suggests that the ossified ceremonial religion of the *Brahmins* was another reason for the spread of the *bhakti* movement.[90]

The reign of the Kalabhras, between the sixth and ninth centuries CE, was a time when both Buddhism and Jainism, formerly considered heretical religions, received royal patronage and consequently attained greater prestige and influence. Appasamy notes that both Buddhism and Jainism were present in South India at the beginning of the Christian era and had peacefully co-existed for centuries with the local religions. But the rise of the Kalabhras and their concerted efforts to spread the two newer faiths made a response from the Hindus inevitable.[91] Stephen Neil points out that their very existence was now threatened.[92]

Buddhism and Jainism became unacceptable because both denied the existence of God as well as the Vedas, the holy scripture of the people. Additionally, the Jains were rejected due to their opposition to art and disrespect of women, among other points of contention. The growth of the popular *bhakti* movement served to curtail Buddhism and Jainism and in turn paved a way for the rejuvenation and resurgence of Hinduism across the southern Indian sub-continent.

As mentioned previously, the two *bhakti* traditions were those of the *alwars* and *nayanars*. *Alwars* were Vaishnavites, whose supreme deity was Vishnu. According to Robertson, N. Subbu Reddiar identified the etymology of the word *alwar* as deriving from a root with multiple but similar

---

89. Appasamy, *Theology of Hindu Bhakti*, 29.
90. Zaehner, *Hinduism*, 131.
91. Appasamy, *Theology of Hindu Bhakti*, 37. (See also Robertson, *Bhakti Tradition*, 24.)
92. Neil, *Bhakti*, 54.

## Doxology and Theology

meanings, including: "one who is plunged in God-enjoyment, or a diver in divinity,"[93] one who has experienced a "deep plunge into the ocean of divine consciousness,"[94] or someone wholly immersed in "the beauty and glory of his Lord." Robertson also offers other definitions of *alwar* as meaning "drowned in God-love," "Sunk in deep ecstasy," or "Lovers of God by God's grace" and so on. "In general," he writes, "*alwar* is the one who has gone deep into inseparable God realization."[95] *Alwars* were so immersed in the Divine that their lives were a ceaseless stream of Divine communion and their hearts were the dwelling-place of Narayana, the Divine. "Their passion poured itself into torrents of Love at the feet of Narayana. Their eyes saw everywhere, in all, in every event Narayana. Their hands worshipped Narayana with pure flowers. Their soul was wedded to Narayana. Their life was the breath of Narayana."[96]

It is generally believed that there were 12 original *alwars*, itinerant saints and torch-bearers devoted to renewal of the Vaishnava faith in the face of Buddhist and Jainist ascendancy. They came from various castes, including seven *brahmins*, one *kshatriya*, two *sudras* and one outcaste (untouchable); at least one was a woman.

They were poets of deep faith and intense religious commitment. Appasamy points out that they "were fervent *bhaktas* who were immersed in the love and knowledge of God and who poured forth the rapture of their experience in songs which have come down to us as an essential part of Tamil literature."[97] He goes on note that they were poets whose hymns "reflect the various moods through which they pass" in their experience of the Divine. "They have ineffable glimpses of God which stir in them lofty emotions. While they do not seek to construct a system of religious philosophy, certain theological ideas are necessarily implied in their hymns."[98]

*Alwar* compositions were entirely in Tamil, as Kerala was still part of Tamilakam. At the time, Malayalam was only in the process of evolving into a separate language. In his book *A History of Indian Philosophy* (Vol. 3), Surendranath Dasgupta refers to two *alwars* having been born in Periyar, which would now be a Malayalam-speaking area. Chapter 1 referred to the Chera

---

93. Robertson, *Bhakti Tradition*, 78.
94. Bharathi, *Alvar Saints*, 2.
95. Robertson, *Bhakti Tradition*, 78.
96. Bharathi, *Alvar Saints*, 3.
97. Appasamy, *Theology of Hindu Bhakti*, 29.
98. Ibid., 30.

King, Kulashekara Varman, who was also known as Kulashekara Alwar and ruled over what became Malayalam-speaking areas.

The main corpus of *alwar* hymns is called *nalayira prabandham*, or A Collection of Four Thousand, and its contents are widely used to this day by the Vaishnavas in temple worship and other occasions all over South India. Appasamy cites comments on these hymns by a Mr. Hooper:

> A yearning after the divine fellowship stands out as the chief characteristic, in comparison with this, the best that the world can offer is valueless: wealth, sensual indulgence, the exercise of kingly authority, the bliss of svarga itself, are all treated with contempt. It is not a vague absorption into the divine essence that is here desired; it is a personal relationship, illustrated largely by the relationship between a man and the woman he loves. The object of man's love is not a neutral abstraction but Vishnu, Narayana above all.[99]

The following verse from a hymn by Kulashekara Alwar illustrates this undying love of God which Vaishnavas believed was the sole source of alleviating the miseries of earthly existence.

> Though thou wilt not remove my woe,
> My heart melts not save at thy boundless love.
> Thy servant more and more wilt set my mind on thee,
> Though thou wilt not remove my human misery.[100]

Studies of *alwar* poems suggest that they reflect Vedantic philosophy but explain it in personal, intimate terms. A significant feature of the movement was its absence of caste structure, since the *alwars* themselves came from various castes, and one had no caste at all. Rao emphasizes that this was a marked difference between the *bhakti* movements in the South and North.[101] Historically, where Malayalam came to be spoken, the *brahmins* had been in power since the ninth century CE and caste was rigidly entrenched and observed in those areas.[102]

Another facet of the *bhakti* movement was the de-Sanskritization of hymns and other literary materials. As noted earlier, until then all religious texts were in Sanskrit, and temple worship was also conducted in that upper-caste language. During the early tenth century CE, the Vaishnava

---

99. Ibid., 37.
100. Varadachari, *Alvars of South India*, 72.
101. Rao, *Bhakti Theology*, 26.
102. See chapter 1.

*acarya* (religious teacher, instructor or mentor) Nathamuni founded the first school to use both Tamil and Sanskrit. Farquhar notes that Nathamuni also began using the *nalayira prabandham* hymn collection in his school.[103] Such initiatives further popularized the *bhakti* movement, giving more non-*brahmins* opportunities for education and leadership. De-Sanskritization increased inclusivity, allowing those from other castes to be part of the movement at all levels.

In the foreword to S. M. Srinivasachari's *Philosophy and Theistic Mysticism of the Alvars*, S. K. Ramachandra Rao writes: "Alwars not only heralded a significant movement of devotion but prepared the ground for a great philosophical system, later crystallized by the eminent Acaryas, Nathamuni, Yamuna and Ramanuja."[104] The evolution of devotional literature as a religious literary genre was another result of the *alwar bhakti* movement.[105]

Just as the *alwars* led the *bhakti* movement among the Vaishnavites, the *nayanars* fulfilled the same role for followers of Siva. From the sixth through eighth centuries CE, the *nayanars* were active in the revival of Hinduism in order to ward off the perceived threat of Buddhism and Jainism. Hymn-singing was also a feature of their movement that kindled followers' enthusiasm and passion. Of the reputed 103,000 *nayanar* hymns once in circulation, only 795 remain. Appasamy comments that "The earnestness of the Nayanars, the sweet and melodious hymns they sang, the gift of healing they exercised, the zeal with which they practiced and propagated their religion, brought about new life to Hinduism."[106] Like the *alwars*, the itinerant *nayanar* saints traveled all over Tamilakam, visiting religious shrines and singing devotional songs.

Among the most distinguished *nayanar* saints are Appar, Jnanasambandar, Sundarar and Manikkavacakar. One of Appar's verses, quoted by Appasamy, gives an insight into the saint's faith and his experience of being freed from fear:

> Bound to no man are we,
> Death hath no terror for us,
> nor can the horrid hell hold us
> We are free from fear set free,

---

103. Farquhar, *Outline of the Religious Literature in India*, 241.

104. Ramachandra Rao, cited in Srinivasachari, *Philosophy and Theistic Mysticism of the Alvars*, ix.

105. Robertson, *Bhakti Tradition*, 92.

106. Appasamy, *Theology of Hindu Bhakti*, 38.

and we shall hold our head high.
Illness and pain shall be alien to us.
We shall forever dwell in joy, and
feel sorrow no more.
( . . . )
His glorious feet, soft like gathered
flowers, we have come unto,
as our sole refuge.[107]

Manikkavacakar, a ninth-century-CE Tamil poet and hymn-writer, lived just after the rise of Shankara (788–820 CE), the great Indian philosopher whose *Advaita Vedanta* would soon gain prominence among the intelligentsia over all other interpretations of the Hindu faith. Although accomplished in many fields, Manikkavacakar disagreed with Shankara's concept of identifying oneself with the Ultimate Reality.[108] He chose instead to submit to the grace and mercy of a personal God. Manikkavacakar's songs are collected in the *tiruvachagam*.[109]

The *nayanars* also used the local language of Tamil and like the *alwars*, their movement was devoid of caste; in the later Malayalam-speaking areas, however, it has been pointed out that caste and Sanskritic brahmanism had not yet become socially established.

## An Indian Christian Interpretation of Ramanuja's Explication of Bhakti: Appasamy

In the development and formulation of the doctrine of *bhakti*, the Hindu theologian Ramanuja (1017–1137 CE) occupies a prime position. While the ancient concept of *bhakti* unfolded and flowered through hymns and legends of the *alwars* and *nayanars*, it is through Ramanuja that one first sees an articulation of the doctrine that embraces "fully all the philosophical implications of *bhakti*."[110] Ramanuja constructed an elaborate philosophical system expounding upon the themes of God, humanity, *bhakti* and *moksha*.

---

107. Ibid., 39.
108. Shankara's *Advaita Vedanta* was monistic and had no place for a personal god.
109. *Tiruvachagam* could be translated as "divine words."
110. Appasamy, *Theology of Hindu Bhakti*, 44.

## Doxology and Theology

Ramanuja emerged after Shankara's *Advaita Vedanta* had achieved renown and eminence.[111] Shankara taught that God was to be seen as absolute and without attributes. Even where Brahman was spoken of as having attributes, this was explained away as *maya*,[112] which collided head-on with the *bhakti* concept of a personal god and the call for believers to have an intimate relationship with Narayana. Ramanuja countered this discord with the understanding that God was specifically endowed with the attributes of power, knowledge, love and bliss. To Ramanuja, it was through absolute *bhakti* (submission) to this personal God that one received salvation and that even at the highest stage of spiritual existence one continued to derive bliss in relationship with the Ultimate. To Shankara, salvation was the realization that a person was one with the Ultimate.

Aiyadurai Jesudasen Appasamy (1891–1975) an early twentieth-century Indian theologian whose work has been previously cited in this chapter, explored the concept of *bhakti* from a Christian perspective. He was Bishop of the Coimbatore Diocese of the Church of South India and his interest led him to study Ramanuja and his philosophical system. Appasamy was convinced that there was much of value in the pre-Christian spirituality of India and felt that Indian Christians should claim the best of this heritage.[113] He was especially drawn to the Hindu *bhakti* poets' devotion to a personal god of love and grace and their intense longing for communion with the Divine. Appasamy was convinced that the *bhakti* movement, from among other Indian traditions, had the closest "affinities with Christianity and could surely be used as a way leading to a fuller Indian understanding of the Christian faith."[114]

In his book *The Theology of Hindu Bhakti*, Appasamy highlights the characteristics of the movement as seen in Ramanuja's interpretation, examining his description of *bhakti* as a meditative state requiring moral preparation, bliss, and exclusivity.

---

111. Shankara lived during in the eighth century CE and Ramanuja during the twelfth century CE.

112. *Maya* could be translated as "illusion."

113. Mathai, "Indian Interpretations," 75.

114. Ibid., 72.

## Meditation

*Bhakti* is primarily a continuous reflection on God. In explaining Ramanuja's phrase, "Meditation is in the form of continuous recollection uninterrupted like the flow of oil,"[115] Appasamy argues that final freedom, according to the scriptures, is only possible through meditation. He goes on to compare such contemplation as being similar to visioning, or *darsana*. "When He, who is Supreme, is seen, the knot in the heart breaks, all doubts shatter and deeds perish."[116] It is only through the practice of constant, continuous meditation that the *bhakta* is able to attain this spiritual goal. Through meditation, one attains knowledge, a concept which parallels the priority of *lex orandi* over *lex credendi*: right worship and right prayer lead to right knowledge and doctrine. Thus for Ramanuja, *bhakti* and the inner self have priority over *jnana*, or intellect and knowledge.

As both meditation and *bhakti* involve continuous recollection of the Deity, leading to an ability to see the Divine, Appasamy explains that, "being like a vision means that the object becomes present to the eyes (*pratyaksha*) . . . This soul cannot be attained by teaching or by knowledge or by much hearing. Whom he chooses, only he can attain him; only to him, this soul manifests His own form."[117]

Thus love for the Supreme is the determinant for having a vision of the Divine, "(t)o those who worship me from love with the desire to be united always with me I grant that measure of understanding, by which they reach me."[118] Here, love is seen as the most important factor in the vision and attainment of God. Appasamy emphasizes that to Ramanuja, the contemplative life was not a vague or confused reality. His knowledge of God is as emphatic as if he had seen the Divine in a vision.[119] Appasamy understands Ramanuja's spiritual perception as being clear and luminous as a vision. Contemplation of God takes one to a point where one experiences the Divine, not as transcendent but as immanent, one who dwells within. "God is very close to us," Appasamy asserts. "He is not an inaccessible, far-off Being, dwelling in remote heavens. His presence is everywhere; as Spirit He pervades the whole universe . . . Not a moment passes but his presence

---

115. In Appasamy, *Theology of Hindu Bhakti*, 72.
116. Ibid., 73.
117. Ibid.
118. Ibid.
119. Ibid., 74.

envelopes us like the air we live in ... If we go in search of Him only outside of ourselves, it will be but wasted labour."[120]

In terms of how to meditate, a *bhakta* is to contemplate the Supreme Soul as if it were one's own soul. As Ramanuja explains, one "who dwells in the soul and is its inner being, whom the soul does not know, whose body the soul is, who controls the soul from within, He is thy soul, the inner ruler and the immortal one." In his book *Christianity as Bhakti Marga*, Appasamy discusses Ramanuja's disciple, Ranga Ramanuja, and his commentary on the *Taittiriya Upanishads*, emphasizing that the Supreme One can be known only in the heart of the world.[121]

Contemplation and meditation are not to be periodic or temporary exercises; rather, our desire ought to be to dwell in the presence of God throughout each day of our lives. The Supreme reality must always pervade our soul.

Appasamy emphasizes that Ramanuja's understanding of divine meditation is about being infused by a deep love for God, where the *bhakta* "lovingly and constantly" dwells on God's excellent qualities. Such a discipline is not the consequence of any pressure or coercion upon the devotee, but comes from the *bhakta's* sheer love for God. "He loves God in and for Himself, not for any wonderful gifts He may give, such as health, knowledge, money or even immortality."[122]

## Moral Preparation

Ramanuja's next focus, according to Appasamy, was on one's moral preparation for the state of *bhakti*. He lists seven prerequisite virtues: "Meditation becomes possible only when there are 1. clearness, 2. freedom, 3. practice, 4. action, 5. goodness, 6. absence of dejection and 7. absence of rapture."[123] Elaborating on these virtues, they also include: purity of body; detachment from desires; frequent execution of the meditation practice; doing righteous actions; being truthful; being straightforward; being merciful; being generous; and not coveting.

Ramanuja emphasizes the obligation of moral duties due to the traditional Indian cultural understanding of *karma*. One's *karma*, whether

---

120. Appasamy, *The Gospel and India's Heritage*, 76.
121. Appasamy, *Christianity as Bhakti Marga*, 41.
122. Appasamy, *Theology of Hindu Bhakti*, 77.
123. Ibid.

good or bad, continuously follows the soul through a potentially infinite cycle of births and deaths. Brahman decrees that people are to be born into certain lives and circumstances, according to the *karma* of their souls. Consequently, Appasamy notes, "(n)ot only do their karmas determine men's births but also, if they are evil, they prevent the birth of the knowledge or love of Brahman, both love and knowledge being considered the same by Ramanuja."[124]

Ramanuja demanded moral uprightness from the *bhaktas*, yet sinful deeds are bound to be met on the way to enlightenment. Thus Ramanuja introduces the concept of *nishkamyakarma*, or doing deeds without the desire for reward. Rather, works must be done because they are ordained by God and because God, being full of love, knows what is right and proper for us. We are called to faithfully perform work, regardless of our inner feelings, whether they are of joy or grief.

### Bliss

Ramanuja teaches that continuous recollection of God brings joy to the point of bliss, or *moksha*, the result of the *bhakta's* attainment of the Divine. The "Supreme Soul itself is bliss," and the attainment of the Supreme One brings the believer into a state of bliss.

> The Supreme Soul is the abode of unsurpassable and innumerable good qualities. Without any blemish, possessed of unlimited precious sovereignty, He is the ocean of supreme kindness, beauty and love. He himself is universal Lord, with the individual soul as His subject. On the realization by the individual soul of this mutual relationship the Supreme Soul becomes an object of extreme love and Himself leads the individual soul to reach Itself.[125]

This realization of the individual soul's mutual relationship with the Supreme Soul leads to extreme love and joy, in which the *bhakta* considers the Lord as a friend in whom all trust and loyalty can be placed.

In his book *What is Moksha?* Appasamy defines the term as: ". . . a continuous contact with Reality, personal, conscious and radiant with joy. It is like the life of Jesus with God. It is not the realization of identity but

---

124. Ibid., 78.
125. In Appasamy, *Theology of Hindu Bhakti*, 81.

the experience of a moral harmony with the Holy and righteous Father."[126] Bliss is seen as the "harmony of the individual soul with the Divine Soul in thought and imagination, in purpose and will, in humble deed and adoring devotion."[127]

Appasamy points out that to Ramanuja, religion is primarily a joyous experience and that one who has attained bliss, or *moksha*, is a "well of joy continually bubbling with a fresh and ever new supply . . . (Ramanuja's) life in God meant a constant joy to him and he dwelt in the bliss that this life gave."[128] He continues:

> We have a constant reiteration in the traditional lives of Ramanuja, which have come down to us that he was steeped in the Tamil Vaishnava hymns of the Alvars. There is no reason why this fact should be doubted. It is a quite interesting fact that a deeply intellectual man like Ramanuja who lived so fully the life of thought and philosophy should have drawn so much of his inspiration from these hymns. We have in the hymns of the Alwars a remarkable outpouring of poetical sentiment, expressing in striking image and picturesque phrase the joy and reality of a life lived in God.

Appasamy emphasizes that the hymns of the *alwars* were the source and inspiration of Ramanuja's own religious philosophy. His concept of bliss was not about frenzy or ecstasy, as some popular religious expressions have come to be. Conversely, Ramanuja's "love for God was balanced by his profound exercise of his intellectual faculties."[129]

### *Bhakti as Exclusive*

Ramanuja explains exclusiveness in terms of the object of one's adoration and its purpose. *Bhaktas* are to adore (worship) God with the sole purpose of pleasing God. From time immemorial, prayer has been enacted mainly for the purpose of achieving temporal blessing. Ramanuja quotes from the *Gita Bhashya* to explain the exclusive character of *bhakti*. "The righteous men who worship me, O Arjuna, are of four kinds—those who, having lost their possessions, desire to have them again; those who desire to attain

---

126. Appasamy, *What Is Moksha?*, 6.
127. Ibid., 68.
128. Appasamy, *Theology of Hindu Bhakti*, 82.
129. Ibid.,

knowledge; those who desire to obtain the wealth which they do not possess; and those who possess knowledge."[130]

Ramanuja points out that the first and third groups could be considered the same because both of them want worldly goods. The second group is comprised of those who desire to become their real selves through attaining knowledge. Here Ramanuja seems to be countering adherents of Shankara's philosophy. But he notes that it is the fourth group of people who know that their true purpose consists in service to the Lord. "Not satisfied with the mere enjoyment of his soul, even though it is separated from the body (the fourth kind of righteous man) . . . decides to attain the Lord, convinced that the Lord alone is his great goal."[131]

The *bhakti* tradition, more than any other on the Indian subcontinent, used the medium of song as a primary expression of faith. In reference to early *bhakti* movements surveyed in chapter 1, it was observed that *bhajans* (free-form devotional songs) were the primary mode of religious expressions of faith, the *locus* of their own theology. As Appasamy rightly points out, the songs of the *alwars* were the foundation of Ramanuja's theological structure.

---

130. Bhagavad Gita vii. 5 in Appasamy, *Theology of Hindu Bhakti*, 86.
131. Appasamy, *Theology of Hindu Bhakti*, 86.

# Chapter 3

## Moshe Walsalam (1847–1916)

ARULANANDAM, MOSHE WALSALAM'S FATHER, was a second-generation Christian, whose parents had converted from Hinduism and were members of the Catholic Church. He was influenced by LMS missionaries with whom he came to contact while teaching at a Christian school near his home.[1] Although he also began his career as a teacher, Walsalam later went on to become an evangelist.

Arulanandam was also an evangelist, as well as being very active in the leadership of social justice movements among his people, such as the movement against *uzhiyam*[2] (enforced servitude). In 1850, he came into conflict for objecting to the illegal upper caste practice of having Christians do *uzhiyam* on Sundays. This incident is recorded in J.W. Gladstone's and Mrs. Arthur Parker's biographies of Walsalam,[3] where Arulanandam suffered the physical torture of having his beard pulled out for his activism. John Cox, a local missionary, successfully intervened on behalf of Arulanandam and the Christians. Not only were the perpetrators of the anti-Christian violence punished, but the upper castes' violation of laws preventing *uzhiyam* ceased and this led to a complete eradication of the practice later on.[4]

1. Arulanandam was earlier named Anthony and received his new name when he became a Protestant. *Nadar* caste converts to Christianity normally took on a new biblical or English single name; as there was no practice of having a family name, one's given name came after the father's name. Samuel Mateer first encouraged *Nadar* Christians to adopt family names and suggested meaningful Sanskrit names for this purpose. Walsalam was the name Mateer suggested to Moses (or Moshe) as his family name. See Gladstone, *Moshe Walsalam Sastrigal*, 38–39.

2. Enforced servitude to upper castes, government, or other authorities (See chapter 1).

3. Parker, *Bharathiya Christu Bhakthar*.

4. Gladstone, *Moshe Walsalam Sastrigal*, 27.

In 1855 Arulanandam undertook an evangelistic preaching tour among the St. Thomas Christians to the north and continued his teaching and evangelism on his return to South Travancore.[5]

## Birth

Moshe Walsalam was born to Arulanandam and his wife in 1847 at Trivandrum. When he was three months old, they brought him to missionary John Cox, who took the child in his arms, blessed him, and named him Moses, praying that just like Moses of the Old Testament, he would grow up to be a servant of God.[6] In 1883, at the age of 36, he received the additional name *sastrigal* from Mar Dionysius, Metropolitan of the Orthodox Church, after he heard Walsalam at a concert in Alleppy and recognized his excellence in music. Dionysius issued a circular on February 9, 1883 to this effect; thereafter he would be known as Moshe Walsalam Sastrigal.[7]

## Early Life

From an early age Moshe showed special aptitude for learning languages and music. As a young child he'd already mastered Malayalam and Tamil and began studying Sanskrit by the age of 10. At 13, he was learning English under Metropolitan Mar Athanasius, a reform leader in the Orthodox Church, while his father taught at the Syrian Christian seminary.[8] At 15 he was enrolled at the seminary in Nagercoil run by LMS missionaries. Besides theology, he studied Greek, Latin and Hebrew, and also learned to sing Tamil songs.

---

5. Many from regions that were once part of the old Travancore Kingdom still refer to those areas as North, Central and South Travancore.

6. Parker, *Bharathiya Christu Bhakthar*, 79. ("Moshe" is Malayalam for "Moses.")

7. The Malayalam term *Sastrigal* refers to one who is learned and expert in a particular area or skill. Dionysius' circular and its translation are in the archives of Kerala United Theological College, Kannanmoola, Thiruvanandapuram, Kerala, India.

8. Jose, "Dakshinendhyan." St. Thomas Christians are also referred to as Syrian Christians because of their historic connections with Syria.

In 1868 he married Rahel from the Manaveli family of Nellikkakuzhy. In his diary he wrote: "My prayer when I tied the *thali*[9] was that God would make our lives peaceful. God has answered this prayer."[10]

## Moshe Walsalam as Composer and Evangelist

Like his father, Moshe Walsalam became an educator and thanks to his skill in languages, he was invited to teach for a brief period at the Orthodox Seminary in Kottayam. He also taught at the LMS school in Neyyattinkkara and while there continued his musical training and learned to play the violin. During this period he also studied poetry in various languages.

His meeting in 1872 with the son of renowned Tamil Christian poet and song-writer Vedanayagam Sastriyar inspired Walsalam to use the medium of music in his ministry.[11] He was convinced that the appropriate use of songs was an ideal vehicle for spreading the gospel. To this end, he composed many songs based on biblical stories and set them to traditional classical Indian melodies, presenting them in *kathakalashepam*[12] performances that were well accepted.

Samuel Mateer, another LMS missionary, arranged for Moshe to receive further training in classical music and appointed him to work in the mission office at Trivandrum. During his stay at Trivandrum, he formed a musical ensemble that toured throughout the LMS mission areas and beyond, holding *kathakalashepam*s and gospel meetings that included slide shows using transparencies that he'd painted himself. He ministered to fellow Christians and also evangelized among people of other faiths. Walsalam was aided in his travels thanks to a Scottish woman who'd heard of his work and presented him with a bullock cart to make transportation easier. The "gospel cart" soon became his travelling trademark.

Moshe Walsalam's growing acceptance as an evangelizing musician is reflected in multiple performing invitations received from the Syrian

---

9. The *thali* is a gold pendant tied around the bride's neck during the marriage ceremony, a cultural practice adopted by many Indian Christians, especially in the South.

10. In Parker, *Bharathiya Christu Bhakthar*, 81, and Gladstone, *Moshe Walsalam Sastrigal*, 32.

11. Gladstone mentions that Walsalam met the Tamil poet Vedanayagam Sastriyar (who died in 1864), but Jose corrects the record to note he actually met Vedanayagam's son.

12. *Kathaprasangam* is performed by an artist using both storytelling and song, while the older form of *kathakalashepam* is a classical Indian vocal performance based on a theme.

Christian bishops, the Roman Catholic Archbishop of Varapuzha, and even the royal family of Mavelikara.

He was also given responsibility for a mission publishing agency that produced Christian books and tracts; he wrote many of these himself, as well as a book entitled *kristhu charithram*.[13] By the end of the 1880s Walsalam was a widely respected writer, musician and preacher. But he also aspired to serve in a congregation, so in 1891 he was appointed as a lay worker for Kattakkada Parish.

In a context rife with animosity among competing castes and religions, Moshe Walsalam succeeded in achieving communal harmony. A social activist like his father, he led the movement to obtain land for impoverished lower caste people; many of the landless poor came to own lands as a result. During his five years at Kattakkada, the parish grew significantly and prospered. On his return to Trivandrum, Walsalam was entrusted with the revision of the hymnal used for local worship, which was published in 1906.[14] Another of his responsibilities was to write a book (which does not seem to be extant) for Western-educated readers explaining classical Indian music and ragas.

From 1913 onward, Walsalam was afflicted with rheumatism and arthritis. When he could no longer move his right hand, he used his left to write with and later dictated songs and tunes that his children and grandchildren transcribed for him, thus preserving his legacy. Moshe Walsalam died on February, 20, 1916. Missionary Arthur Parker eulogized him in a few eloquent words: "The saying 'though dead he still speaks' will be true of [Moshe] for many more years."[15]

## Songs for Worship

Moshe Walsalam's greatest contribution to the church in Kerala and beyond is the body of songs that he wrote, composed, arranged and adapted; today, they are still used extensively by Christians in Kerala. Their greatest virtue is that they appropriately combined tunes and messages for the full diversity of church life and occasions. Gladstone points out that the songs for worship could be divided into three groups—translations from Tamil, translations from English, and songs written in Malayalam.[16]

13. Gladstone, *Moshe Walsalam Sastrigal*, 46.
14. Ibid., 77.
15. Ibid., 80.
16. Ibid., 63.

When Walsalam began writing, Tamil Christian music (through the work of Vedanayagam Sastriyar and others) had already a developed a substantial collection of songs that were used in Walsalam's home region of South Travancore. Encouraged by missionary Samuel Mateer, he translated many Tamil lyrics into Malayalam for worship use.

He was also praised for his skill in translating English hymns. While remaining true to their original meter and melody, he translated their texts so faithfully and naturally into Malayalam that the words flowed as if they had been originally written in that language. Some of the more familiar English hymn texts he translated include: All Hail the Power of Jesus' Name, Abide With Me, When I Survey the Wondrous Cross, O for a Heart to Praise my God, Jesus is Tenderly Calling, Lone and Weary Sad and Dreary, Just as I am Without One Plea, Take My Life, My Faith Looks up to Thee, and Nearer My God to Thee.

Moshe Walsalam's original sacred songs and hymns in his native Malayalam were deeply reflective of his personal vision and faith. Being scripturally based, they touched on most aspects of Christianity, covering an impressive range of topics. The music and words clearly flowed from a constant and profound experience of God in his life. One particularly eloquent song, *ninte hitham pole enne, nithyam nadathiidename, ente hitham pole alle, en pithave en Yahove*[17]—Lead me always according to your will, not as per my will, my father, my Yahweh, was written after Walsalam tragically lost his young son due to a fatal poisonous snake-bite. It reflects the writer's unwavering trust in God, even through the most trying experiences of life.

Besides using melodies from classical Indian music, Walsalam adapted folk tunes for his Christian songs, a habit also practiced by Martin Luther. Classical Indian music can be divided into two primary schools or traditions; Carnatic and Hindustani. Carnatic identifies the music of South India and is mainly practiced by Hindus. Hindustani music is from the North and involves both Hindu and Muslim musicians. The two styles share common origins, but the historic and musicological details of the relationship are debated. Most of Walsalam's classically-inspired music was composed in the Carnatic (South India) style. The few songs he wrote in Hindustani style were an unfamiliar novelty to the southern folks who heard them.

---

17. *Kristhiya aaradhanakkulla paattugalum aaradhanakramangalum* [Hymns and Lyrics and Orders of Service for Worship], 147; *kristhiya kiirthanangal* [Christian Hymns], 141. Referred to hereafter as KAPA and KK, respectively.

## Songs as *Locus* for a Lay Theology

### Devotional Songs

Walsalam also wrote some shorter resources for devotions and spiritual renewal. *Namaskara malika*[18] (1873), is a collection of songs to be used as part of morning and evening meditations for a week. Through song, one could meditate on God, raise one's praise and petitions to God, and also intercede on behalf of one's community.

*Ponmanimaala*[19] (1874) is an invitation to be thankful for all the goodness received through the Lord and to affirm the believer's faith in the One who will return. In *albhudha manjaari*[20] (1874), Walsalam describes the 33 miracles of Jesus and also briefly touches on the cruelty of those who crucified him. *Albhudha malika*[21] (1874) dwells on death, judgment, heaven, and hell.

*Dhyana malika*[22] (1901) is considered the most profound of Moshe Walsalam's devotional writings. Like the hymn *ninte hitham pole enne* it was written following the death of his young son. In grief, he meditates upon the transitory nature of worldly greatness and points to the eternal way of Christ. In total, this major work contains 32 Indian songs in 16 ragas.[23]

### Songs about Christ

*Kristhu charithram*[24] (1878) was Walsalam's largest song collection; it describes the life and divine appointment of Jesus Christ. *Kristhavathara kiirthanam*[25] was another work about Jesus, focusing on his childhood from birth, through exile and return from Egypt, and the boy Jesus settling in Nazareth with his parents.

*Thamburan katha*[26] (1878), is another composition on the life of Jesus and *sriyeshu nama mahathmyam*[27] (1888) dwells on the power and glory of Jesus' name.

18. Songs of Worship.
19. Beads of Gold.
20. Garland of miracles.
21. Amazing Songs.
22. Meditation Songs.
23. Gladstone, *Moshe Walsalam Sastrigal*, 67–69.
24. History of Christ.
25. Song of Christ's Incarnation.
26. Lord's Story.
27. The Power of Jesus' Name.

# Moshe Walsalam

## Songs for Kathakalashepams

Besides those songs written for worship, Moshe Walsalam wrote his music primarily for *kathakalashepams*.[28] Among those specially composed for these performances are the following:

*Kalyanamala*[29] (1875) is a poem that sings about the Lord's presence at the Wedding in Cana and of Christian family life.

*Jalapralayam*[30] (1878) is inspired by the flood narrative from Genesis and uses the story to point out evils that were prevalent in late nineteenth-century South Indian society.

*Agnipralayam*[31] uses the event of a local fire to teach about the final judgment and invites people to put their trust in Jesus.

*Yerusalem puthrimarude vilaapangal*[32] has two parts; the first is about the women wailing at the cross; the second describes women bewailing the destruction of Jerusalem by the Romans in 70 CE.

*Surapaanakutari* and *surapaana parihari* are two writings about the evils of alcoholism and how the solution to overcoming them is found in accepting Christ.

While current hymnals in Kerala, India, still include a number of Moshe Walsalam's worship songs, his other compositions are no longer in general circulation. Some are available in the library archives at Kerala United Theological College, the seminary which primarily trains ministers for the six dioceses of the Church of South India in that state. The last available printing of Walsalam's works is *The Collected Works of Walsala Sastriar*[33] published in 1958 by his grandson, J. John. The 210-page volume includes: *namaskara malika, kalyanamala, albhudha manjaari, sriyeshu nama mahathmyam, ponmanimaala, thamburan katha, yerusalem puthrimarude vilaapangal, jalapralayam, agnipralayam, surapaana parihari, surapaanakutari* and some songs for worship.

---

28. See footnote 12 for an explanation of *kathakalashepams*.
29. Wedding Garland.
30. Deluge of Water.
31. Deluge of Fire.
32. Lament of the Daughters of Jerusalem.
33. John, *Collected Works of Walsala Sastriar*.

Songs as *Locus* for a Lay Theology

## A Theological Exploration of Walsalam's Songs

Systematization was not a characteristic of Indian religious expression. The Shankaras, Madhavas, Ramanujas and others also expressed their theological and philosophical structures in poetic form. Spiritual expressions were primarily based on lived experience and were thus spontaneous in nature. Music is seen as the expression of the heart in India, a sentiment just as true of Indian Christians. To them, the act of passing on one's faith and traditions was oral in nature. In particular, it was the songs—initially translations of Western hymns, followed by the emergence of indigenous sacred lyrics—which provided a means of grasping and expressing their faith.

### *Trinity*

Several of Moshe Walsalam's shorter religious songs succinctly illustrate his understanding of God as Trinity.

> *naadhane en yeshuve halleluiah*
> *thadhanam em daivame halleluiah*
> *ma parishuddhathmave halleluiah*
> *daivame thriyeekane halleluiah*[34]

> O Lord my Jesus, hallelujah
> O God my Father, hallelujah
> My Holy Spirit, hallelujah
> God, three-in-one, hallelujah.

The lordship of Christ, the fatherhood of God, and the Spirit that sanctifies are all praised. Especially notable here is his use of the salutation *thriyeekane* in reference to the Trinity, translated above as three-in-one, or triune one. This is very different from the usage of other Indian Christian writers who have chosen the word *thrimurthy* to describe the Trinity.[35] In

---

34. KAPA, 3; KK, 41. All translations of songs by Moshe Walsalam in this chapter and Kochukunju in the next chapter are mine.

35. In the works of some of the earlier Indian Christian theologians, such as K. C. Sen and Brahmabandhab Upadhyaya, the preferred term to refer to the Trinity is *saccidhananda*. Here *sat* means truth, *cit* means intelligence and *ananda* means joy, where *sat* refers to the Father, *cit* to the Son, and *ananda* to the Holy Spirit. See Boyd, *An Introduction to Indian Christian Theology*. In popular usage, however, the term *thrimurthy* is frequently used. The Malayalam translation of the St. James Liturgy of the Marthoma

the Hindu tradition, *thrimurthy* is associated with the Hindu triumvirate of deities comprising Brahma, Vishnu and Siva (or Shiva); respectively, the Creator, Redeemer, and Destroyer. While some Indian scholars qualify their use of *thrimurthy*, others raise the theological implications of this non-Christian term. Walsalam's choice of *thriyeekane*, while new in the context of hymnody, adequately and faithfully expresses the traditional Christian understanding of the Trinity, pointing to a significant change in language usage.

> *halleluiah, halleluiah, halleluiah, amen*
> *anbu thingiidum nal—anandha pithave*
> *krupa niranjiidum nal—kristhukarthave*
> *vishuddhinalgiidum nal—parishudhathmave*
> *thatha sudhathmavamv—vdaivame thriyeeka*[36]

> Halleluiah, halleluiah, halleluiah, amen.
> O eternal[37] Father, overflowing with love,
> O Lord Christ, full of grace,
> O Holy Spirit, who makes holy,
> God, three-in-one, who is Father, Son and Spirit.

In the above example, Father is seen as the eternal Supreme Being, *anandha*, a close parallel to the *thrimurthy* understanding of *Brahman* as the eternal Supreme Being. It is the Father's love that redeems and manifests itself through Jesus Christ, who as the second person in the Trinity, is seen as being full of grace. The third person of the Holy Spirit is the sanctifier. The writer goes on to acknowledge the unity of the three persons in one godhead.

The song *anandapithaavinu sangiirthanam*[38] also points out to whom our worship is directed:

> Praise to the eternal Father, as it was in the beginning is now and forever.
> Praise to the eternal Savior, as it was in the beginning is now and forever.

---

Church uses both *thriyeekan* and *thrithvam*, which are translated as Trinity in Malayalam dictionaries.

36. KAPA, 2; KK, 41.

37. The word *anandham* is also translated as Supreme Soul. Warrier et al., *Malayalam-English Nighandu* [Malayalam-English Dictionary], 39; hereafter referred to as *Malayalam-English Dictionary*.

38. KAPA, 2.

> Praise to the sweet divine Spirit, as it was in the beginning is now and forever.
>
> Praise to the wonderful three-in-one, as it was in the beginning is now and forever.
>
> Praise is due to the Triune God.

The coeternity of the Father and Son is another aspect of God that is stressed in the above song, being faithful to early creedal statements of the Church. As well, the Holy Spirit is referred to as being "sweet" or *inbam*, being associated with pleasure and intense joy, or bliss,[39] such as the devout *bhakta* enjoys in the presence of the Divine.

## *God the Creator*

The first person of the Trinity is addressed in Walsalam's writing as Lord, Father and Creator. God as Creator is a frequent theme in a number of his songs. Additionally, he addresses God with adjectives such as almighty, holy, true, worthy of praise and victory, exalted, omnipresent, and saving. Of those songs that focus on God, his *nithyavandanam ninakku*[40] touches on most of these themes.

> Chorus: Eternal praise to you, true God
> You are worthy of praise and victory, O exalted one.
>
> Creator of the human race, eternal father,
> We who truly believe in you praise you.
>
> How beautiful are your creations
> How wonderful and great they are.
>
> O, almighty one, who dwells among the cherubim
> Praise to you always, who is present in all the world.
>
> To free humankind from sin
> O, Lord, who erased our sin on the despicable cross,
>
> To grant heaven to all who believe in you
> O, Lord, who went to the heavens,
>
> All honor, all glory and praise,

---

39. *Malayalam-English Dictionary*, 142.
40. KAPA, 8.

Is to you Jehovah, the Supreme one.

Here, and in *aadithya chandraadhikale*[41] while extolling the attributes of God, Walsalam includes the image of God (as Christ) on "the despicable cross" and now in heaven to redeem humankind. This reflects the understanding of both composer and singer that God the Father was with Christ on the Cross—a divine act reflecting the divinity of the one who was crucified. It is belief in this God that imparts *moksha* (bliss, freedom, release) to the faithful, making it clear that God is also the one who saves. The divine salvific act originated out of God's love for us, to free humankind from fear, deception and injustice, and to reveal the universal dimension of God's authority. God created all that is, freeing people from sin and opening the way of attaining salvation.

The song thus invites believers to continually praise this God who is simultaneously Creator, Savior and Lord. In the text of *aadithya chandraadhikale* (cited above), Walsalam affirms that creation was something that happened in a moment, wholly according to God's will: *bodhichadellam kshanathil thikachavanu sthothram*—Praise to the one who created all he wanted in a moment.[42] Here, creation emerged out of nothing, not as *maya* or illusion, as the Advaithic philosophy of Shankara would claim. In *aadithya chandraadhikale*, God is pictured as being in communion with Adam and Eve.

In *parishuddhaparane*[43] God is referred to as the "ocean of love," echoing the *bhakti* tradition in which the Divine is understood in similar terms and where immersion in that ocean brings extreme joy and bliss (*moksha*). Walsalam deftly applies this Hindu usage to refer to God as the Provider who is worthy of worship.

> *nanmakadaline chemme naam sthudhichaal*
> *namukkilla kurachil ennarinju kumbiduviin*
> *iimmaha padhaviye naam ellavarum ishtathodaacharikkam*[44]

> If we aptly worshipped this ocean of love,
> Know that we will have no want and so worship.
> Let us all gladly observe this great honor.

---

41. Ibid., 9.
42. Ibid., see verse 1, line 2.
43. Ibid., 12.
44. Ibid., 12. No. 23, verse 3.

As the text indicates, being a follower of this God is honorable. Believers can depend upon God for sustenance, as they are free from their previous dishonorable state.

> *devanam yahovekkennum sevacheyidhu thosha*
> *puurnam urvuyengum khoshippin*[45]
>
> Serve Jehovah who is God
> Joyfully proclaim him in all the world.

Jehovah is referred to here as *devan*, a term normally used to refer to the various manifestations of God in history. One might ask if this was due to linguistic and poetic license, or if it was an affirmation of the presence of Yahweh among the faithful, through their spiritual and physical struggles on earth. God is also pictured as both shepherd and king; we are sheep and subjects—*aadugal* and *prajagal*.

### God the Son—Jesus Christ

The Christology of Moshe Walsalam's hymns reflects deep knowledge of the scriptures and profound religious experience. The experience of the worshiping community that shaped his own is also reflected in the verses he penned about Jesus Christ. As James Cone similarly points out about African-American spirituals,[46] these songs are also silent when it comes to abstract theological references to Christ. There was no question about who Jesus is and how the divine could become human; these understandings were among the "givens" received in faith. More than anything, Walsalam's songs reflect the collective experience of the community and the received assurance that God was with them in their spiritual and temporal struggles.

For example, the song *yeshupara illee bhavanu thullyam*[47] (Lord Jesus, there is none equal to you), praises the glory and supremacy of Christ.

> *pallavi: yeshu para—ille bhavanu thullyan, ella lokathum cholvan*
> *vallabha, mahesha, nallava devesha,*
> *chollayudha sarvesha, swamin chollayudha sarvesha.*
>
> *ellam ariyum nii, ellyidathum nii,*
> *ekkalavum niiye, swamin ekkalavum niiye.*

---

45. Ibid., 13. No. 25, *pallavi* (chorus).
46. Cone, *Spirituals and the Blues*, 47.
47. KAPA, 48.

*ellam srishtichu nii, ellam azhikkum nii,*
*ille ninnepolarum, swamin ille ninnepolarum.*

*rooparahithane, roopam dharichone,*
*paparahithan niiye, swamin paparahithan niiye.,*

*kodikodi dhoothar, paadisevichiidum,*
*moodiyeerunna rajan nii, swamin moodiyeerunna rajan nii.*

*jiivannudayone, bhuvittuyirnnone,*
*daivakumaran niye, swamin daivakumaran niye.*

*sarva marthyareyum, divyaniithiyode,*
*nii vidhichiidum veegam, swamin nii vidhichiidum veegam.*

*nii kalpicha kaalam, aaya bhuuvin koolam,*
*niikkum nii andhyakaalam, swamin niikkum nii andhyakaalam.*

*Refrain*: Lord Jesus, there is none equal to you in all the worlds.[48]

Lord,[49] Divine One, One who is goodness,
Divine one, Supreme Lord, Divine one.
You are omniscient, you are omnipresent,

You are eternal, Lord, you are eternal.
You created all, you will fulfill all,
There is none like you, Lord there is none like you.

You are without form, you took on human form,
You are without sin, Lord, you are without sin.

Crores on crores[50] of angels praise and serve you,
You reign in splendour, Lord, you reign in splendour.

Lord of life, who rose from the earth,
You are the Son of God, Lord, you are the Son of God.

All humankind, with divine justice,
You will judge soon, Lord, you will judge soon.

---

48. Refers to the three "worlds" of heaven, earth and hell.
49. *Vallabhan* could also mean "dear one."
50. One *crore* is ten million.

At your time, at the end,
you will remove the ways of the world, Lord, you will remove the ways of the world.

This song proclaims the writer's statement of faith in Jesus Christ, whom he refers to as the incomparable supreme one, of indescribable glory, Lord of the heavens. This is graphically presented through his reference to angels waiting on and serving the glorified Christ, whose lordship and supremacy extend over the three worlds, heaven, earth, and hell. He is King and reigns in splendor, even over the realm of the Evil One.

The belief that the Son is also active in creation and an eternal being with the Father stands out in a number of songs, including *bhoolokathe chamacha thrilooka daivasudha*[51] (O Son of God, Lord over the three worlds[52] who created the universe) and *aadhiudan andhavumillathavanu mangalam*[53] (Blessings[54] to the one with no beginning and end).

Christ is the source of all, the beginning (*aadhiyum*) and the end (*anaadhiyum*).[55] All beings of creation find their source in him, who created and adorned (*chamacha*)[56] the universe. The eternal preexistence of Christ is affirmed in the reference to the Son as the source of all things. The acknowledgement, *ekkalavum niiye* (you are eternal, or, you are there through all the ages), reinforces belief in the Son's status as the deathless, eternal one.[57] In this context, Christ is also seen as sharing the attributes of being the source of all knowledge and being ever present.

At times, the distinction among persons of the Trinity as traditionally understood seems blurred in Walsalam's writing. In the eight verses of

---

51. KAPA, 27. No. 50, *anupallavi*. South Indian or Carnatic devotional music normally consists of three parts: the *pallavi* is a refrain consisting of one or two melodic lines in a middle-octave register; the *anupallavi* is the second verse, beginning with notes related to the motif of the *pallavi* (this section contrasts with the *pallavi* by moving into a somewhat higher register); and the *caranam*, the final and longest verse, set to a different melody, but sometimes concluding with melodic ideas from the *anupallavi*. Pallavi and anupallavi would be choruses of the song.

52. Refers to heaven, earth, and hell.

53. KAPA, 27. No. 50, verse 1.

54. The word *mangalam* is translated as auspiciousness and happiness. See *Malayalam-English Dictionary*, 828.

55. KAPA, 27, No. 49, verse 4.

56. Ibid., 27, No. 50, *anupallavi*.

57. Ibid., 212, No. 352, verse 4.

*varasundara paramandala*,[58] he focuses primarily on the incarnation and work of Christ. The first verse is an invocation to Jesus, the noble and beautiful lord of all, to come and bless the assembly. In the line that functions as the song's chorus, repeated after every stanza, he uses the term Jehovah to refer to the one who has been so invoked: *sthuthimangalam jayamangalam ninakke yahovaye* (adorations of praise and victory are to you, Jehovah). The second verse refers to the one who created the heavens and the earth, again using the noun *devan*—a term primarily used in the local religio-cultural context to refer to *avatars* or manifestations of the Hindu deity, Vishnu. It was not about making divine distinctions, however, but rather to express believers' collective experiences of the Divine that mattered most to Walsalam; through Christ, it was the Triune God who was at work.

Walsalam uses the word *mahesha* in a number of instances; it can be translated as auspicious and fortunate one, and is used in Hindu references to Shiva, the Destroyer in the Hindu triad. One reason for avoiding the term *thrimurthi* to describe the Trinity in Indian Christian vocabulary is its association with the Destroyer, rather than an understanding of the Son of God overcoming sin and death for the redemption of humankind. However, one could also understand this as a redefining of the Hindu term into a vehicle for communicating the Christian belief that sin was destroyed on the cross. Jesus is also sung about as the embodiment of goodness and mercy; *karuna niranja kannullonavan*[59] (literally, "he has eyes full of mercy," or "he surveys us with mercy").

While there are many references to the preexistent, coeternal, and co-creative nature of the Son, the main focus of Walsalam's songs for the spirituality of the people who sing them is Jesus' incarnation, life, and ministry. The incarnation is seen as the Divine Son taking on human form; the infinite coming to live among humans and taking on their mortality. The theme of becoming human "like me" is powerfully expressed here. The concept of becoming human is also described in terms of wearing humanity, *jadam dharichu*,[60] or in the guise of a servant/slave, *dasa veshamodu*.[61] Going through Walsalam's songs that are still in circulation and in the hymnals of the Church of South India and Marthoma Church, a noticeable feature is that he describes the incarnation of Jesus as the Son becoming

58. Ibid., 21, No. 38.
59. Ibid., 17, No. 33, verse 1.
60. Ibid., 213, No. 354, verse 4.
61. Ibid., 211, No. 351, verse 1

human, taking on human form, born of the Virgin, born of a woman, being of David's line, and so on, yet never uses the title "Son of Man." The closest observed phrasings are *naradevan*[62] and *naraparan*,[63] both of which translate as human-god.[64] Explanations as to why the common Western phrase "Son of Man" is absent remain unanswered, but could possibly be due to the monistic Jacobite theological position of the St. Thomas Orthodox tradition, or that of the Indian religio-cultural worldview, which did not have such an understanding. Vishnu's avatars were seen as coming down from the divine realm when there was unrighteousness and discord on earth, but unlike Christianity, there was no concept of any beings that were "fully god and fully human."

Walsalam's use of the word *naraparan* is also qualified by him in that Christ came as himself, *thaanaayi vannu*. Whether this was intentional, or a consequence of influences exerted on him, is also open to debate. As previously noted, he describes the Son of Man as *manushyaputhran*, but does not use the title formally. The influence of the south Indian context on Walsalam's theological expression and diction comes to the fore here.

The birth of Jesus Christ was a redemptive act in itself, through which he identified with the contemporary condition of the faith community to which Walsalam belonged. Thus Walsalam uses terms such as *adima*[65] (slave), *dasa*[66] (servant or slave), and *yajagan*[67] (beggar). Communities experiencing pain and dehumanizing conditions were comforted and spiritually liberated by the assurance that the Son of God was indeed one with them.

Understandably, given the context of the time, the ministry of Christ and the purpose of his earthly incarnation is expressed in a number of Walsalam's songs. Christ's incarnation was understood to be sinless, a formless supernatural entity taking on human form, becoming part of the physical created order. *Varasundara paramandala* recalls the birth of Christ in a stable, which is described as taking place in a "dense forest," an image that places the holy birth on the margins of society among the outcast and

---

62. Ibid., 128. No. 225, verse 2.

63. Ibid., 104, No. 185, verse 4.

64. This usage is also seen in Indian theologian P Chenchiah who uses the term God-Man to refer to Christ, being the bridge between God and humanity. Boyd, *Introduction to Indian Christian Theology*, 150–51.

65. KAPA, 212, No. 354, verse 1.

66. Ibid., 211, No. 351, verse 1.

67. Ibid., 212, No. 354, verse 2.

forgotten. This is the context with which Jesus identifies—the God of all peoples, the Savior and teacher of all, becoming human among the destitute.

In *rakshagane ninakku kiirthanam anandam* and other compositions, the centrality of grace through salvation is affirmed:

> *thiruraktham chorinju thinmappetta enne nii, parannu viindedutha maa paksha krupagalkkume, rakshagane ninakku kiirthanam anandam.*
>
> *niidhishuddhi bodham ninthiru nal roopam, chedassil kalpichu thanna divya krupa kadalam, rakshagane ninakku kiirthanam anandam.*[68]
>
> For saving me, an unrighteous one, by the shedding of your holy blood and including me on God's side by your grace, Lord, praise be to you forever.
>
> Ocean of grace, you made me righteous, holy and in your image; Lord, praise be to you forever.

In the song *allelu, allelu yesu nathane*[69] Walsalam also writes of the work of grace in the salvation that Christ offers, where salvation is because of God's grace: "For by grace you have been saved through faith, and this is not your own doing; it is the gift of God."[70] The call of grace invites all to come to the Savior, because without grace it is not possible to experience salvation—*krupayal allatharkkum moksham kitten kazhivilla*.[71] Walsalam further emphasizes that the call to grace originates with Christ himself and is not of human initiation; the response of the sinner is to run into the Savior's embrace.

The purpose of the Son of God coming among us was to be a sacrifice (*bali*) for all human beings; through Christ's five wounds, the curse of sins on humankind was removed. Thus in many of Walsalam's compositions, the cross as an image for sacrifice or atonement for sin stands out. This sacrifice was ordained from of old[72] and Christ fulfilled it for all.[73] The shedding

---

68. Ibid., 22, No. 40, verses 1 and 4. Verse 4 literally translates as, "you made me conscious of righteousness, holiness and your image."

69. Ibid., 31–32, No. 58, verse 4.

70. Ephesians 2:8.

71. KAPA, 104. No. 185, verse 6.

72. Ibid., 222, No. 368, verse 2.

73. Ibid., 21, No. 38, verse 5.

of Christ's blood was a fulfillment of God's righteousness and justice[74] for he came as Lamb of God, *daivakunjadu*, to take upon himself the sins of the world and be sacrificed on the cross in a supreme act of love. Thus in Walsalam's song texts, one can identify the aspects of both substitution and propitiation, as in the following example:

> *en peerkkukonda adi murivukalum—kaayam*
> *engumm nurungi raktham oodiyathum*
> *en peerkku vitta diirkashwasangalum—ellam*
> *iipapi ennum dhyanichiha vasippen*

> All the wounds and beatings you suffered for me,
> All the wounds and the blood flowing,
> All the sighs you made for me,
> this sinner will always meditate on and live on this earth.

Christ's suffering was not only endured for the sake of the sinner, but also in place of the sinner. The sinless one, pure of all experience of sin, nevertheless suffered for the sake of humankind, a vicarious ordeal undertaken to meet the penal requirements of God's justice.

In contrast, however, Christ's resurrection and ascension assured believers that beyond physical death, one would continue to praise him again and again.

> *dharini vittuyare, parane kandavane*
> *maranathin pinbum sthothram cheiven, cheiven.*[75]

> The Lord was seen in the heavens above the earth
> Even after death (we) will praise, will praise.

Christ's resurrection was seen as the victory that broke the powers of death and evil; in reference to this triumphal event, Walsalam describes "crores[76] of devils" running in fear. The term *pey*,[77] which he sometimes uses for Devil, refers to spirits traditionally worshipped by the *shanar* community; however, the word *pishaju* is more common in the culture to refer to the devil. Earlier pre-Christian religions were concerned with appeasing these spirits and keeping them happy. Gladstone points out that a distin-

---

74. Ibid., 128, No 225, verse 5.
75. Ibid., 19, No. 35, verse 5.
76. See footnote 49.
77. KAPA, 30, No. 56, verse 2; KAPA, 20, No. 36, verse 2.

guishing feature of *nadar* religion was the direct worship of demons.[78] Walsalam counters earlier religions by affirming the universal lordship of Jesus Christ over the spiritual realm that formerly held the people in bondage.

The mediating role of Christ is also touched upon in *oodivaa krupayaam nadhiiyarikil*,[79] a song that portrays the Son of God searching intently for sinners, suffering on the cross and earning salvation for humankind, then raised back into his Father's presence to mediate and plead on humanity's behalf.

The various Christological titles used in Walsalam's songs succinctly reflect his deep understanding and belief in Jesus Christ. Among them, one often encounters King, Righteous One, God's Holy Son, Savior, Messiah, Supreme Lord of the Universe, *maheshan*, *devan*, Formless One, Sinless One, God, Leader, Christ, Lamb, Strong One, and so on.

## God the Holy Spirit

In the hymn *maa parishuddathmane*,[80] (Great Holy Spirit), Walsalam describes the work of the Holy Spirit, here also addressing the Spirit as God:

> *pallavi: ma parishuddhathmane,*
>     *shakthiyerum daivame,*
>     *vannu rakshikkeename—veegam*
>
> *paapiyennullil nyayangal*
> *vaadhichunarthiiduga en*
> *papa vazhigal thonnikkuka*
>
> *paapabhodham nalkuka nii*
> *niidhinyaya thiirppineyum*
> *pakshamodingorma nalkuka*
>
> *yeshuvodu cheruvanum*
> *sathyam grahichiiduvanum*
> *enne aagarshichaduppikka*
>
> *nalla jiiva vishvasavum*
> *moksha bhagya mudrayathum*
> *nalkuka viindum jananavum*

---

78. Gladstone, *Protestant Christianity*, 29.
79. KAPA, 100. No. 180.
80. Ibid., 36, No. 69.

## Songs as *Locus* for a Lay Theology

*parushuddanakkukenne*
*padippikka daiva hitham*
*parane vazhi nadathenne*

*balahiinatha varumbol*
*thunachashvasippikkenne*
*paralokanandam kattuka.*
  *Refrain:* Great Holy Spirit,
    Almighty God,
     Come soon and save me.

In me a sinner your ways
teach and rekindle;
show me my sinful ways.

Give me an awareness of sin,
of justice and righteousness
bring to my remembrance.

To be united with Jesus,
to perceive the truth,
attract me and bring me close.

True faith and life
the seal of the fortune of heaven,
give also rebirth.

Make me holy
teach me God's will.
Lord, lead me.

when I am weak;
help and comfort me;
show me the joy of heaven.

 This song powerfully affirms the role of the Holy Spirit in the salvific work of God; who is the indweller, occupying a key place in the lives of Christian *bhaktas*. Here, an understanding of the Spirit as comforter, edifier, counselor, embodiment of truth, guide, sanctifier, teacher (and many other aspects) is central to the faith experience of the believer; consequently, a number of these attributes are reflected in the above verses by Walsalam. It is as God that the Spirit saves and it is the Spirit that enlightens and enables one to be united with Jesus Christ. The Spirit actively continues the work of Christ in the Church through saving, teaching what is holy, bringing believers to an awareness of sin, making them mindful of justice and righteousness, uniting believers with Christ, understanding them fully, assuring them of salvation, and offering comfort.

The chorus or refrain after each stanza is a prayer to the Spirit, who is also God, to come soon and save the people. The continuing work of God's grace within the believer, through the Holy Spirit, is recognized when Walsalam's words acknowledge that the Spirit is the agent that brings about awareness of one's sin. Humans are seen as being in a state of total depravity and unable to do anything about sin by themselves, or even become aware of their sinful condition. In the song *vaa, vaa, vishudhathma en nenchakathil*,[81] Come, come, Holy Spirit, to my Heart, Walsalam stresses that it is the Spirit that brings about our awareness of sin and repentance; *paapabodhavum anuthaapavum undaakuvanum*. He further dwells on the assurance of salvation and the experience of being born again as also belonging to the work of the Spirit. While none of his songs dwell on Christian baptism as such, the practice of infant baptism would point to this prayer as indicative of the Spirit's activity in the individual believer's daily experience of baptism as ongoing redemption. It is the Spirit that evokes mindfulness of our sinful nature, but also makes it possible for us to rise into new life in the daily experience of rebirth. One of the things prayed for is that the Spirit close the springs or sources of sin—*paapathin urava adakkename*.

It is in this that the Spirit sanctifies, by bringing about an awareness of sin and enabling one to experience new birth. The song *viindum janippikka*[82] describes what being born again means and how the indwelling Spirit sanctifies and gives life to those who are dead in sin.

> *Refrain*: Let me be born again great/noble Holy Spirit
> Great/noble almighty Spirit of God
> Let me be born again by the word, Spirit of God.

Because of great sins I was dead and without strength;
Sided with Satan and became unclean.

I lost my sight, hearing, sense of touch, taste and happiness;
Lord finish me in your image.

---

81. Ibid., 35, No. 66.
82. Ibid., 43, No. 80.

## Songs as *Locus* for a Lay Theology

I became as dry as bones and was without life;
O, Great Wind, blow on me.

Make clean my legs, hands, tongue, ears, eyes and heart;
Let me live for the glory of the Lord.

Create in me love for God, hate for sin and make me righteous;
Divine Holy Spirit, you live inside of me.

In this composition Walsalam expresses the experience of being born again as the enlivening of one who had been aligned with Satan and was thus spiritually dead because of sin. The life-giving activity of the Holy Spirit is also the theme of *ennullil ennum vasichiiduvan*. In this song, Walsalam calls the Spirit *jiivippikkum karthane*,[83] or the Lord who brings to life. And in *penthakosthin vallbhane*, he affirms that if it was not for the Spirit's breath we would be mere lifeless forms—*nin shvasam illa engil, nirjiiva roopam njangal*.[84] The believer's experience of the Holy Spirit takes one to narratives of the Spirit of God hovering over the waters and the breath, or wind, of God giving life to creation as in Ezekiel's vision of the Valley of Dry Bones. The idea of the indwelling Spirit, the *antaryamin* as Appasamy terms it, brings out the indwelling role of God as the Inner Controller through the *bhakta's* faith.

The prayer *karthane nin roopamaakki thiirkkukayenne*, Lord, make me in your image, draws a parallel to the Indian theologian Chakkarai's understanding of the Holy Spirit. To Chakkarai, Christ continues to be present as the *antaraatman* through the Spirit. Thus the incarnation moves from the historical to the spiritual, in the continuing work of the Spirit.[85] Walsalam is able to address the Spirit and pray that he be given the Spirit's image.

In *penthakosthin vallbhane*, the Spirit is also addressed as the hope of those who seek refuge, pointing to Walsalam's understanding of the Spirit's presence in the experiences of liberation and freedom within his own community. It was the presence of the Spirit that led the song and also had a vital role in bringing about unity in the church. By contrast, when the Spirit was absent, every mind turned its own way, and the strength derived from being of one mind is not there anymore—*ella manusukalum, ooroonila thirinju, oru manmenna sakti, ozinjupoyallo swami*. Unity throughout the body of Christ is the work of the Spirit.

---

83. Ibid., 33. No. 61, verse 1.
84. Ibid., 38. No. 71, verse 1.
85. Boyd, *Introduction to Indian Christian Theology*, 242.

Another aspect of the Spirit that stands out in Walsalam's songs is its power to enliven the believer to continue the mission of Christ. The Spirit works within the individual, motivating him or her to search after the rule of the kingdom of God, and to perform justice and true service: *daivathin raajavum niithiyum sathyaseevayum cheyithiiduvan*.[86] The Spirit breathes upon believers so that its fruits are made manifest.

The role of the Spirit in learning and perceiving the Word is also affirmed, for the Spirit removes *avidya*,[87] ignorance or darkness, and illuminates the soul, imparting awareness and knowledge of truth—*sathyathin bhodham enikku tharuvan*.[88] Once freed from ignorance, the believer is able to know the Word and the mystery of the cross, knowing that all who believe find rest for their souls and thus experience salvation in this world: *mukti ii bhumiyil*.[89]

## Sin and Salvation

Sin in Moshe Walsalam's songs is understood as human beings being deceived into disobeying God. The incarnation of Christ was therefore necessary to free a deceived, imprisoned and fearful humankind—*aadhi maanushyan chadhivil aayadhine kandu, bhiidhi bhuu bhavanathilninnu poovathinayikkondu*.[90] In the song *innum ennenneekkum yeshu mathi*, Today and Forever, Jesus will Suffice, he writes *krura chathiyanam peeyin kenikalam*[91]—in the traps of the cruel deceiver *peyi* (Satan). To sin was to fall into the deceiver's trap and be drawn into the ways of Satan.[92]

The death or sacrifice of Christ is seen as the remedy to Adam's original sin of eating the forbidden fruit, which caused the rest of humankind to be inherently born into sin.[93] Theological argument over humanity's originating sinfulness can be traced back to debates between St. Augustine and

---

86. KAPA, 37. No. 70, verse 3.

87. The term *avidya* is used in the Indian concept of *jnana marga*, the way of knowledge, to refer to ignorance which prevents one from gaining knowledge of the Divine and thus attaining *moksha*, or salvation.

88. KAPA, 35. No. 66, verse 1.

89. Ibid., 37. No. 70, verses 4 and 5.

90. Ibid., 27. No. 50, verse 2.

91. Ibid., 126. No. 223, verse 2.

92. Ibid., 127. No. 223, verse 4.

93. Ibid., 27. No. 50, verse 2; KAPA, 206. No. 117, verse 1.

Pelagius during the fifth century CE. Augustine affirmed that by virtue of organic unity, the entire human race existed within Adam at the time of his transgression. Adam's will was understood as being the will of all humanity; thus in his freely chosen act of disobedience, all human will revolted against God, and human nature became corrupted. Augustine's premise was that all people existed as one moral person in Adam, making Adam's sin everyone's sin. Luther also took this position, contrary to the Roman Catholic assertion of concupiscence, arguing that humans are born into sin and are inherently sinful. Walsalam's understanding also affirms that in Adam we are all sinful as a consequence of our first ancestor's sin:

> *eedhan thoottathil aadham thinnoru*
> *paathapaphala paathakam*
> *meedhini vittozhinju pookuwan*
> *mrithyuveetta dayaapara*[94]
>
> Of the fruit that Adam ate in Eden
> the destructive fruit's curse,
> to leave the earth
> you died, O, Loving One.

Walsalam's interpretation of sin is very different from the traditional Hindu one. In India, the average Hindu is well aware of his or her *karma*[95] but may have very little feeling of sin. In Sankara's monistic Advaitic thought, there is no concept of sin; inherent sin is irrelevant because the human *atman*, or soul, is eternal and, moreover, identical with the Supreme Soul, or *paramatman*. In discussing the theology of Appasamy, Boyd points out that in the theistic *bhakti* tradition, the concept of sin and any focus on it are also very rare. Appasamy himself did not dwell much on sin and sinfulness, but rather talked about freedom from the fear of *karma*, a freedom for which all Hindus long.[96] One can be reborn into any caste, or even as an animal, depending on one's actions; this is described as *karma marga*.[97] Good actions would result in having a better birth; that is, being born into a higher caste. The only way one is released from this cycle of birth and

---

94. Ibid., 206. No. 117, verse 1.
95. The fruit of one's actions.
96. Boyd, *Introduction to Indian Christian Theology*, 131.
97. The way of works.

rebirth is if one is born a *Brahmin*. In *karma*, it is the concept of good and bad actions that are in play rather than any concept of sin.

In this light it is interesting to observe Walsalam's position on sin and its consequences. His emphasis on human sin as being the act of our first ancestors and passed on through the generations seems a very Augustinian stance. The phrase *aadhimaanushan pizhacha paathakathe ooharicha, bhoothalam*, for example, refers to the created order that inherited the sinful error of the first human.[98]

In his compositions Walsalam often describes being in sin as comparable to being in a state of death:

> *marichu njan kidannen, naari uruwazhinjeen*[99]
> I lay dead, a stinking corpse.
>
> *dine dine njan chaakunnu . . . njan paapi ennathre*[100]
> Daily I die . . . I am a sinner.
>
> *eettam paapathal marichu shaktikettu poyeen*
> *. . . ellupolunangippoyeen jiivanillathayeen*[101]
> Because of great sin I was dead and without strength;
> I was dry as a bone, and without life.

*Raksha,* salvation, in this context consists in being enlivened by Christ through the Holy Spirit. Christ himself is addressed as life and it is at his feet that the sinner finds refuge. His description of the sinful state as being one of allegiance to *peyi* (Satan) also points to his understanding of sin in terms of relationships. Satan's deception results in our rightful allegiance to God being placed elsewhere; thus *moksha*, salvation or bliss, is a restoration of that relationship and its price was paid on the cross:

> *kodikalaaya peykal kodukuude devarum*
> *kuudoode peedichoodum thiru*
> *balathal naadukalakhilavum namichiidum thirunamam*
> *narakularakshakan vaazhenam melkumel*[102]

---

98. KAPA, 27. No. 50, verse 2.
99. Ibid., 22. No. 40, verse 2.
100. Ibid., 33. No. 60, verse 3.
101. Ibid., 43. No. 80, verses 1 and 3.
102. Ibid., 30. No. 56, verse 2.

> Crores of demons and crores of gods too,
> Will flee in fright;
> At your strength all the world will bow at your name;
> The Savior of humankind will reign.

The defeat of the powers of darkness realigns relationships and allegiances. From this example, one can infer that Walsalam understood sin as a break in one's relationship with God and the attachment of one's allegiances to other gods and demons:

> *vittidunneen pishajin naanaavidha vyartha vazhikale njan*
> *kittanam eettavum maahaathmyamulla kristheeshuvam*
> *mahaamuthenikaakayaal*[103]
>
> I leave Satan's various vain ways
> and will receive the most glorious gem of Christ Jesus for myself.

Sin is also described as blindness, lacking the ability to perceive God's ways or will; conversely, salvation is described as receiving, or being restored to sight—*kurudanaayirnnen thottu kazhcha thannu nii*, I was blind and you touched me and gave me sight. This act of receiving sight is also parallel to the removal of the "leprosy of sin," *kushta paapathe*.[104]

In the song *niiyozhige niiyozhige*[105] Walsalam describes Christ as being family, pointing to the intimacy of the relationship between them: *niiyen raksha, niiyen bandhu, niiyenikkasha,* you are my salvation, you are my kin, I desire you; *jiivanekkal nii valiyon aakunnenikku,* you are more important[106] than life to me; and *bhangamilla bandhuve,* you unfailing family member/relative.[107] The word *bandhu* can be translated as meaning family or relative or kindman, a term that emphasizes the place and role of relationships (formed, sustained, or broken) in the understanding of sin in Walsalam's songs.

Salvation is seen as freedom or liberation from the spiritual and social powers that hold one in bondage (these themes are dealt with later in more detail).

---

103. Ibid., 127. No. 223, verse 4.
104. Ibid., 22. No. 40, verse 3.
105. Ibid., 124. No. 220.
106. Literally, larger or bigger.
107. KAPA, 124. No. 220, verses 1, 3, and 5.

## Moshe Walsalam

### *Love*

Walsalam understands divine love as that attribute of God that does not give up on sinful human beings, but instead works out a plan of salvation; this theme is scattered throughout his compositions.

> *dayaketta pey ingu narareppathalathil*
> *chathichu kondodunnathu maname*
> *kandu daya krupa sneehavum niranja paran vannu*
> *sathya vedan arulam maname*[108]

> Unmerciful Satan in this hell, reigns over humans in deception.
> Seeing this, the Lord full of mercy, grace and love, came to declare the truth.

God is the fountain from which endless love flows; thus Walsalam addresses God as one who is full of, or bursting with, love—*anbuthingiidum nal ananda pithave*. He refers to Christ, the incarnate one who died on the cross, as the personification of divine love—*sneha roopan*.[109] In Christ, love lived among us in human flesh and blood. God is the preserver, or *palakan*, of love, igniting a reciprocal flame of love in the believer's heart.

> *sneehathin paalakane nin kaatinaal snehaagni jwalippikka*
> *iha nin sishyaril yeshu naamathin mahathwam kandiiduvan.*[110]

> Preserver/source of love, let your wind ignite the flame of love,
> that your disciples could see the glory of the name of Jesus.

In the song *niiyozhike, niiyozhike*[111] Walsalam addresses Christ as the embodied fullness of love, *sneha mayan*, dwelling on the consequences of Christ's outpouring love. This love saves, unites one with God, gives hope, and makes possible the constant and intimate presence of Christ; in fact, there is no relationship more intimate to the devotée.

> *pallavi: niiyozhike, niiyozhike aarumilliisho*
> *anupallavi: snehamayame vishuddhi niithi nirave*
>
> *niiyen raksha niiyen bandhu nii enikkasha*
> *niiyen swanthamaayi vannadhen mahabhagyam.*

---

108. Ibid., 128. No. 225, verse 4.
109. Ibid., 230. No. 381, verse 1.
110. Ibid., 37. No. 70, verse 2.
111. Ibid., 124. No. 220, *anupallavi*.

*ennum engum yeshu nii ennodu kuudave*
*annirunna shakti krupayodu vazhunne.*

*jiivanekkal nii valiyon aakunnenikku*
*bhuvil arivan ninakku thulyam mattille.*

*thannu sarvavum enikkuveendi niiyallo*
*ninnaruma naamam adiyaanu samastham.*

*mangalame en dhaname kshema dathave*
*bhangamilla bandhuve maha shubhavane.*

> *Refrain*: Except you, I have no one, Lord.
> *Sub Refrain*: Abounding in love, fullness of holiness and righteousness.

You are my hope, you are my family, you are my hope.
It is my great fortune that you became my own.

Daily, everywhere, Jesus you are with me.
You reign in grace and might.

You are greater than life to me;
on earth there is none equal to you.

You gave everything to me.
Your beloved name is everything to me, your servant.

Praise to you, my treasure and Protector,
Unifier, kinsman, great Auspicious One.

This song reflects the intimacy between God and the devotée as well as the devotée's dependence on God. In *yeshuve thirunaamam ethra madhuram*[112] Walsalam further intensifies that intimacy by addressing Christ as his husband, suggesting a spousal love and reinforcing the idea that Jesus is forever one's closest companion.

As Appasamy points out, in *bhakti* tradition love, *vatsalya*, is the most important factor in the believer's vision and attainment of God. However, the direction of love here is different, being directed to God as a cow would relate to its newborn calf.[113] Walsalam remains true to the traditional Christian understanding that sinful humankind cannot compare in any way

---

112. Ibid., 158. No. 277, verse 4.
113. Sundara Rao, *Bhakti Theology*, 51.

with the Divine, the source and fountain of infinite love. He reinterprets the concept in his songs to suggest that love between God and the devotée is primarily directed to humanity, like the love between parent and child; he does not usually use the term *vatsalyam*, but instead chooses *sneham*, the term used for love in Malayalam translations of the Bible. This love of God searches out sinners and suffers for their sake. In love, divine blood was shed for the sins of humankind and thus the Son of God became the incarnation of Divine love. In the following excerpt, love is also seen as a quality of the believer:

> *visvasam sneham aashayum agathikalkku meelilninnayakkename.*[114]
> Send to those that seek refuge in you faith, love and hope.
>
> *daivasneham paapadvesham niithiyum undakki*
> *divya vishuddhathmave nii vasam cheyken ullil*[115]
>
> Give love of God, hate for sin, and righteousness, and
> Divine Holy Spirit you live within me.

Here, the believer prays for the inbreaking and indwelling love of Christ, affirming that love for God and others is a response of the love of God through Christ. In the song *pirupiruppeedhumilladhe*,[116] he describes God's love in Christ as the Son giving up heaven, taking up the cross of atonement for human sin, shedding his blood, and coming in the form of one who has nothing, *daridran*, in order to save all. Our response to this love is the invitation to live in God's way; that is, in Christian love. The invitation is to identify with and live the life of Christ.[117]

The song *sneha virunnaubhavippan* affirms that we are to be marked by the love of Christ, according to the command given by our Lord.[118] This is the special kind of love that distinguishes followers of Christ from others.

## Trust

The song that epitomizes Walsalam's complete and unflinching trust in God is *ninte hitham pole enne nithyam nadathiidename*, According to Your Will

---

114. KAPA, 38. No. 71, verse 1.
115. Ibid., 43. No. 80, verse 5.
116. Ibid., 175. No. 299.
117. Ibid., 102. No. 182.
118. KK, 188. No. 315 (See the section on Liberation for a detailed look at this song.)

## Songs as *Locus* for a Lay Theology

Lead Me Ever, still one of the most popular and widely used of his compositions among Malayalam-speaking Christians. There are various opinions as to when this song was written, but the most widely accepted is that this is one of the pieces he wrote after losing his young son to a fatal snake bite.[119] Here, he summons up great faith and courage to commit himself to the will of God. In his commentary on the song, Gladstone writes: "The Word through the death of Christ on the cross reveals the lofty nature of dedication. To find . . . such dedication in experiences of life is what this song challenges one to (do)."[120]

> *pallavi: ninte hitham pole enne nithyam nadathiidename*
> *anupallavi: ente hitham pole alle, en pithave, en yahove*
>
> *inbhamulla jiivithavum, eere dhana maanangalum*
> *thumbamatta sowkyangalum, chodikkunnille adiyan*
>
> *neeru nirappam vazhiyo? niinda nadayo kurudho?*
> *paaram karanjodunnadho? paarithilum bhagyangalo?*
>
> *andhakaaram bhiidhikalo, appane prakashangalo?*
> *endhu nii kalpichiidunno, ellam anikkaashirvadham.*
>
> *eedhu gunamennarivan, illa jnana mennil nadha*
> *nin thiru naamam nimitham, niidhi margathil thirichu*
>
> *agni mekha thuunugalal, adiyane ennum nadathi*
> *anudhinam kuude irunnu, appane kadakshikkuge*
>
>> Refrain: According to your will lead me ever.
>> Sub refrain: Not according to my will, my Father, My Jehovah.

A life of pleasure, plenty of wealth and prestige,
unending comforts, I do not ask

A straight flat road? A long path or short?
Abundance? More fortunes on earth?

The fearful darkness, or Father, the light.
Whatever you command, they are all a blessing to me.

I do not have the intellect to know what is good.
Because of your name I turned to the path of righteousness.

---

119. Gladstone, *Moshe Walsalam Sastrigal*, 66.
120. Ibid.

By pillars of cloud and smoke, you led your servant always.
Every day be with me and look upon me with favor.

The believer's experience of trust is grounded in the reality of the exodus by the Israelites and being led by God in every way. This was a "coming out of and going into" experience for the community. The freedom it signified had both temporal and spiritual dimensions: freedom from the religion and religious structures that had held them in bondage, as well as from the social structures that oppressed them. Walsalam uses imagery from the exodus experience of the children of Israel to emphasize the ongoing guidance and sustenance the community receives from God.

The devotée's trust and faith in the Divine is complete and unwavering, seeking nothing of the material world or otherwise, but only to be subject to the will of God; "whatever is commanded" is a blessing. The recognition that this is not something of the believer's own doing also stands out. Human ignorance in perceiving God's ways is acknowledged, along with the recognition that faith and trust alone draw us to the path of righteousness. This echoes the teaching of Ramanuja that the *bhaktas* were to be upright and do what was pleasing to the Divine, as well as the concept of *nishkamyakarma* (discussed in chapter 2) as an attribute of the *bhakta*, who did all solely to please God.

The *bhakta's* absolute trust in and dependence on God is reflected in a number of Walsalam's other songs, such as: *niiyozhige, niiyozhige aarumilliisho*,[121] I have none beside you; and *ha yeshu rakshakaane, ninnil aashrayichen paahimam . . . vere sharanam ille ente paaraye raksha parichaye*,[122] Protector of the godly, I take refuge in you . . . I have no other refuge, my rock and defensive shield.

The reason for unwavering and unquestioning trust in God is given in the song *veeroraashrayamilla*,[123] which points primarily to the Divine grace that saves, calling sinners to put their trust and refuge in God. To those dying in unrighteousness, Christ provides life and help. This song is also a response to the love of God manifested through Christ, grounded in the belief that the Lord of the Church is Lord over all, and prevails even over the forces of evil. It also reflects the perception of human insignificance before God, in which the believer self-identifies as a *puzhu*, worm.

---

121. KAPA, 124. No. 220.
122. Ibid., 123. No. 218.
123. Ibid., 117. No. 206.

## Songs as *Locus* for a Lay Theology

### Liberation

As the spirituals which evolved from African-American slave culture reflected the social consciousness and aspirations of an oppressed people, one can also trace in Moshe Walsalam's compositions the social consciousness and aspirations of his own community. In context with the latter decades of the nineteenth century, Walsalam was not far removed historically from major social upheavals such as the Upper Cloth protests, advocacy for freedom from enforced labor, *uzhiyam*, the access of lower castes to the use of public roads, and so on. Caste discrimination, though illegal by Walsalam's time, was far from being eliminated. While Christians now had more opportunities to be educated and enlightened, to become more aware of their rights and privileges, they were still very much enmeshed in the struggle for emancipation along with fellow caste members and other lower Hindu castes.

Reflecting this context, some of Walsalam's songs stand out for their theological perspective on the evils prevalent in society at the time. James Cone notes about black American spirituals that they were musical stories of the "black people's historical strivings for earthly freedom, rather than otherworldly projections . . ."[124] This is also true of Walsalam's songs, in that they focus on the work of Christ, the cross, the life of faith, and mission in the light of the community's here-and-now worldly experiences, rather than emphasizing the hereafter. The overall reflection is that of present social realities expressed through faith, in song.

*Sneha virunna nubhavippan*,[125] which is sung during Holy Communion in many Malayalam-speaking churches, is a song that most vividly pictures the aspirations of the oppressed and marginalized:

> *pallavi: sneha virunna nubhavippan, sneha*
> *daiva makkalellarum kuuduvin jayam jayam namukke*
>
> *anupallavi: paka thingi loka makkal*
> *pala kulam jathikalayi pirinju nalkunal*
> *paranodethirkunnu*
>
> *namukkoru pithavu thanne*
> *namukkevarkkum jiivan aruliidunnathum daivathmavu thanne*
> *namukkeka rakshakanaam*
> *namukeevarkum kuudi irippathinini swargam onnuthanne*

---

124. Cone, *Spirituals and the Blues*, 15.
125. KK, 188, 315.

*namukkeeka bhojaname*
*namukkeevarkkum nizhal velicha thuunathum yeshu nayakane*
*vazhi vaathil snanamonne*
*kristhu vidhi chollunneeram namukellavarkum valathubhagamonne*

*snehakkuri thottidenam naam*
*niyamam itheeshuvin janangalkkeevarkkum niyamicheshuparan*
*paka peeyude kuriyam*
*paraneere sangadam koopavum varum pinangum lokarode*

*kristhan thiru chintha dharippin*
*kurisheduthu thazhmayodavan pinchelluvin thiru krupa labhippan*
*eeka manassode japippin*
*avasaanatholavum nilaninniiduvin varum bhagyam namukke*

  *Refrain*: To experience the love feast
    let all loving children of God gather; victory is ours.
  *Sub refrain*: Full of hate, the children of the world
    separate themselves into clans and castes and defy God.

We all have one Father;
The Holy Spirit gives life to us all;
We all have the same Savior;
For all of us to stay together we have the same heaven.

We have the same feast;
We all have the Lord Jesus as our light;
The way, the door, and baptism are one;
When Christ judges we all have the one right side as our reward.

We all have to be marked by love.
This commandment was given by Jesus for all his people.
Hate is the mark of the devil.
The Lord will be sorry and angry and will become hostile.

Wear the holy mind of Christ;
In humility take the cross and follow to obtain divine grace.
Pray with one mind;
Be faithful to the end, blessedness will be ours.

 This song, given the context within which Walsalam lived, ministered and wrote, is powerfully pregnant with symbols of liberation. The *pallavi* and the *anupallavi* lay the thematic foundation, in which the call for all to sit together at the table was a radical concept in such a caste-conscious society. Normally, sharing a table—especially with those from lower castes—was absolutely not done. Most lower caste people would not even be allowed into the homes of higher caste families. Thus, a shared table signifies acceptance, equality, and dignity for the one who would otherwise not have been there. To Walsalam, this would be a victory because it was from God. In the *anupallavi* he is much more direct, openly referring to clans and castes, which he believed were sinful divisions directed against God.

Succeeding verses go on to express the theme that God is the one and only parent to all of us; we all find our life-source in God, whose Spirit enlivens us. God as the Creator and Sustainer of all does not distinguish among clans and castes; all are equally deserving of God's love, just as the children of any loving parent. All of us have just one Savior, and as his children, we are assured that our future lives beyond this earthly one will be in heaven, sharing the same space with him. Within the above-quoted song, Walsalam's text makes strong inferences about divisions within the faithful, perhaps an indictment of problematic historical practices among the Christians of South India themselves.[126]

In the second stanza he again reminds the faithful that we have just one feast; that is, all of us as children of God have a place at the table, share the same baptism, and are promised the same heaven in the hereafter. The word *snehakkuri* in stanza three stands out in particular: while it can be literally translated as "mark of love," *kuri* alone means simply "mark" and is the same word used to indicate the caste mark on a Hindu's forehead.[127] By the

---

126. The St. Thomas Christians, who had found their own niche among the higher castes, did not consider lower caste converts as their equals and did not even worship with them. These two segregated Church of South India congregations exist to this day in Thiruvanandapuram—Christ Church, for those from the original St. Thomas Christian roots and Mateer Memorial Church, primarily comprising lower caste *nadar* Christians; they are just a couple of blocks from each other. Christ Church is not part of the South Kerala Diocese even though it is located within its geographical jurisdiction; instead, it is affiliated with the Central Kerala Diocese which predominantly consists of St. Thomas Christians. This historical division has been a difficult issue wherever members from Central Kerala Diocese have established congregations in diaspora. Yet the reasons given for their separation do not include caste! This state of denial is not only a feature in the Church of South India but also of the Marthoma Church where until recently, lower caste converts were segregated into their own congregations and did not have the same rights as other "Syrian" congregations. Interestingly (and somewhat ironically), this song is among the most frequently used in Marthoma Churches during Holy Communion!

127. *Malayalam-English Dictionary*, 289.

shape of the mark one could identify the caste to which a person belonged. Here Walsalam exhorts all believers to wear instead the mark of love commanded by Christ; this love ought to be the only mark of one's identity. Hate, as manifested in divisions of clan and caste, is a mark of *peyi*, Satan, the devil or demon. To continue in that condition can only bring sorrow, anger and estrangement from the Lord.[128] While referencing liberation from the evil divisions within worldly society, the song also points to freedom within oneself, once the walls of prejudice are demolished by Christian love.

The path to liberation is also the path of the cross; thus we are called to put on the mind of Christ, a mind that humbles itself and transgresses social boundaries, in order to be faithful to him. This again is an act made possible only by grace. Unity in prayer and in the Church are the yearned-for fruits of faith, which includes breaking down or destroying the divisions of casteism; *jaathi bheedangal mudikkanam*.[129]

Walsalam's songs reflect the incarnation itself to be a liberating experience because Christ identified with all people on society's margins; the deprived, oppressed, vulnerable and under-privileged. This is why Christ took the form of a servant or a slave, a *dasan*[130] or *adima*.[131] Jesus is even referred to as a beggar, *yaachagan*.[132] The believer, in identifying with the incarnate Christ, becomes a kinsman with him on the cross. In this context, the resurrection was not so much a victory in the spiritual realm, as it was the overcoming of oppressive and marginalizing temporal space. By dying on the cross, Jesus Christ brought salvation and raised the humblest of humanity from a demeaning state—*marichu thaan, namukku mokshathe varuthi thaan . . . eliya koottare uyarthi thaan*.[133]

## Mission of the Church

The mission of the Church is understood as the action of spreading the gospel and establishing the reign of Christ over all the earth. The power of the gospel will overcome evil within the structures of both religion and society, putting an end to all forms of oppression.

---

128. A better translation might be, "the Lord will become unfriendly," rather than "hostile."

129. KAPA, 170. No. 294, verse 2.

130. Ibid., 211. No. 351, verse 1.

131. Ibid., 212. No. 354, verse 1.

132. Ibid., verse 2.

133. Ibid., 170. No. 294, verse 3.

## Songs as *Locus* for a Lay Theology

*jayikkume! Suvishesham lokam jayikkume!*
*peyude shakthikal nashikkume!*
*sakala lookarum Yeshuvin naamathil vanangume*
*thala kunikkume athu bhahu santhoshame.*[134]

The Gospel will win over the earth;
the strength of the devil will be destroyed.
All the earth will bow at Jesus' name,
will lower their heads; that is cause for happiness.

This mission involves destroying the powers of the devil that were inherent in believers' earlier allegiances and loyalties; in Malayalam these are referred to as *pey*, the term Walsalam uses here. Among the evils to be destroyed are those of caste distinctions and discriminatory social structures. The removal of caste divisions establishes the flag of love.[135] Only when this is accomplished will the reign of Christ become a reality.

To more vividly illustrate the transformation of society through Christ's love, he uses imagery from Isaiah 11:6-9, which describes the wolf living with the lamb, the leopard grazing alongside the kid, and children playing fearlessly with the adder.[136]

Justice is another issue Walsalam deals with in light of the church's mission. Typically, he uses the idea sparingly, but in *yeshu paran vaanidum*[137] the establishment of the reign of Christ and the universality of the gospel are paralleled with justice, equity, and freedom as manifestations of God's righteous justice.

In his more formal *kathakalashepam* compositions, Walsalam approached other social evils more directly, especially the issue of addictions, as in the last verse of *surapaanaparihari*:

*aayussu kallinu vilkkathe nithyam*
*aanandathoodu mokshe sukhippan*
*maayakali ellam vittuvechu raja*
*mannanin pinnadiyil nadappin*[138]

---

134. Ibid., *pallavi*.
135. Ibid., 173. No. 297, verse 3.
136. Ibid., 174. No. 298, verse 3.
137. Ibid., 172. No. 296, verse 5.
138. John, *Collected Works of Walsala Sastriar*, 170.

Don't sell your life to alcohol.
To enjoy the bliss of heaven,
reject all illusions.
Walk in the ways of the King.

The traditional trade or occupation of the *shanar/nadar* community was toddy-tapping, extracting the sap of certain palm and coconut trees to produce a local alcoholic brew; this was considered part of the *varnashrama dharma* of their caste.[139] Two of Walsalam's compositions, *surapaanaparihari* and *surapaanakuttari*, directly urge followers of Christ to reject this occupation and free themselves from a social evil that had been imposed on them; such evils were a consequence of Christ's absence among their forebears; thus it was important to scare these demons away.

While Walsalam's songs do refer to the gospel becoming universal, it should be noted here that the purpose of the church's mission as he understood it was not to establish its hegemony,[140] but rather to establish the freedom offered in Christ.

## Walsalam—An Indian Christian Bhakta

Various aspects of the *bhakti* tradition are reflected in Moshe Walsalam's writings. The basic characteristic of a *bhakta* is the individual believer's intimate relationship with the Divine, which is reflected throughout his songs. He writes that the name of Christ is paramount—*christhuvin naamam maathramen gaanam*,[141] and that he takes refuge at the feet of Jesus, his deliverer—*paadhathil paninjore nithyavum paalikkunnoone*.[142]

As noted in chapter 2, *bhakti*, as an expression of one's total religious experience, was grounded in an emotional encounter with the Divine. This intimate relationship was expressed in various ways. In Walsalam, we see it vocalized in the terms he uses to refer to Christ. He even uses the word for "husband" to indicate the depth of that relationship. Christ is also imaged as the "ocean" of love and grace.

Another aspect of *bhakti* reflected in Walsalam's songs is his rejection of social divisions in society. Historically, the *bhakti* movement originated

---

139. Their duty under caste responsibilities.
140. KAPA, 173. No. 297, verse 1.
141. KAPA, 19. No. 35, verse 4.
142. Ibid., 22. No. 41, verse 5.

in the casteless society of the early and mid Sangam period,[143] thus a feature of the movement in its later stages was a continuing rejection of caste, along with a tradition of using the vernacular (language of the people) rather than high caste Sanskrit. Walsalam's songs reflect his nostalgic yearning for a previous era in which people were free of social oppression, as well as for a liberating future when the love of Christ will reign.

In Walsalam and others of his time, one can trace the origins of local Malayalam expressions in Christian song. Earlier believers had only the choice of songs written in, or translated from Tamil, or translated hymns from the Church of England. Since language is the chief mode of expression for any culture, only that which evolves in a local place and context can faithfully reflect the inner feelings, emotions and experiences of that community. That being so, these songs in the local language of Christian singers became truly authentic expressions of their faith.

---

143. See chapter 1.

# Chapter 4

## Sadhu Kochukunju Upadeshi (1883–1945)

SADHU KOCHUKUNJU'S ANCESTRAL HOME, the Muthampackal *tharavad*,[1] is located on the banks of the Pamba, one of the sacred rivers of Central Travancore, in the present state of Kerala. The small village, Edayaranmula, was close to Aranmula and Maramon, two places of cultural and religious significance. The Aranmula Sree Parthasarathy Temple is one of the most ancient in Kerala and Maramon was the home town of the Orthodox Church reform movement leader Abraham Malpan. Kochukunju's family was part of the reformed Orthodox group, and belonged to the Lakha Marthoma Church in Edayaranmula.

Kochukunju's father, Itty, was a farmer and known for being a "kind and good-hearted" person. He was also known as a devout Christian, involved in the activities of his congregation. Kochukunju's mother, Mariamma, was also from Edayaranmula. She was known for her efficiency and generosity to the poor. K.M. George notes that her ability to face all challenges with true commitment and faith had a strong influence on her son.

Itty and Mariamma's first son drowned in the Pamba River when he was just a toddler, about two-and-a-half years old. After losing him, they had six daughters in succession. In those days, having a son to continue the family legacy was a top priority. The couple became objects of ridicule with so many girls and no boys, so they prayed fervently for a son. When Kochukunju was born, Itty and Mariamma believed God had answered their prayers.

---

1. The ancestral home of a family, here the ancestral home of the Muthampackal family. The name *packal* means "abode," or "where one lives" and *mutham* could be translated "precious." The land the family was located in was very fruitful, hence the name. George, *Sadhu Kochoonju*, 20.

## Birth and Early Life

Kochukunju,[2] M. I. Varghese, was born on November 29, 1883.[3] He grew up in a very devout Christian family atmosphere and attended a Christian school close to his home at Kunnumpuram,[4] Edayaranmula. The young Kochukunju was influenced by the school's head teacher, K.V. Cheriyan, who was well known as a scholar and spiritual guide.

He was a diligent student; if anything caught his interest he would carefully study it. As was the custom among some St. Thomas Christians at the time, Kochukunju was married in 1895 at the age of just 12, to Aleyamma[5] of Vattappara House, Kurianoor. When fellow students taunted him because of his marriage, he refused to attend the local school.

But fortunately, Poovathoor School, an English medium (language of instruction) institution, opened across the river from his home that year. He eagerly enrolled and continued to excel in his studies. Sadly, Poovathoor School closed after about two years and Kochukunju had to end his formal education at age 14. But his life and work thereafter show that he continued to be a student as long as he lived. His search for knowledge led him to master maths and other disciplines on his own.[6]

Around the same time, Kochukunju's father was in failing health and could no longer maintain the farm and his family's affairs. As the only surviving son, 14-year-old Kochukunju had to take on the responsibility of heading the household. In between his farm chores, however, he would spend time reading under the shade of a tree. He was also diligent in studying the Bible, praying, and participating in gospel meetings held at the local church.

---

2. St. Thomas Christians of the area had the custom of naming their children officially with the family name, father's given name and one's own given name in differing orders; family and close friends would also address one by a "pet" name. His full official name was Muthampackal Itty Varghese and family and friends called him Kochukunju, the name by which he came to be addressed by everyone.

3. *Vrichigam* 14, 1059, of the Malayalam calendar. There are differences about the accuracy of the Malayalam date, with two biographers giving it as *Vrichigam* 22; however, his tombstone is inscribed as *Vrichigam* 14. Kochukunju's granddaughter remembers that he died the day of, or day after, his birthday; if true, *Vrichigam* 14 would be the more accurate date.

4. While this name seems to refer to a place, it could also be a reference to the school's physical hilltop location: *kunnu* means "hill" and *puram* means "on."

5. Elizabeth.

6. George, *Sadhu Kochoonju*, 28.

K.M. George notes that the family underwent severe financial hardship due to the costly dowry tradition that prevailed among St. Thomas Christians. This was especially difficult for families like Kochukunju's where daughters so greatly outnumbered sons.[7] After the marriages of four of his sisters, the family owned much less land than before. Adding to the hardship of this time Kochukunju's mother Mariamma, who had been a rock of stability through many a crisis, passed away. As a 16-year-old, Kochukunju continued to minister to the needs of his ailing father and his other siblings. As farming alone no longer earned enough income to support the family, he ventured into a textile business. As Matthew Daniel notes, it ended in failure because of Kochukunju's generosity to those in need.[8] He then taught at the school near his home for a while and also sold local farm products at market in the nearby town of Chengannur. K.M. George describes how neighbors commented that the teenage Kochukunju would carry portions of the Bible tucked in his cap when he went to the farm so that he could read and pray during breaks. At 17 he experienced two profound turning-points in his life; he became a father and also dedicated himself to evangelistic ministry.[9] During this time he became more involved in his congregation, organizing prayer groups, developing children's programs, and teaching Sunday school. In 1903, when Kochukunju was 20, his father Itty died.

Kochukunju spent hours in prayer and made important decisions only after prolonged meditation and reflection. On one such occasion in 1905, he wrote in his diary:

> Decided to offer myself and everything in my care to my Savior. I offered myself to the Lord; I entrusted my wife to the Lord; I gave my children away to the Lord; I gave over to him the wealth in my possession; I handed over my debts to Him; I submitted myself to Him to utilize me in His service in the Lakha Parish; I left all my desires in his hands. At the Eastern end of Pathampuram I fell on my knees. This day is a memorable one in my life.[10]

This decision would set the tone for his lifelong work and ministry in the Church. A singular pattern one can see in Kochukunju's personality is that whenever he believed he had failed, he would rededicate himself afresh. This is further reflected in his deep and intimate relationship with Christ.

7. Ibid., 31.
8. Daniel, *Sadhu Kochukunju: A Biography*, 3.
9. George, *Sadhu Kochoonju*, 34.
10. Daniel, *Sadhu Kochukunju: A Biography*, 5.

Songs as *Locus* for a Lay Theology

## Ministry

After this incident, he became a more active participant in the Parish Mission at Lakha Rev. Thomas Anikat and K.V. Simon[11] were two local leaders who befriended Kochukunju there, where the three worked to advance spiritual and social reformation in the community. In 1905 they formed the Edayaranmula Christian Fellowship Unity, with Simon as chairperson and Kochukunju as secretary. They organized study classes, public meetings, and prayer groups, as well as ministering to the people and visiting them in their homes.

The years between 1910 and 1913 were full of trials and hardships for Kochukunju, marked by poverty, sickness, and especially the death of his second-born son, Samuel. The family was in such dire straits that his wife and children had to move in with Kochukunju's in-laws for a time. He called these difficult years the "Valley of Baca," referring Psalm 84:5.

But these years were also a time of intense meditation and scriptural study for Kochukunju. He spent many hours in solitary prayer and study in the attic or grain cellar of the house. Focusing on books such as Ecclesiastes, his experience of the Lord as his beloved became very real. The gloom of these sequestered places was transformed for him by the light of divine revelation. Daniel refers to it as a mystical or *yogic* experience, in which the *Sadhu* found extreme bliss in the presence of his God. In 1913 he discerned the call to be a preacher and this is how he spent the rest of his life, hence the suffix *Upadeshi* to his name which is translated as "preacher."[12]

Despite his studious ways, Kochukunju sometimes acted on impulse. In 1913 he underwent a "believer's baptism." The motivation for this could be traced to pietistic influences in the Marthoma Church, which came through British preachers with Brethren leanings. But within ten days of being baptized, he writes about questions arising regarding permanent peace and happiness in Christ, as well as his fear of death; he seems to be quickly questioning the validity of his second baptism.[13] But he does not

---

11. Simon and Kochukunju were neighbors and friends from their school days. Simon also went on to become a literary figure and leader in the Kerala Church. He was awarded the title *mahakavi*, or great poet, for his *veda viharam*, a poetic rendition of the book of Genesis.

12. He is known as Sadhu Kochukunju Upadeshi.

13. George, *Sadhu Kochoonju*, 72. He notes that the believer's baptism took place on Edavam 3, 1088 of Malayalam Era and on Edavam 13 Kochukunju wrote the note about his doubts.

give in to these doubts, seeing in them instead an opportunity for rejuvenation and renewal. There are songs that indicate he welcomed suffering and through it identified with Christ.

With a very definite recognition of his call, Kochukunju began the ministry of public preaching. Earlier, he had devoted evenings to his spiritual vocation after working on the farm by day, but now he did it full-time. The prefix *Sadhu* to his name means mendicant or sage in Indian languages. After his decision to take up evangelistic preaching as a full-time call, he also devoted himself to living the ascetic life of a sage, following ancient Indian tradition. He took five vows to which he remained faithful for the rest of his life.

1. Vow of renunciation: He renounced sex and all carnal relationships, considering this step as one of great spiritual gain. The reasons for this particular vow, he pointed out, was to ensure that his ministry among women would be a blessing and that the vow would further his desire for *bhakti*.

2. Vow to read books: For Kochukunju, reading many books and gaining knowledge only for its own sake was not spiritually beneficial; instead, one should derive strength only from God. Thus, all his reading would be directed only for this purpose.

3. Vow to set aside the desire for children: Kochukunju felt content with the children he had and desired only to have spiritual children henceforth; he writes that his wife Aleyamma supported his decision.

4. Vow of meaningful work: He decided that he would be content to farm only the land inherited by him and not on leased lands, giving him more time to devote to preaching.

5. Vow of abstaining from unnecessary food: Kochukunju wanted to concentrate primarily on the needs of his inner, or spiritual, person and thus adopted a very strict dietary discipline. He would eat only to meet the body's physical needs and suppress the body's desire for enjoyable foods. He followed this regimen very diligently; if he felt he was developing a fondness for a particular food, he stopped eating it. He ate only once a day, after 10 p.m., allowing himself only 14–19 meals a month—less than the number most people consume in a week. During daylight hours, he did not even drink water. And if he ate for 10 days in succession, he fasted on the 11$^{th}$ as his tithe. Kochukunju also

considered fasting as a time when one could draw away from the desires of the world and focus more intently on God.

Kochukunju's preaching journeys took him to all parts of Travancore and Kochi kingdoms. George points out that he wrote and rehearsed all of his sermons even though he did not always stick to his script while preaching. Another observed characteristic of his style is that the earlier sermons were more intellectual, while those of his later career were simpler in language and presentation. As his reputation grew, Kochukunju was invited by many different churches to speak at their gospel meetings. It was "rare to find a Protestant Christian in Travancore that had not heard him,"[14] writes George. He frequently made preaching trips to Tamil-speaking areas as well, held meetings in the Telugu-speaking areas of present-day Andhra Pradesh and Telengana, and also went twice to Sri Lanka.

South Travancore (where Moshe Walsalam was from) was a very special mission field. Kochukunju was well accepted and popular among *nadar* Christians of the LMS congregations there. A major reason for his popularity was the volunteer work he did among the *nadar* Christians during a cholera epidemic that struck South Travancore in 1929. Among the volunteers he worked with was C. M. John, who later became Juhanon Marthoma, Metropolitan of the Marthoma Church. Juhanon Marthoma was also a vice-president of the World Council of Churches at the New Delhi Assembly. The relief activities the group did under Kochukunju—including the establishment of orphanages for children who'd lost their parents in the epidemic—endeared these volunteers to the local people.

Kochukunju's work frequently kept him away from home from Thursday through Sunday evening most weeks; in fact, as both George and Daniel point out, this was his usual schedule for at least 30 years. Kochukunju also started annual Christian conventions in a number of Travancore towns that continue to this day.

During a period in 1915, however, he was denied permission to preach in Marthoma churches due to theological disagreements, especially concerning his baptism. Kochukunju was allowed to explain his position and was reinstated. His loyalty to the church was unwavering, even when his close friend, K.V. Simon, joined the Brethren Church. Being rooted in the traditions of the church is reflected in many of his songs, which will be explored later in this chapter.

14. George, *Sadhu Kochoonju*, 72. He also includes the Marthoma Church as part of the Protestant tradition.

Besides preaching and teaching, Kochukunju also served the church in various other capacities. Beginning in 1924, he was General Secretary of the Mar Thoma Voluntary Evangelists' Association,[15] a position he held for 21 years. His corrective voice was heard for many years in the *mandalam*, the National Assembly of the Marthoma Church. He also served on the church's Mission and Clergy Selection committees.

During the course of his ministry, Kochukunju established three orphanages, the first being (as noted above) in Marthandam for orphans of the South Travancore cholera epidemic. He also founded monasteries, schools, and institutions for the well-being of the poor and needy.

After some three decades of faithful and ceaseless ministry, Kochukunju was aware that his body was weakening and wearing out; he knew the end was near but approached it with meticulous preparation, even to the details of how he wished to be dressed for burial. He left this earthly abode on November 30, 1945, after a brief illness. George mentions that his last words were: "Is this death . . . not dying . . . let me rest."[16]

## Sadhu Kochukunju's Writings

Kochukunju was primarily an evangelist and, unlike Moshe Walsalam, not formally trained in the nuances of Indian music. In fact, his biographers mention nothing about him being trained in Indian music, but family contacts suggest that he acquired his musical interest and skills from Hindu friends and the proximity of a Hindu temple near his home.

He wrote a number of booklets on social evils, as well as on Christian faith and living, but the most popular of his writings is *aashwaasagiithangal*,[17] meaning Songs of Comfort, which will be examined in more detail later. Here is a brief overview of Kochukunju's other religious writings:

*Bhaktirasam*[18] is a booklet recounting his own religious experience and how one's experience of the Kingdom of Heaven can produce extreme happiness, or bliss—*moksha*, as a *bhakta* would say. Kochukunju emphasizes that Christians must avoid overindulgence in the pleasures of the flesh and gives practical suggestions and guidance on how to achieve this.

---

15. The voluntary mission wing of the church.
16. George, *Sadhu Kochoonju*, 240.
17. The full title: *yahova bhakthanmaarkulla aashwaasagiithangal*.
18. Kochukunju, *bhaktirasam*.

*Paramachristhyaanithwam*[19] (Essence of Devotion) was written in 1923, during the aforementioned dark period that Kochukunju refers to as his Baca Valley ordeal. On the cover he writes, "The Divine Teachings of my Gracious Lord during My Baca days."[20] This reference originates with the Song of Solomon, whose imagery he uses to illustrate the revelations he received from his Savior.

*Paramaananda christhiiyajiivitham*[21] (Joyful Christian Life), published in 1925, is a commentary on the earlier chapters of the Song of Solomon. The theme is on the joy a follower of Christ will have, in spite of the trials endured in this world. Kochukunju writes that only the love of newlyweds can compare to the love between a devout believer and the Savior.

*Vyapaaradharmam*[22] (The Way of Trade), published in 1926, addresses the business community, urging merchants and entrepreneurs to be just and honest in their ways and conduct themselves in a Christian manner. Kochukunju also includes general instructions about proper ways of doing business and instructions to customers on how to relate to traders.

*Sthreedhanathyagam*[23] (Sacrifice of Dowry), published in 1927, presents Kochukunju's stand against the dowry tradition, which had caused his mostly-female family so much financial hardship during his youth. The booklet explains how to conduct marriages and all such landmark celebrations in a Christian manner. When Kochukunju organized a protest opposing the practice of dowry, this booklet was used to promote the cause.

*Leelachittidoosham*[24] (Evils of Subscription Lottery), published in 1929, exhorts Christian believers to resist the evil of subscription lotteries and also discusses the pros and cons of the banking system of his day. Here Kochukunju warns his readers about greed; how it causes discord within families, the breaking of friendships, and the confusion of deceit.

*Paramaartha christhyaani*[25] (The Sincere Christian), published in 1930, is a devotional on various aspects of the Christian life and how one can become a sincere follower of Jesus Christ. Kochukunju explains the

---

19. Kochukunju, *paramachristhyaanithwam*.
20. George, *Sadhu Kochoonju*, 154.
21. Kochukunju, *paramaananda christhiiyajiivitham*.
22. Kochukunju, *vyapaaradharmam*.
23. Kochukunju, *sthreedhanathyagam*.
24. Kochukunju, *leelachittidoosham*.
25. Kochukunju, *paramaartha christhyaani*.

nature and consequences of various vices, such as idolatry, adultery, lying, drunkenness, greed, and selfishness.

*Yahova bhakthanmaarkulla aashwaasagiithangal* (Songs of Comfort for the Devotées of Jehovah)[26]: as mentioned at the beginning of this section, this remains Kochukunju's best-known and most popular work. In 1947, George wrote that no other publication in the Malayalam language had sold as many as 50,000 copies in 25 years.[27] It points to the popularity of *aashwaasagiithangal*, which by 1985 had been reprinted 22 times. Copies of the original 1922 edition are no longer available.[28] The book contains 235 songs, of which just 27 are by writers other than Kochukunju. The most recent printings were done in 2002 by Kerala-based publisher CSS, followed in 2007 with an edition published by Kochukunju's family.[29]

In his Foreword to the 1939 edition, Kochukunju describes these songs as a "collection of the truth/creed[30] revealed from above." They are further described as the fruit of the writer's deep spiritual experiences, which touch hearts and rouse lofty desires.[31] Kochukunju wrote songs on various occasions, whether travelling, meditating, or simply observing the world around him; if he was inspired, he would jot down the lines that came to him. George notes that he did this even while preaching and would later refine and revise what he had written. Then he would set his words to music on the harmonium,[32] which his daughter played for him.

The songs also reflected his response to life experiences and how he faced them as a person of faith. He had a hymnal with notes in it about the circumstances under which he had written some of the songs. A few of these are included in the 2002 edition of *yahova bhakthanmaarkulla*

26. Kochukunju, *yahova bhakthanmaarkulla aashwaasagiithangal*.

27. George, *Sadhu Kochoonju*, 161.

28. The earliest publication I could track down was a 1928 reprint owned by his granddaughter.

29. Unfortunately, the tunes to most of the songs in the book has been lost. Except for two recent editions of the Marthoma and Central Kerala CSI Diocese hymnals, worship books provided only words, not musical scores. In contrast, most of Moshe Walsalam's songs are preserved along with their musical scores by his family. It is my hope and intention to transcribe the scores of all tunes that have survived in their original arrangements with the assistance of family and children of close associates of the composer.

30. The word *pranaamam* would be a combination of what the words mean in English.

31. George, *Sadhu Kochoonju*, 161.

32. A compact reed organ, whose keyboard is played with one hand and bellows pumped with the other.

*aashwaasagiithangal*, edited by Daniel. In an earlier book on Kochukunju, he has included many of the notes Kochukunju had jotted down. One of these songs, *dukkathinte panaapathram*, The Cup of Sorrow, was written when he saw a nine-year-old boy helping on their farm, the same age as his own son who had died of sickness. This song resonates deeply in the hearts and minds of all Malayali Christians to this day.

Kochukunju's songs do not appeal primarily to the intellect, but to the inner person, which made them accessible to folks from all walks of life. Their pietistic style generated deep religious consciousness, as did his many other writings. Being so little removed in time from the reforming influence in Travancore of mission preachers from non-traditional churches in England and elsewhere, Kochukunju's songs found ready acceptance among local congregations. A close affinity with Abraham Marthoma, head prelate of the Marthoma Church during the latter part of Kochukunju's life and advocate for mission as the church's primary mandate, greatly influenced his writings. A number of songs from *aashwaasagiithangal* have found their way into the hymnals of various denominations from both traditional and non-traditional churches among Malayalam-speaking communities.

## A Theological Exploration of Kochukunju's Songs

As mentioned earlier, the believer's perception of God and other aspects of faith are major themes that arise in song. The mystical character of Kochukunju's experience and compositions has been commented upon by all who have written about him and who remember him.[33] While Moshe Walsalam's songs reflect his formal theological training and are typically written specifically for worship and special occasions, this was not the case for Kochukunju. His songs were generated by a more spontaneous upwelling of his deep spirituality and life experiences.

### *Use of Scripture*

A striking feature of Kochukunju's hymnal is his use of and reference to scriptures. Earlier editions of *aashwaasagiithangal* printed some songs with scriptural references next to the specific verses inspired, or validated by

33. Since I could not travel to India for direct research on this project, I have had theologically trained contact persons do interviews for me; a close associate who worked with Kochukunju, as well as members of Kochukunju's family, were interviewed and recorded.

them. In the song *anandamundenikkaananadamundeni*[34] (I Have Joy, I Have Joy), which is titled[35] *karthavu nammude ashwasamaakunnu*[36] (The Lord is our Comfort), the *pallavi* (refrain) is based on Psalm 16:11b, "in your presence there is fullness of joy."[37] All the verses in this song have a noted reference.

> *pallavi: anandamundenikkaananadamundeni*
>   *yeshu maharaja sannidhiyil*
>
> *lokam enikkoru shashwathamallennen*
> *sneham niranjeshu cholliitunduh*
>
> *sorloka naatukaarkkikshithiyil pala*
> *kashta sangadangal wanniidunnu.*
>
> *Refrain*: I have joy, I have joy,
>   In the presence of Jesus the sovereign king.
>
> That the world is not eternal
> was told me by Jesus who is full of love.
>
> For the citizens of heaven on this earth
> suffering and sorrow will be a part.
>
> Very truly, I tell you, you will weep and mourn, but the world will rejoice; you will have pain, but your pain will turn into joy. When a woman is in labor, she has pain, because her hour has come. But when her child is born, she no longer remembers the anguish because of the joy of having brought a human being into the world. So you have pain now; but I will see you again, and your hearts will rejoice, and no one will take your joy from you.

The verse above is based on John 16:20–22. The rest of the song includes direct references to: 1 Tim 1:19; 2 Tim 4:18; Ps 84:6–7; 2 Cor 5:1; 2 Cor 9:8, and John 16:33. Other songs with scriptural references given by Kochukunju include: *ente daivam mahathvathil, ente ella vazhikalum*

---

34. Kochukunju, *aashwaasagiithangal*, 1. No. 1.
35. Kochukunju has titles to each of his compositions.
36. Unless otherwise mentioned, the first lines of songs are used to refer to them, but Kochukunju gives separate titles to his compositions based on the scripture passage that each refer to.
37. Bible references, unless otherwise noted, are from the NRSV.

*daivaputhran ariyunnu, raavile naam withakka, anukuulanai varika,* and *visrama naadine kandu.*

*Nalpathi anjaam sangiirthanam,*[38] Psalm 45, is an example of Kochukunju's inimitable way of interpreting the psalms.

> *athil rajaavum rakhnjiyum thozhimarum kuude*
> *swargiiya kottaram puukunnanugraha jyo*
> *thisu wilasunnu santhoshame*
>
> In it the King, Queen and consorts together
> are happy in the radiating of the blessed happiness
> the heavenly palace blesses them with.

He then goes on to refer to the king being Jesus, elaborating on his qualities. Kochukunju uses this psalm to point toward the incarnation, as well as to the relationship between the king, his queen, and the consorts, who represent believers.

He also composed songs about various Bible narratives. *Oru makan varunnu,*[39] A Son is Coming, is based on the parable of the Prodigal Son. In Kochukunju's use of scripture we see a coming together of the Word and our experience of the living Christ's revelation. The community's present and past revelations combine to pave the way for new insights and inner understanding.

In *paramachristhyaanithwam,* Kochukunju describes scripture as being the illumination of spiritual experience. He talks of the importance of testing one's experience in the light of received teachings or instructions, *upadesangal.*[40] He goes on to point out that scripture is the living Word and it is through scripture that Christ continues to enliven, convict, and transform—*jiivanullathu, chaidanyamullathu, thulachu kayarunnathu, vakathiruvunalkunnathu.*[41] By affirming the place of scripture and the knowledge of the divine in one's spiritual life, he uses song as a medium to help believers perceive their faith more deeply and raise praises to the Holy One.

---

38. Kochukunju, *aashwaasagiithangal,* 128. No. 154.
39. Ibid., 38. No. 45.
40. Kochukunju, *Paramachristhyaanithwam,* 24–26.
41. Ibid., 38–40.

## Sadhu Kochukunju Upadeshi
### *Experience of God as Father and Mother*

Kochukunju's experience of God as father and mother is reflected in a number of his songs. The concept of God as mother is not new to the Indian worldview, which has a long tradition of female manifestations of the Divine. In Hinduism, the mother goddess is the supreme Divinity, even before the Thrimurthy; she is considered the source of life and sustenance. In *ente daivam swarga simhasanam thannil*,[42] Kochukunju refers to God as sovereign of the entire universe, the provider, sustainer of creation, and father and mother to the destitute.

> *pallavi: ente daivam swarga simhasanam thannil*
> *ennil kaninjenne oorthiidunnu*

*maathaa pithaakkalum viidum dhanangalum*
*vasthu sukhangalum karthavathre*
*paidal prayam mudhalkkinneevareeyenne*
*pottipularthiya daivam mathi*

*aarum sahayamillellaavarum paaril*
*kandum kanaatheyum pokunnawar*
*ennaalenikkoru sahayakan vaanil*
*undennarinjadtilullasame*

*nalloruthaathan pithavillathoorkkawan*
*pettammayekkavinjadrazaanum*
*vidhawakku naadhanum sadhuvinappawum*
*ellaarkkumellaamen karthaawathre*

> Refrain: My God who reigns on the heavenly throne
> has mercy on me and thinks of me.

My mother, father, home, wealth,
property and pleasures is my Lord.
From my childhood years to date
The one who raised me is enough for me.

There is none to help; all on earth
go on whether they see or not.
But to have a helper in heaven,
the knowledge is cause to rejoice

---

42. KK, 155, No. 249.

## Songs as *Locus* for a Lay Theology

> He is a loving Father to the fatherless,
> more loving than the mother who gave birth.
> He is Lord to the widows and the provider of the poor;
> my Lord is everything to everyone.

Another song that uses the feminine address calls God "mother God who gave me birth," *petta thalla daivame*.[43] In the very next phrase, God is called a priest "who accepted me." The sovereignty of God over the universe also stands out in this song,[44] with God referred to as the glorious and merciful one, *ente daivam mahathvathil aadhravaanai jiivikkumbol*.[45] Here, Kochukunju uses the phrase *ha mahesha karunesha ponnuthathaa nii enikkai*—God as the auspicious one, kind provider, gracious one, loving protector, etc.[46] He also uses the same term interchangeably to address Jesus Christ. As found elsewhere in Kochukunju's writing, God's sovereignty is understood to extend over all worlds—*unnatha, daivame, thrilooka rajane*,[47] Exalted one, God, king of the three worlds.

Divine sovereignty is understood in the light of God's attributes as Creator and Sustainer of the universe—*kodaakoodigoolamellam padachavanellaatinum veendathellaam nalki*;[48] that is, the One who created everything in the universe and gave creation all it needed. In the same verse, Kochukunju goes on to describe God as the source of joy to all of creation—*srishtikalkokkeyum aanandadaayakan*. He also refers to creation as having been formed out of nothing, *onnumillayimayilninnu*.[49] As Vitor Westhelle points out, "(p)enitence and the conviction of being under judgment are indeed part of doxological experience."[50] Westhelle uses 2 Maccabees 7 to illustrate his observation:

> When the tale of the martyrdom of the seven brothers and their mother is told in 2 Maccabees 7, we observe that each son, refusing to succumb to the power of the king, affirms that faith with words of praise to God. After the first three brothers have been tortured

---

43. Kochukunju, *Aashwaasagiithangal*, 102. No. 117, verse 10.
44. Ibid., 66. No. 76.
45. Ibid., 2. No. 2, verse 1.
46. Ibid., 3. No. 2, verse 9. The use of this term in reference to Christ was discussed in the previous chapter.
47. Ibid., 127. No. 152, verse 10.
48. KK. 155, No. 249, verse 5.
49. Kochukunju, *aashwaasagiithangal*, 188. No. 209, verse 4.
50. Westhelle, "Creation Motifs," 152.

and killed, the king attempts to persuade the mother to convince her last son to obey him. The mother reminds her son that he should not be afraid, even in the face of this total destruction, for God has made heaven and earth 'not out of existing things' and humanity in the same way (v. 28).[51]

He points out that such an affirmation of creation as being out of nothing, *creatio ex nihilo*, could only result from an experience of total negation. The compositional context of some of Kochukunju's songs has been noted by Daniel and this song is not on the list. But could this thought have been affirmed by his Baca Valley experience which, as noted earlier, was an encounter with negation? This also draws attention to the Indian understanding of creation being a *lila* of God; that is, having come into being at God's pleasure. Creation is expected to praise and proclaim its creator,[52] because God is not only its Creator, but also gracious and merciful.

This raises the theme of sinful humanity's dependence on this gracious and merciful God. Throughout his hymnal, Kochukunju refers to the devotée as *sadhu*. In the Indian context, mendicants or *sadhus* depended on society-at-large for their sustenance and survival. Here, however, the *sadhu* depends only on God to provide every need.

In describing the sovereignty of God down through history, Kochukunju uses the Exodus narrative and the Hebrew name of Yahweh. In the song *ente daivam*, he affirms that this God is on his side. God as Judge is another aspect of divine authority that is reflected here.

> *loka raajaakanmaarellaam sarveshanmunbhilaayi ninniidenam*
> *neerulla thrassinmel maha daivam thuukkiidum mannavare*
> *sookskapadigal kondavaravar karmathe*
> *suukshmamaayi thuukkiittu than widhicholliidum*[53]

> All kings of earth ought to stand in front of the King of Kings.
> Almighty God will weigh humans on a true scale,
> In careful manner each one's actions,
> Will be weighed and judgment proclaimed.

He emphasizes that the judgments of God are to be feared. God is holy and "wears" justice, *dharichoon*, shows no partiality, wields a scepter,

---

51. Ibid.
52. Rao, *Bhakti Theology*, 84.
53. Kochukunju, *aashwaasagiithangal*, 160. No. 184.

and judges all in righteousness.⁵⁴ Moreover God's judgments are always just—*ooroouthanum vidhi nyayamayi nalkiidum*.⁵⁵

The last verse of *ente daivam* points to Kochukunju's assertion that God is on the side of the weak and powerless. He is Father to the orphan, the one who loves and provides for widows and the weak.

God's being is not seen by Kochukunju and other Indian writers in terms of divine essence, but rather in terms of relationship. For them, God *is* because God is relational. As John Zizioulas points out, it is that relating quality of God that takes priority because it is only through relationship that one can become known.⁵⁶ This is especially applicable to the mystic and Christian *bhakta*. God is a heavenly Father and Mother to whom the *bhaktas* look for help. Kochukunju frequently uses related terms such as *bhaktan*, *bhaktanmar*⁵⁷ etc., to refer to the believer.

An intimate and personal love is what characterizes the relationship between a devotée and God. The song *nithyakaala rajaawe*,⁵⁸ that he titled *prema dhyanam*, Meditation of Love,⁵⁹ dwells on this intimate relationship with God.

> *nithyakaala rajaawe bhakthanmaarku mathaawe*
> *ennenneekkum ninnil njan en premam waikkunnu*
> *kashtameere vannaalum ellaam nashtamayalum*
> *mrithyuvenmeel vannaalum daivam ente ashrayam*
>
> *hanockenna vishwasi aayishkaalamokkeyum*
> *daivathoodu koodawan premam poondu nadannu*
> *loke ninnu pooyawan ennanneekkum thejassil*
> *chavin yordanoolangal bhakthanaayawan kandilla*
>
> *moabkari ruuthine israelin maathawai*
> *thiirtha prema shakthiye nine vazhthipaadum njan*
> *ellam vittu snehathal pinne vanna kashtangal*
> *thazhmayoode sahippan daivam krupa nalkiye*

---

54. Ibid., 138. No. 163, *anupallavi*.
55. Ibid., 163. No. 187, *anupallavi*.
56. Zizioulas, *Being as Communion*.
57. *Bhaktanmar* is the plural of *bhaktan*; in Malayalam, the word is *bhakta*, from Sanskrit.
58. Kochukunju, *aashwaasagiithangal*, 71. No. 82.
59. *Premam* in Malayalam indicates sensual love between two lovers.

> Eternal King, Mother to the devout,
> I put my love in you forever.
> Even if I have severe trials and I lose everything,
> even if death overcomes, God is my refuge.
>
> The believer Enoch, through his whole life
> fell in love with and walked with God.
> He went from the earth to glory forever;
> he was fortunate and did not see the banks of death.
>
> You who made Moabite Ruth Israel's mother
> O, power of love, I will praise you
> Left everything, in love to humbly suffer
> the trials that followed, God gave grace.

This is another example of Kochukunju's way of expressing intimate love with God, in which his use of biblical characters and events bring out the themes on which he focuses. It is interesting to see how in the same line, he addresses God as both King and Mother, intensifying the intimacy of this unique relationship. The overarching themes of suffering and trial characteristic of his songs are also evident here. He identifies Enoch and Ruth, male and female, to illustrate the believer's relationship with God, as well as the desire for a future in God's presence.

The song *mannawane mahoonnatha*,[60] Sovereign and Glorious Lord, also points to the devotée's total dependence upon God, who is addressed as the only refuge of the faithful. God as a holy being is worthy of worship, while we humans are barely worthy of singing God's praise. The singer then pleads for grace, to be drawn closer to God.

### God the Son: Jesus Christ

Of Kochukunju's songs about the Son of God, *karthave nin roopam*,[61] Lord your image, beautifully portrays his experience and understanding of Christ.

> *karthave ninroopam enikkelyaipozhum santhoshame*
> *swargathilum bhumiyilum ithupolillor roopam were*
>
> *arakkashinum muthalillathe thala chayippanum sthalamillathe*
> *muppathimuunnarakollam paarthalathil paarthallo nii*

---

60. Kochukunju, *aashwaasagiithangal*, 32. No. 39.
61. Ibid., 158. No. 182.

*janma sthalam vazhiyambalam shayya graham pulkuudakki*
*vazhiyaadhara jiiviiyayi nii bhuulookathe sandharshichu*

*ellawarkum nanma cheyiwan ellayippozhum sancharichu*
*elladathum daivasneham weliwaakki nii maranaholam*

*sathaane nii tholppichawan sarwaayudham kawarnallo*
*sadhukkalkkor sankeethamayi bhulookathil nii mathrame*

*dushtanmare rakshippanum dhesham kuudaadhakkiidanum*
*rakshithawayikshithiyil kaanapetta daiwam niiye*

*changill chora gethashamenil vechundaya poraattathil*
*thulli thulli viyarthathal daiva kopam niingipoyi*

*yehuudhanmaarkkum romaakkaarkkum pattalakkar allaathorkkum*
*ishtampole endhum cheyiwan kunjadupol ninnalloo nii*

*krushinmel nii kaikaalkalil aani eettu karayunneram*
*narakathin thiramaalayil ninnellareem rakshichu nii*

*muunnaam naalil kallarayil ninnudthaanam cheyithathinaal*
*maranathinte parithapangal ennenneekkum niingippoyi*

*priya sishyar madhyathilninnuyirnnu nii swargathilaaya*
*shiikkram waraamennallo nii galiilyarodurachathu*

*thejasinte karthave en pranapriya sarwaswame*
*galiillyarin sangeethame viindum veegam vanniidane.*

Lord your image is always a joy to me;
on earth and in heaven there is none comparable to you.

With no riches and with no place to lay your head
you lived on earth for thirty-three-and-a-half years.

Your place of birth was an inn and your resting home was the manger;
as a homeless person, you traveled around in this earth.

One who did good to all, traveled everywhere,
everywhere you revealed God's love until death.

You defeated Satan and stole his mighty sword.
You are the only refuge to the faithful on earth,

## Sadhu Kochukunju Upadeshi

To save wicked people and to make them righteous.
You are the God who was on this earth as the Savior.

In the conflict in Gethsemane, your blood
Was shed drop by drop which removed the anger of God.

For the Jews, Romans, soldiers, and others
to do anything , you stood there like a lamb.

When you were weeping on the cross with nails in your hands and feet,
you saved all from the destruction of hell.

Because you rose up from the grave on the third day,
the effects of death were removed forever.

You rose from the midst of your dear disciples into heaven
and promised to the Galileans that you would come back soon .

Lord of glory, my beloved, my all in all,
refuge of the Galileans; come again quickly

This song explains in detail the writer's perception of the Incarnation. It begins with Kochukunju's declaration of love for Jesus Christ, pointing again to the intimacy of a relationship in which the devotée finds sole joy and spiritual fulfillment in Christ. It is also a declaration of the unique nature of Christ; there is no one else like him, none can compare to what he did, and does. He is for all time, God's Son, *daiva sudhan*. In referring to the defeat of Satan and the destruction of his sword of evil, one can detect in Kochukunju an echo of the Classical or Triumphalist theory of atonement. As a *bhakta*, Jesus gives anyone who comes to him supreme happiness, *endhanandam*, as the song *ponnu karthavine kaanunna nazhika* states.[62]

Jesus is unique in that he is also the Savior. He, the sinless one,[63] *nirmalan*, came to remove the sins of the world, to save humankind from the punishment for sin,[64] suggesting that the suffering of Christ was vicarious in nature. This theme is amplified in the songs through texts such as, *ente paapam cheyidha dosham kaanunnu njan kruushingal, ente priya*

---

62. Ibid., 117. No. 189. The word *endhanandam* literally means "what great joy," and the title translates as "The moment of seeing the dear Lord."

63. Ibid., 122. No. 148, verse 1. Kochukunju's images of the lamb and dove further emphasize sinlessness.

64. Ibid., 108. Nos. 123, 124.

*ninakkidhu varuvan njan kaaranam*,⁶⁵ I see the harmful effects of my sin on the cross; my beloved, I am responsible for making you to suffer so. This salvific act of God through the Son was unique to Christ, and it was this that endeared Jesus to Kochukunju, who in his own struggles drew strength and sustenance from this closeness to his beloved Savior.

In referring to the Incarnation, Kochukunju states that the Son of God came among us as one with nothing, not even a place to lay his head.⁶⁶ He also identifies Christ with the poor and neglected, moving through society as one without riches. In the song *oru manohara sainyam*,⁶⁷ A Beautiful Army, verse four affirms that identification of Christ with the poorest of poor—*eettam saadhuthwam ulla*. Kochukunju also uses the imagery of a servant and slave, or *dasa*⁶⁸ in Sanskrit, to refer to Jesus' humanity. The place where he was born—the stable of an inn—and who he was during his entire life on earth, place Christ at the margins of society. It was this personal Lord of the marginalized that Kochukunju worshipped and followed.

When George and Daniel discuss his songs, they direct one's attention to those that "call for social change,"⁶⁹ reflecting his involvement in campaigns for improving quality of life for the impoverished and providing aid to those in distress. The booklets and tracts that Kochukunju wrote were briefly discussed earlier in this chapter. The call to "do good" that permeated his prose works similarly stands out in his musical compositions. In fact, Kochukunju was unique in that he wove together the formative elements of pietism and social consciousness in carrying out his vocation. In addition to his involvement in various relief and rescue⁷⁰ operations, his songs also voice condemnation of the caste system and its social evils.

> *yeshu warunnihe thante raajyam sthaapippan*
> *naashamilla raajyamathile raajanum thane*
>
> *jaaathi bhethamo illavidaarilum thanne*
> *jaathi bhethamokke yeshu niikkum snehathal*

---

65. Ibid., 15. No. 16.
66. Luke 9:58.
67. Kochukunju, *Aashwaasagiithangal*, 57. No. 67.
68. Ibid., 56. No. 66, verse 1.
69. Daniel, *Sadhu Kochukunju: A Biography*, 40; George, *Sadhu Kochoonju*, 171.

70. George mentions that Kochukunju and his volunteers went into cholera-infected areas where no others would go; they even rescued babies found still feeding at the breasts of their dead mothers.

*desham deshamayi yeshu bharanam cheyyumbol*
*mooshakkaarennivide kandor kuude vaanidum*[71]

Jesus is coming to establish his kingdom;
He is the king of the kingdom that knows no decay.

There are no divisions of caste there;
Jesus will remove caste divisions through his love.

When Jesus establishes his reign
the ones who are now looked down upon will reign with him.

In the song *karthawin waakthvatham nammalkkundu,* We Have the Lord's Promise, Kochukunju's text affirms *kakshithwa doshamo jaathivikalpamo, illalloo raksahkan pakshakkaarku,*[72] meaning that the evil of group separation or caste distinction is banished from those on the Lord's side.

In the song *karthave nin roopam,* Lord Your Image, its five verses dwell on the death of Christ and what it means to a believer. The cross and suffering are very central to his thought. Kochukunju sees the death of Christ in terms of Satan's defeat; he offers salvation to the wicked, makes the sinner righteous, turns away God's anger, suffers in atonement for others, and saves humanity from hell. What stands out in Kochukunju's *theologia crucis,* (theology of the cross, is that it stands in complete antithesis to the Hindu religious understanding of the confrontation between good and evil. In the theistic form of Hinduism, the wicked are destroyed; love for sinners is a wholly alien concept for a faith in which love is directed only to the *bhaktas.*

Kochukunju's most popular song about Christ's crucifixion is *krushinmeel, krushinmeel,*[73] On the Cross, on the Cross, in which he affirms that Jesus' death was for the sake of sinful humans; through the cross he removed the curse on humankind. While human sin made the cross necessary, it also signifies the utmost expression of God's love.

*Sarwapaapa karakal thiirthu,*[74] Removing all Stains of Sin, is another song in which Kochukunju focuses on the redemptive role of the cross.

*sarvapaapa karakal thiirthu narare rakshiichiiduvan*
*uurvi naathan yeshu deevan chorinja thiru rakthame*

71. Kochukunju, *aashwaasagiithangal,* 149. No. 173, verses 12, 13, 17.
72. Ibid., 162. No. 186, verse 5.
73. Ibid., 31. No. 38. See appendix vi for tune.
74. KK, 98. No. 148.

## Songs as *Locus* for a Lay Theology

*yeshuvoodii lookar cheyitha thorka ii puungaavane*
*veedhanaayoodeeshudeevan chorinja thiru rakthame*

*kaattu chennayi kootamaayooraadine pidichapol*
*koottamayi dushtaradicha ppol chorinja rakthame*

*mullukondullor mudiyal mannavan thiruthala*
*kullilum purathumaayi panja thiru rakthame*

. . .

*vanjaka saathaane bandhi chandakaaram niikkuvan*
*anchu kaayangal vazhiyai vazhinja thiru rakthame*

To save humankind and remove all stains of sin,
the Lord of the universe, the Lord Jesus, shed his blood.

Remember now what the people did to Jesus,
O, the blood shed in pain by Lord Jesus.

Like wild wolves catching a sheep together,
O, the blood that flowed when beaten by the wicked ones.

The Lord's head was crowned by a crown of thorns,
O, and the blood that flowed inside and out.

To bind deceitful Satan and to remove darkness,
O, the blood that flowed from the five wounds.

This song and others on the same theme reveal that Christ's sacrifice on the cross was necessary in order to remove the stain of human sin. As in the writings of Moshe Walsalam, Kochukunju here points to sin as something that stains human beings and is inherent in them. Thus for the removal of this collective stain, the Savior himself had to suffer and shed his own blood. Sin had brought the curses of death and hell to humanity and Kochukunju asks the challenging question; "Hey sinful man, what will you do?"[75]

The shedding of blood, understood as the sacrifice on the cross, is a powerful theme in a number of Kochukunju's songs. The image of a blameless and pure lamb sent to slaughter points to the sinless one offered up for the redemption of humankind. It is the sacrificial blood of Jesus, the Lamb of God, which cleanses and purifies.[76]

---

75. Kochukunju, *aashwaasagiithangal*, 14. No. 14, verse 4.
76. Ibid., 110. No. 180, verse 3.

In the song *karthave nin roopam*, Lord Your Image, he affirms that Christ's resurrection guarantees the salvation he attained for us on the cross; it is in the resurrection that the believer is assured of eternal life. Salvation is to be found in Christ, and Christ alone. The intercessory role of the Son is also touched upon in some of his songs: *sadhu enne oorthu nithyam thaathanoodu yaachikunnu*[77] means that Jesus Christ is always interceding with God the Father on behalf of the *sadhu*. Another theme is that of the Second Coming, with a prayer that Christ, the Beloved One, will return soon.

## *Christian Life*

K.M. George observes that most of Kochukunju's songs deal with Christian life and hope[78] and divides them into groups under the categories of: earthly life's insignificance (transitory nature), hope in the Second Coming, love expressing mystical thoughts, the call for social change, and stirring one to meditative thinking. Among these topics, the transitory nature of mortal life is especially noteworthy. The song *anandamundenikkaananadamundeni*, I have Joy, I have Joy,[79] affirms this thought in a number of places.

> *pallavi: anandamundenikkaananadamundeni*
> *kkeshumahaaraja sanniidhiyil*
>
> *lokam enikkoru sashwathamallennen*
> *sneham niranjeeshu cholliitundu*
>
> . . .
>
> *vishwasa kappalil sorpuram cheeruvan*
> *chukkan pidikkane ponnunadha*
>
> . . .
>
> *koodara vasigalaakum namukkinnu*
> *viidenno naadenno cholwaanenduh*

---

77. Ibid., 13. No. 13, *anupallavi*.

78. George, *Sadhu Kochoonju*, 162. K. M. George, Kochukunju's nephew, was a writer and literary figure in India who received many awards and much national recognition. In the biography of his uncle, he comments on the language and literary beauty of the songs in *aashwaasagiithangal*; however, the aesthetic aspects of Kochukunju's work are not attempted in this project.

79. Kochukunju, *aashwaasagiithangal*, 1. No. 1, and KK, 17. No. 1. This song was also referred to in the section discussing Kochukunju's use of scripture.

...
*karthave nii wegam wanniidane njangal*
*kkoorthaalii kshooniyil mahaa dukkam*
   *Refrain*: I have joy, I have joy
      in Jesus the Sovereign king.

The world is not permanent for me
says my loving Jesus.

To reach the other side in the ship of faith,
hold the rudder, dear Lord.

For us who are tent-dwellers
there is no home or place.

Lord, come soon,
because we are in great affliction.

In other song lyrics, Kochukunju writes that he very much longs to leave this world and see his heavenly abode: "I am marked a stranger and foreigner, for heaven is mine."[80] In his songs and theology, expectation of the Second Coming is very strong, for as a *bhakta* one is only a sojourner in this world. Daniel suggests that this understanding was the motivation for Kochukunju's ascetic way of life, a daily personal discipline based on the vows he took to resist the desires of the material / physical world. His religious discipline became much stronger toward the end of his life. In a 1940 article for the journal *prabhadhadoothan*, he wrote; "O, blessed land of my hope! If only my heart was large enough to grasp you!"[81] One reason Kochukunju gives a number of times in his writings for abstaining from so-called worldly pleasures was that his Lord did not have anything and lived as a servant and homeless person. As noted earlier, he emphasizes that this world is transitory; the only true reality is our sure hope and promise of a future life in the presence of Christ.

*ente desham iidharayalla, anyanayi sadhu*
*haamin desham vittu pokunnu*
*melilerushaleemennecheerthukolva norungiithan*
*shobhayerum waadhilukalenikkayi ttuyarthunnu*[82]

80. KK, 156. No. 249, verse 7.
81. Daniel, *Sadhu Kochukunju Upadeshi*, 73.
82. Kochukunju, *aashwaasagiithangal*, 13. No. 13, verse 5.

## Sadhu Kochukunju Upadeshi

> My home is not here; as a stranger Sadhu
> [I] am leaving the land of Ham.
> The heavenly Jerusalem is ready to welcome me
> and the shiny doors are being lifted.

Kochukunju's desire to be close to his Savior is expressed in the wish to be free of all worldly attachments—*ellam vedinju naam, ellam marannu naam melootunookkikondaanandikaam*[83]—giving up everything, forgetting everything, let us look heavenward, and rejoice. He goes on,

> *thamburanee yeshunadha ponnukantha ente*
> *sangadangal ennu thiirum cholliidane*
>
> . . .
>
> *inbameerum parudhiisil wannuwazhan*
> *njangalkkethra kaalam meedhiniyil kashtam nadha*
>
> *swargasiiyon appurathil kaandhanoode*
> *njangalkandhamillaa waasamaashu nalkiideenam*
>
> *dayavu thonni thamburaane vegam wannu*
> *ninte kleshidharaam njangale nin maarvil cheerka.*

> Lord Jesus, Beloved One,
> tell me when my sorrow will end.

> To come and reign in joyful paradise,
> how much longer do we have to suffer on earth?

> In heavenly Zion with my beloved,
> grant to us eternal abode.

> Be kind Lord, come soon.
> Take us who are weary into your embrace.

Although Christian life is to be sought here on earth, it is the promise of eternity that makes it meaningful. Kochukunju's unwavering hope in the Second Coming of Christ encouraged him to regard the trials of this world as trivial. He was therefore a true *bhakta*, seeking happiness only in the presence of Jesus, the Beloved, upon whom he wholly depended.

Whether Kochukunju's intensity of dependence and devotion in his relationship with Jesus could be compared to Schleiermacher's understanding

---

83. Ibid., 61. No. 71, verse 19.

of absolute dependence is a valid issue to raise. In *On Religion*, while arguing against religion as just "knowing," Schleiermacher asserts that "true religion is essentially contemplative."[84] In another study, *The Christian Faith*, he describes religion as a consciousness or feeling of absolute dependence on God.[85] The *bhakta's* absolute dependence and complete devotion to the Divine is part of the Indian tradition of *bhakti marga*, or the Way of Devotion. As mentioned previously, the influence of *bhakti* on the spiritual and religious context of Kerala was profound. Its impact, especially on the doxological tradition of song-writing, is prominent in the style and expressions of Walsalam and Kochukunju, both of whom derived their melodic traits from the Hindu tradition, while being rooted in Christian theology. In Kochukunju's lifestyle and songs, however, once can identify more of the classical traits of a *bhakta*. Viewed through a Western lens, he seems to fit Schleiermacher's definition of religion very closely, especially in those song texts that express a theology of absolute dependence.

## Love

The songs of Kochukunju reflect his understanding of Christian love, *kristhiiya sneham*, which he expresses as *premam*, as in the sensual-erotic relationship between two human lovers; in this case, it is between the mystic *bhakta* and the Lord, his beloved.

The Song *krishtiiya snehame*,[86] Christian Love, dwells on the greatness of the love of Christ, whose outpouring is the model for the love Christians should have for one another. Although Kochukunju refers to "Christian love" in each verse, he elaborates eloquently about the various manifestations of Christ's love in the world. In his biography, George notes that *krishtiiya snehame* was inspired by Kochukunju's compassion for a widow and he wanted to offer her some solace.[87] In this context, he refers to Christian love as the mother of all loves; there is nothing to compare with its joy. He then sums up all the experiences of a believer as being undergirded by the love of Christ.

---

84. Schleiermacher, *On Religion*, 36.
85. Cross, *Theology of Schleiermacher*, 121–22.
86. Kochukunju, *Aashwaasagiithangal*, 94. No. 110.
87. George, *Sadhu Kochoonju*, 166–67.

## Sadhu Kochukunju Upadeshi

O Christian love! Mother of all love,
Is there anything on earth as delightful as you?
You are mother to the poor, you are queen to the world,
you are the overflowing river, you are the fire that enflames.

O Christian love! Power that makes holy.
What ocean is as pure as you?
In the ship of faith sail the devout;
O Ocean of bliss, you have no end.

O Christian love! Hope of the poor.
Who is on the side of the broken as you?
Medicine to the sick, clothing to the naked,
bread and wine to the hungry are you.

O Christian love! Refuge of the widows.
Who is there as companion to the lowly like you?
Father and mother to the orphans,
well-being to the oppressed, you are Christ's love.

O Christian love! Strength to the weak.
None has the strength to combat you in conflict.
Even if mountains be submerged by the waters of the flood,
eternal flame of love, you are the light to the devout.

O Christian love! Refuge to the wanderers.
Who is such a mountain of refuge as you?
Even in enemy territories, on the mountain tops,
you are the delightful wind that sweetly blows.

O Christian love! Song in times of danger.
When confronted by trials you remove all afflictions.
Even if all is lost, the world pushes one aside,
you are the breast that comforts, you are the life in the desert.

O Christian love! The power that saved me.
Refuge to the sinner, door to heaven,
grant me the favor to live for you,
to be a salvation to all walks of people.

As the words of the song so vividly portray, it is the love of Christ that saves and sustains the believer, and is the hope of all the distressed. This composition aptly summarizes the writer's experience of the love of Christ. The response of the sinner is a work of the love of Christ; that is, it is a work of grace. Christ's love is the ocean of bliss or *moksha* and in it the *bhakta* finds boundless and eternal delight and contentment.

As we have seen, the *bhakti* literature of India places great emphasis on love. Kochukunju pictures God as the supreme source of overflowing love for humankind and the created order. *Bhakti* (or devotion) is the continual flow of love from the *bhakta* to God. In turn, the *bhakta's* outflow of love is directed both to God and to the world around, since believers are understood to be images of Christ on whose love their devotion is modeled. Kochukunju draws attention to love as the sustenance of creation in the song *ente daivam swarga simhaasanam*.[88]

> *karayunna kaakkakkun, vayaile roosakkum*
> *bhakshyavum bahngiyum nalkunnavan*
> *kaattile mruugangalaatiile malsyangal*
> *ellam sarveeshane nookkiidunnu*
>
> *kodaakodi goolamellaam padachavan*
> *ellaattinumm veendadhellaam nalki*
> *srishtikalkkokkeyum aananda kaaranan*
> *dushttanmaarkkeettavum bhidhiikaran*

> To the crying bird and the rose in the field
> He gives food and beauty.
> Animals in the forest and fish in the rivers
> all look to the Almighty.
>
> The one who made the universe,
> He gave everything to all.
> The reason for joy to all creation,
> the biggest terror to the wicked.

In Kochukunju's songs, God's love clearly encompasses the entire universe. To him, the created order was also a means of God's revelation. As a *bhakta* who looked forward to being in the presence of his Beloved, Kochukunju repeatedly composed lyrics about the transitory nature of this

---

88. Kochukunju, *Aashwaasagiithangal*, 66. No. 76, verses 4 and 5.

world and the redemption of the created order. God gives all of creation hope for redemption.

As noted above, a unique aspect of Kochukunju's songs is their expression of love for God using terms normally associated with intimacy between two human lovers, or *premam*, rather than traditional images one might usually encounter between God and a believer. Thus in addressing Christ, he frequently uses phrases such as *praananaathan* (Lord of my life), *premanaathan* (Lord of my love), *priiyakaanthan* (dear lover), and *priiyan* (my love). The poetically sensual Song of Solomon was a favorite Old Testament book of Kochukunju's; both in his songs and devotional booklets, he uses intimate images found there to describe the relationship between God and the believer.

In the song *swargiiyadhambadhimaarude sambhaashanam*,[89] Conversation Between the Heavenly Couple, Kochukunju likens the relationship between Christ and a devotée to that of a couple waking up and expressing their devotion for one another in passionate love-making.

> *shooleemiye premakanthe nin mukhan njan kandiiduwan*
> *veegam ezhunneelkkuka vaa en kuude nii*
> *kaalam paazhilaakkuvadhendhu sangadamii nilayikku nii vannadhendhu*
> *prema daaham vedinjayyo praavee nii*
> *ninte saakshi naadam kelpathinu kaalamai*
>
> *varshakaalam kazhinjithaa shiithamaari niingipooyi*
> *sneha chuudoodezhunneelkka soodhari*
> *ente sangadangalil vankadalkkare vannu nookkuka viithi*
> *aazhameeruveekkaal uyaravumallayoo*
> *njan ente krushil nine snehichathennoorkka nii.*

O beautiful one, my love, for me to see your face,
get up soon and come to me.
Why do you waste time? It is sad. Why come in such a state?
Did you give up the thirst for love?
It is time to hear your voice.

The rainy season is over, the cold rains moved on.
Get up with the strong passion of love, sister.
In my sadness I come to the great ocean and see;

---

89. Ibid., 28. No. 35.

it is not wider, deeper, or even higher
[I] remember the love with which I was loved on the cross.

This is yet another song that throws light on the intensity and intimacy of the love between God and the *bhakta*, through its comparison with two lovers, or bride and groom. It again affirms that one's response to God can only be through love. The core of the *bhakti* relationship with God is an attitude of total surrender, and so the believer pleads with the Beloved to once again respond with intense passion. The song later moves toward directing one's love to others, but it is in being with the source of love that brings the *bhakti* most intense joy.

> *ponnu karthaavine kaanunna naazhika*
> *endhaanandam enathmave ha endhaanandam enathmave*
> ...
> *kaadhanoodonnichulaavunnadhoorkkumbool*
> *endhaanandam enathmave ha endhaanandam enathmave*
>
> When I see my dearest Lord,
> how joyful is my soul; O, how joyful is my soul?
> ...
> Resting with my lover,
> how joyful is my soul; O, how joyful is my soul?[90]

In the song *mannavane mashihaye*,[91] the intense yearning of the *bhakta* to be with the loved one is expressed as a series of pleading questions: *ennu kaanaam, ennu kaanaam* and *ennu varum, ennu varum*—when will I see you? when will I see you? and when will you come? when will you come? The devotée's heart is torn apart when the lover is perceived as being absent. Here, Kochukunju also addresses the Lord as his "husband"[92]—*prema sukhan poole veere sukham endhu, daiva premasukham pole veere endhu*[93]—what joy is there to compare with the joy of passionate love? what joy is there to compare with the joy of the passionate love of God?

He looks forward to the day when he will go to his *preemasakhi*,[94] or love-companion, to lean on the Beloved's breast and forget everything else.

---

90. Ibid., 117. No. 189, verses 1 and 4.
91. Ibid., 39. No. 47.
92. Ibid., verse 2.
93. Ibid., 58. No. 68.
94. Ibid., 88. No. 104, verse 9.

## Sadhu Kochukunju Upadeshi

### *Trust*

Absolute trust and dependence are continuously interwoven through the writings of Kochukunju, especially in compositions from his Baca years, during which he faced and responded to the trials and suffering that came his way. One of his best-loved songs is *dukkathinte panaapathram*,[95] The Cup of Sorrow. As mentioned earlier, it was written after the death of his second child, Samuel, at age nine. In the note he jotted down at the time of composing this song he wrote; "seeing my wife asking a boy, our dead son's age, to dig in the land I repented and sang this song."

> *dukkathinte panapaathram karthavente kaiyill thannaal*
> *santhoshathoodathuvangi halleluyah padiidum njan*
>
> *doshamaayittonnum ennoodente thaathan cheyikayilla*
> *enne avan adichaalum avanenne snehikkunnu*[96]
>
> If the Lord gives to my hands the cup of sorrow,
> I will receive it joyfully and sing halleluiahs.
>
> My Lord will do nothing harmful to me;
> even if he beats me, he still loves me.

This reflects Kochukunju's absolute trust and dependence on his Lord, whatever life's circumstances may be. In loving God, the *bhakta* surrenders wholeheartedly to the Divine, another concept that is variously understood in Indian thought. Two prominent schools of opinion among the followers of Ramanuja differ in their understanding. One group sees it in terms of a baby monkey clinging to its mother as the *bhakta* clings to God under all circumstances; the onus is on the *bhakta* not to let go. The other group uses the analogy of a cat carrying its kittens to explain the *bhakta's* relationship with God; the *bhakta*, like the passive kitten, does nothing but simply gives up the self entirely to the Divine.

These images also help in understanding the work of grace in one's surrender to God. From the analogies noted here, parallels can be drawn between the first group, baby monkey, and the concept of salvation by works, while the second group, the carried kitten, more closely reflects salvation through grace. The Southern School, as the second group is called,[97] is

---

95. Ibid., 38. No. 45. See appendix v for tune.
96. Ibid., verses 1 and 2.
97. Appasamy, *Theology of Hindu Bhakti*, 108.

reflected in Kochukunju's songs that describe the Lord as a *bhakta's* saving strength, holding one against the Lord's breast—*paapamellam pookki enne, maarvil cheertha amma nii paripaalakaa vandanam,*[98] you are my mother who removed all my sins and embraced me to your breast, O, protector, praise to you. In the song from which this reference comes, he continues:

> *aarude meelum aasrayam vechal*
> *avrellaavarum name thallium*
> *yeahuvinmel naam aasrayam vechal*
> *avanil thanne sakalavum undu*
>
> ...
>
> *ninnepoolillarumenikku*
> *varanee veegam enne kaanan*
> *haa enikkasrayamaarumille*
> *varane veegam enne kaanan*

> Whoever we place our trust in,
> all of them would reject us.
> If we place our trust in Jesus,
> He has everything in him.
>
> ...
>
> I have none like you;
> please come to see me soon.
> I have none else as my help;
> please come to see me soon.[99]

## Ecclesiology

The song *endhendhu santhosham, endhendhu santhosham,*[100] How Joyful it is, How Joyful it is, delineates Kochukunju's image of the people of God. He refers to the worshiping community as a holy fellowship of love—*parishuddanmar sneeha kuuttamaai cheerunna*—as well as a rejoicing community, *aanandamulla.*[101]

---

98. Kochukunju, *aashwaasagiithangal*, 52. No. 63, verse 2.
99. Ibid., 85. No. 100, verses 1 and 5.
100. Ibid., 161. No. 186.
101. Ibid., verses 1 and 2.

Satan's influence or feelings of despair
will not exist among the Holy ones.
In the Lord's love, in friendship with one another,
the saints together sing.

Selfish behavior or egotism;
how blessed are the saints who are not touched by these.
They bear each other and
are happy because of Jesus.

The evils of groupism and division of caste
do not belong to those on the Lord's side.
They are a fellowship that evolved
from their oneness in Christ.

Rich or dreadfully poor,
those in positions, or those that are simple;
from the time they are in the Lord,
in genuine unity they are one.

To share wealth with those in need
is a joy to those in Christ.
The gifts of mercy that the Lord gives
to share with the needy are a blessing to one.

If there are deceivers among the holy,
like Ananias and Sapphira,
the Lord will pass judgment on them.
O, terrible will be their plight.

The holy ones will leave this earth and
will sing together in the Holy One's presence.
Eternal is their joy and happiness;
Lord Jesus is their joy.[102]

Through this poetic catalogue of their characteristics, Kochukunju portrays the people of God as a holy community, a community of love, a generous community, a joyful community, and a community with no distinctions or divisions of class and caste.

---

102. Ibid., verses 3–9.

## Songs as *Locus* for a Lay Theology

In *swargasthapithaavaam daivame*,[103] Father in Heaven, he also describes the people of God as a worshiping community—*thirunaamathil koodi varunna*[104] and continues with a description of this blessed community as one that prays and praises together. He also points out that it is a repentant and learning community, in which young and old receive instruction in the Word of God.

In spite of holding a very fundamentalist theological position, which resulted in periodic conflict with ecclesiastical authorities, Kochukunju remained faithful to the Marthoma Church and its traditions. The sacraments and the altar itself signified to him the holiness of God, a topic featured in the songs *dukkathinte panapathram*, The Cup of Sorrow and *sathyeeka daivame ninte kuudaarathil*,[105] One True God, in Your Tabernacle. In both, he describes the altar, the presence of the Eucharistic elements, the rising of the incense, and the curtain.[106]

In the first of these examples, *dukkathinte paanaapathram*, after declaring his total trust in God, Kochukunju in the persona of the believer identifies with the suffering of Christ; he does not look forward to anything but to bear the mark of the cross. He describes God's glory filling the sanctuary, along with the fragrance of prayers of the faithful rising to God. For him, the altar symbolizes the sacrifice of Christ for our salvation.

In *sathyeeka daivame*, the second example, Kochukunju compares the believer to the altar itself, praying for faithfulness and sustenance to do God's will. Just as everything prepared for the altar reflects God's divine purpose, the believer's prayer is to be so prepared by God. The song goes on to reference the cross of Christ, for it is because of the sacrificial altar that sinners find daily redemption. Referring to the screen or curtain before the altar, Kochukunju notes that worshipers often forget that it represents the cross, which made salvation possible.

In both these songs, he expresses the comfort and sustenance the believer experiences through such nearness to the altar and sanctuary. Here, Kochukunju prays for grace to be a human embodiment of what the altar and sanctuary represent.

---

103. Ibid., 120. No. 146.

104. Ibid., verse 1.

105. Ibid., 59. No. 69.

106. The Marthoma and Orthodox traditions still place the altar behind a curtain, as is the Orthodox tradition..

## Sadhu Kochukunju Upadeshi

### *Social Concerns*

Kochukunju's involvement in social justice and activist causes for improvement to the lives of the poor has often been acknowledged by those familiar with his work and writings. One can discern throughout his ministry a continual effort to use the Gospel to transform and reform society. Among his songs on the theme of social change the most widely known is *karthavin pakshathaar*,[107] Who is on the Lord's Side? It is a long composition with 31 verses, listing the various vices seen in society. He condemns them all and declares their dreadfulness. In this and other songs, such as *kaalam apakadathilaayirikkunnu*,[108] The Times are in Danger, he comes out strongly against business and banking practices that exploit the poor and needy.

To Kochukunju, the work of the cross was not just about actualizing a transformation of the inner person, but equally of reforming a society which he believed was under the dominion of Satan, the evil one. Salvation, however, is accessible through the cross which transforms society, freeing us from the Devil's power. In this song, excerpted below, he asks:

> *karthavinte pakshathu nilppaan ividethra mahathmaakkalundu,*
> *krushil maricheesukristhan kenchunnu nammaloodinnum,*
> How many great souls are here to be on the Lord's side?
> Jesus Christ, who died on the cross, beseeches us even today.[109]

To drive home his points, Kochukunju refers to God the Son in several of his songs, outlining his position against caste and class distinction, calling it an evil practice and deception of Satan. There will be no place for any kind of societal division and bigotry when the sovereignty and love of Christ encompass all of humanity. In the presence of God, where Satan has no power, the community will be free of these sins.[110]

### *Suffering*

Kochukunju personally welcomed suffering as a means of identifying more profoundly with Jesus Christ. He writes, *kashta nashtameeri vannal bhagyavaanai thiirunnu njan, kashtameetta karthaavodu, kuuttaaliyai thiirunnu*

---

107. Kochukunju, *Aashwaasagiithangal*, 88. No. 105.
108. Ibid., 21. No. 25.
109. Ibid., 88–89, No. 105, vv. 1–2.
110. Ibid., 70. Nos. 67 and 68.

*njan*[111]—I am fortunate if my tribulations and losses increase; I become a kinsman of my Lord, who also suffered. Similarly the suffering of the faithful, according to him, has a redemptive purpose and character. Tribulation and loss were both understood as being natural consequences of following Christ—*bhakthanmaarku bacayin siioon margamaakunnu*,[112] to the godly, Baca is the way to Zion. Thus for Kochukunju, the faithful Christian's calling is to give up and forget all that pertains to earthly happiness and to find one's joy solely from above.

As mentioned earlier, Kochukunju's own physical-material and spiritual way of life exemplified suffering as a primary mark of being Christian; his daily ministry was shaped and molded by it. To summarize, the cross was central to his faith and living. Westhelle reminds us that the cross is "always the other side" of the resurrection; if not for the cross, we would never experience the resurrection.

## Kochukunju: A Sojourner Bhakta

The dominant theme of Kochukunju's life and work was the understanding that he was only a wanderer, a spiritual nomad on earth who looked forward to his eternal home and a promised future in the presence of Jesus, the Beloved One. Through him, one can trace the coming together of Indian spirituality, the Marthoma Church tradition, and Western-influenced systematic theology. While some of his songs raise a critical voice against recent (early twentieth-century) tendencies in theological thinking, especially higher critical thought, Kochukunju's use of Western literary tools and other resources was accomplished and refined. Despite receiving formal education only until the age of 14, he continued his quest to continually inform himself of developments in various fields.[113] In his writings and songs, for example, he often makes references to reformers from the West and their influence on him is reflected in his work.

The intimate relationship of this unique *bhakta* with his Beloved One permeates his entire output. Kochukunju fully expected to be with his lover, the Lord Jesus, and to find eternal bliss in repose on his breast. This was the ultimate experience of the *bhakta*. As a true *bhakta*, we see in his

---

111. Ibid., 38. No. 45, verse 3.
112. Ibid., 40. No. 48, verse 3.
113. Copies of the covers of the parallel Bible and commentaries he used were sent to me.

writings an intense sense of God's passionate nearness, but also those occasions when this nearness seems to be lost—*nallavane vallabhane ennu nine vannu kaanam*,[114] Good One, Almighty One, when can I see you?

Kochukunju's intense and intimate spiritual experiences are openly expressed throughout his sacred songs. Along with his ministry of preaching, it was these songs that voiced his interpretation of scripture and his vision for church and society. Their words flow in memorable verse from the depths of his heart. As such poetic expression is the literary tradition in India, looking for and attempting to systematize these versified theological concepts in prose remains a challenging, and at times frustrating, endeavor. As Daniel points out, in Kochukunju one detects the language of the heart expressed as "music of the mind."[115]

---

114. Ibid., 30 No. 36, verse 1.
115. Daniel, *Sadhu Kochukunju: A Biography*, 44.

# Conclusion

SONGS, AS MELODIC EXPRESSIONS of a worshiping community's faith experience, are also its theological statements. They encompass that community's understanding and interpretation of the Word and how it reflects their praise to God. Hymns, in a very profound way, reflect on the mystery of faith as experienced by both their writer-composers and their receiving faith communities. They stand up to theological scrutiny and endure over time as a medium for communicating the Word, creedal beliefs, and traditions of the Church.

As the previous two chapters on Moshe Walsalam and Sadhu Kochukunju illustrate, hymns affirm and sustain a denomination's theology, taking the place of confession in communities that do not have an established tradition of formulaic confessional statements. Walsalam belonged to a mission church that was an outgrowth of the London Missionary Society's work in Southern Travancore, while Kochukunju belonged to the reform movement of the Jacobite Orthodox tradition in Central Travancore. For both of these fledgling movements hymnody, more than anything else, carried the faith and beliefs of the laity which collectively recognized the value of their continued use in worship.

Another important attribute of these hymns is their ecumenical nature. They cut across denominational lines, being used for communal and personal praise by Orthodox, Reformed Orthodox, Protestant, Anabaptist, and Pentecostal traditions. *Ninte hitham* and *dukkathinte panapathram* are classic examples of how these songs have been adopted by different communities.[1] Topically, both could be classified as being about trust and hope, and were written during very trying and sorrowful times for their authors.

---

1. Discussed more fully in chapters 3 and 4.

## Conclusion

Both also contain formative Old Testament imageries. *Ninte hitham* refers to the pillar of fire by night and pillar of cloud by day leading the Israelites—*agni meekha thuunugalal*. In *dukkathinte panapathram* there is the image of the tabernacle, *kuudaram*, which also means a tent. Communities whose members came from oppressive and exploitive conditions would see the liberating hand of God leading them on in *ninte hitham*, while more liturgical groups would see their traditions affirmed in *dukkathinte panapathram*, whose imagery of the tabernacle would be understood as representing both the altar and elements of the Eucharist.

Both Moshe Walsalam Sastriar and Sadhu Kochukunju Upadeshi were pioneers among Malayalee hymn-writers and were very much products of their times. Colonization was the overarching and hegemonic influence during that period and this reality also included contemporary religious movements of late nineteenth- and early twentieth-century India. In this context, viewing the writings of exemplars such as Walsalam and Kochukunju as being postcolonial in nature merits closer examination. As R.S. Sugirtharajah observes:

> Anti-colonial reading is not new. It has gone on whenever a native put quill pen to paper to contest the production of knowledge by the invading power. Postcoloniality begins when subjects find themselves thinking and acting in certain ways. What is distinctive about the current enterprise, however, is that it is not locked into the colonial paradigm where the colonialists set the ground rules, but, more importantly, it concedes the complexity of contact between the invader and the invaded. It goes beyond the binary notions of colonized and colonizer and lays weighty emphasis on critical exchanges and mutual transformation between the two.[2]

## Colonialism

Colonialism has been variously described and defined through history. In its earlier usage, it referred to the movement of people from one geographical area to another in search of a better economic, religious, or political life—often a combination of these aspirations. Such migrant peoples historically established communities in their new lands but maintained "citizenry bonds" with their countries of origin.[3] Over time, however, the meaning and implications of colonialism have undergone radical change.

---

2. Sugirtharajah, "A Brief Memorandum," 3.
3. Young, *Postcolonialism*, 20.

Until the early nineteenth century, the word was used in a positive rather than pejorative sense. In the culture of the time, bringing higher civilization to "less-developed" peoples through colonization was seen as a praiseworthy enterprise. Originally, definitions of colonization did not include the elements of power and subjugation, focusing rather on settling in a foreign land and not dominating or enslaving its residents. Taken in this way, the word did not have the negative connotations it acquired later on.

But this process of settling in an alien land was not without consequences to its indigenous people, since it resulted in the "un-forming" and "re-forming" of the local population at all levels of existence—social, economic, religious, intellectual.[4] Edward Said's *Orientalism*[5] (1978) is widely credited with inaugurating colonial discourse as a new field of academic inquiry. In this book, as well as his 1993 study, *Culture and Imperialism*,[6] Said is among the first to argue that colonialism is not only an economic and political phenomenon, but also includes culture—the assertion of control over a territory beyond political or economic agendas in order to exert cultural and imaginative power.[7]

In current usage, the tendency is to use the term colonialism to refer to 500 years of European global domination, from the 1400s through 1800s. While this phenomenon certainly happened at other points in human history, the extent and impact of European expansionism during these centuries was much greater than at any previous period. Consequently, criticism from "colonized geopolitical sites" has also been greater.

After half a millennium, however, the global empires built by once-powerful European nations began to fall apart, beginning with the 13 American colonies breaking away from Britain, culminating in the 1776 U.S. war of independence. This pivotal event was followed by a succession of Latin American and Caribbean nations gaining independence from Europe during the nineteenth century. Following World War II (1939–1945), another wave of independence occurred in Asia, Africa and Oceania. Researchers often pinpoint 1947 as the beginning of the end for the era of colonial empires. But the collapse actually occurred over three centuries, due to various campaigns of anti-colonial resistance and rising nationalist movements. The period since that time has come to be known as the Postcolonial Era.

---

4. Loomba, *Colonialism/Postcolonialism*, 2.
5. Said, *Orientalism*.
6. Said, *Culture and Imperialism*.
7. Boehmer, *Colonial and Postcolonial Literature*, 5.

## Conclusion

### Notion of Postcoloniality

The term *Post*colonial seems to suggest the dual connotation of something coming chronologically afterwards, as well as that which supersedes it, i.e. the *colonial*.[8] Fernando Segovia is among those who argue for understanding this term both ways. He sees postcolonial as including "a temporal (what-follows-the-colonial) as well as a critical application (what-questions-the-colonial)."[9] This explanation for both definitions seems quite straightforward; the era of formal colonial control is no longer a reality and points to the historico-political reality that follows the colonial one—that "period of time following the formal separation or 'independence' of a 'colony' or group of colonies from a governing 'empire.'"[10]

Yet the reality of colonialism continues in various non-formal structures even to this day.

> Other forms of domination, largely driven by a globalizing capitalism, quickly replaced the formal structures of empire. The concepts of 'neo-colonial,' 'imperialist,' and 'neo-imperial' articulate this condition of informal subjection of a sovereign state to a superpower and/or to transnational corporate priorities. Forms of formal colonialism, however, also survive along with neo-colonial ones.[11]

With colonies continuing to be a present-day fact in different parts of the world, historico-political and chronological definitions do not adequately portray this reality. Here is where Segovia's second definition deserves more examination. One can argue that the notion of superseding the colonial is little different from an unequal exercise of power and must be rejected. Conversely, his notion of "post" in non-chronological form suggests "a critical idea, and so indicates the intention to go beyond the colonial in all its forms."[12] Expressed this way, the concept is not bound by chronology, but rather by place and context in relation to the continuum of colonialism. In Postcolonialism, dwelling on colonization's "historical effects" has a place in the discussion, but only for the purpose of shedding light on its aftermath. A more inclusive and wider definition of Postcolonialism would describe it as a "discourse of resistance to projects of dominance."

8. Chrisman and Williams, "Colonial Discourse and Post-Colonial Theory," 3.
9. Segovia, "Interpreting Beyond Borders," 12.
10. Ibid., 12.
11. Keller et al., *Postcolonial Theologies*, 7.
12. Ibid.

Sugirtharajah also notes that Postcolonialism is a contentious term:

> Considering its relatively recent entry into the Western academy, it has successfully brought to the hermeneutical agenda the overlapping issues of race, empire, diaspora, and ethnicity. It must be stressed that it is not a homogeneous project, but a hermeneutical salmagundi (*mish-mash or miscellany*), consisting of extremely varied methods, materials, historical entanglements, geographical locations, political affiliations, cultural identities, and economic predicaments . . . The current postcolonial criticism takes the critique of Eurocentrism as its central task . . . It signifies three things—representation, identity, and a reading posture, emerging among the former victims of colonialism.[13]

He goes on to discuss the diversity of the Postcolonial enterprise, also emphasizing that this is a task undertaken by the victims of colonization. As noted in my earlier citation by R. S. Sugirtharajah, when "the natives" put pen to paper, by that very act they challenge the assumptions and representations of the colonizer; thus, Postcolonial expressions happen.

In his article "From Orientalism to Postcolonialism," Sugirtharajah highlights the main characteristics of Postcolonialism. Primarily it involves the "Other," the people who were colonized, "insisting on taking their place as historical subjects." Those once relegated to the periphery as inconsequential, now make themselves heard as "confident, indomitable, and indispensable" partners in the dialogue, as well as collaborating with those similarly dispossessed and disadvantaged in the West. In such an exercise, the Orient-Occident, Colonizer-Colonized boundaries that once segregated them are torn down; those formerly on the margins make themselves heard and felt at the very center of society.

Currently, Postcolonial studies are theoretical attempts to engage with a particular historical situation. But what characterizes the notion of Postcoloniality in this context? Most now see it as far more complex than the transitional and often turbulent conditions that attend the aftermath of colonial occupations. In Keller, Nausner and Rivera's *Postcolonial Theologies: Divinity and Empire*, distinction is made between the chronological historico-political approach to understanding the term *post* in Postcolonial, and the critical idea that informs an "intention to go beyond the colonial in all its forms."[14] I would argue for classifying as *Post*colonial any discourse

---

13. Sugirtharajah, *Asian Biblical Hermeneutics*, 16.
14. Keller et al., *Postcolonial Theologies*, 7.

## Conclusion

(even if the intent is not explicit) that counters the cultural and discursive domination of the colonial. As Westhelle points out:

> Postcolonialism indicates a crossing over the boundaries of the colonial world, simultaneously incorporating some of its values and accomplishments while abandoning others in a dynamic process . . . Postcolonialism receives a distinct and definable character which, however, cannot be precisely identified because its own self-expression is evasive in its hybridity; its language is not conceptually pure. The language of Postcolonialism is characterized by 'heteroglossia,' an intersection of different semantic fields producing unexpected communicative effects.[15]

Unlike much of Western theology, the non-systematic nature of Indian religious expression has made it possible for variant voices to be heard. In the process of making the Christian message relevant, or serving it in an "Indian cup,"[16] one can indeed perceive Westhelle's crossing of boundaries and the emergence of something new, which during Walsalam and Kochukunju's time was, by its very nature, subversive.

M. M. Bakhtin, writing in *The Dialogic Imagination*, explains "hybridity" as a mixture of two social languages within the limits of a single utterance; that is, an encounter within the arena of an utterance between two different forms of linguistic consciousness, separated from one another by an epoch, by social differentiation, or by some other factor.[17]

Homi Bhabha sees hybridity as a counter-narrative in which the liminal, or in-between spaces give rise to an interstitial (or in-between) perspective. He contends that a new hybrid identity, or subject-position, emerges from interweaving elements of the colonizer and colonized, so as to challenge the validity and authenticity of any essentialist cultural identity.[18] In his article "Hybridity in the Third Space: Rethinking Bi-cultural Politics in Aotearoa/New Zealand," Paul Meredith references Homi Bhabha, highlighting that in Postcolonial discourse, the notion of any culture or identity being pure or essential is disputable. Rather, the indeterminate spaces between subject-positions are where the disruption and displacement of colonial narratives of cultural structures and practices occur. Bhabha refers to this liminal in-between space where hybridity occurs as

---

15. Westhelle, "Multiculturalism, Postcolonialism," 3–13.
16. As expressed by Sadhu Sundar Singh, an Indian Christian Theologian and mystic.
17. Bakhtin, *Dialogic Imagination*, 358.
18. Bhabha, *Location of Culture*, 2–4.

"the third space"—a space intrinsically critical of all essentialist positions of identity and conceptualizations of so-called "original culture." It is, as Bhabha puts it, an "interruptive, interrogative, and enunciative" space of new forms of cultural meaning that blur existing boundaries and call into question established categories for both culture and identity. Bhabha characterizes this hybrid third space as an *ambivalent* site, where cultural meaning and representation have no "primordial unity or fixity."[19] With their innate knowledge of "transculturation," their ability to traverse dual (or multiple) cultures, as well as their capacity to translate, negotiate and mediate affinity and difference within a dynamic of exchange and inclusion, those who inhabit this hybrid space represent the power of potential. They have encoded within them a counter-hegemonic agency; thus, at the point when the colonizer presents a normalizing, hegemonic practice, the hybrid strategy opens up a third space in which to re-articulate concepts and meaning.

As Westhelle points out; "If the definition of hybridity lies in the crossing and displacing of different cultural, semantic, economic, ethnic or social spheres, its distinctiveness lies in the crossing of them, in the act of transgressing their domains and not in their unifying blending or in their binary coupling or non-organic assembly of different entities."[20]

In the very act of composing religious songs, Walsalam, Kochukunju and their contemporaries intentionally crossed colonial boundaries to claim their own space in which to express their faith; this act, as much as their writing itself, established their legacy and asserted their cultural characteristics. As previously noted, Indian Christian hymnody is not just a syncretism of Eastern and Western tradition; nor is it Christian practice taking on an Eastern garb. It was in fact the evolution of something new, where old practices took on new meanings and the new, while inclusive, asserted its own unique identity and characteristics. An example of such transformation, seen in the work of both Walsalam and Kochukunju, would be their distinctive understanding of *bhakti* and the relationship between the *bhakta* and the Divine. While redefining the perception of *bhakti* and the direction of *prema* or love in this relationship, the concept now inclusively embraced social and communal dimensions where it formerly signified only the personal. The use of the love feast by Walsalam to point to the universal parenthood of God and

---

19. Ibid, 37.
20. Westhelle, "Displacing Identities."

## Conclusion

an equitable, nondiscriminatory and just kingdom at the same time, affirms the liberating dimension of the Eucharist.

The notion of mimicry or dissimulation is discussed by a number of Postcolonial writers. In this context, survival for the colonized depended on their ability to resist; this was manifested through mimicking or dissimulating the colonizer where mimicry, as Bhabha explains it, is the "ambivalence of colonial discourse," the desire of wanting to be something and at the same time wanting to be its opposite.[21] The real threat of mimicry is not the concealment of one's identity behind a "mask," or even direct opposition to colonial discourse, but rather the disruption of colonial authority; mimicry is also potentially mockery.

In his article "Liberation Theologies as Hybrid Theologies," Westhelle compares dissimulation to "allergy-causing parasites gnawing at this process of domination."[22] The only ways the colonized could express themselves were in ways the colonizer expected to see and so they hid behind given or imposed masks. But mimicry was also a protective strategy against "overwhelming supremacy" on the colonizers' part. As Westhelle points out, "[t]he success of dissimilation or mimicry lies in the fact that it makes the colonizers blindly believe that their project of turning the colonized into their image is working. They often do not realize that they are spectators of the mimicry of their own projections and expectations."[23] As beautiful parasites, dissimulators belong to no one, existing in the place of their choice.

In this light, the emergence of a distinct genre of music within India's colonized Christian communities would have been looked upon with approval. But these compositions, while mimicking what already existed, were also laying the groundwork for a clearly distinct identity of their own. Some early mission hymnals, for example, contained translations of Western hymns and songs set to Western music, grouped together in front; local worship songs, called "Lyrics," were gathered in a separate back section. Today, however, most hymnals are not segregated this way and local (vernacular) compositions dominate. It was the local songs, rather than imposed colonial hymns, that triumphed in establishing the worshiping community's own particular way of articulating its doxology.

That which exists at the liminal edge or threshold of practice does not belong to the center of either, which typifies those narratives that express

---

21. Bhabha, *Location of Culture*, 85.
22. Westhelle, "Is There a Universal Theology?," 97.
23. Ibid.

the interstitial perspective, but then transgress their domain and cross over. Referring to Bhabha, Michael Nausner points out that the boundary itself becomes a margin of hybridity where differences come into contact, and sometimes into conflict. Rather than being places meant for separation, boundaries or margins become relevant places for the evolution of new meaning and expression. Within these hybrid and fluid places, differences and commonalities are constantly negotiated, resulting in the experience of newness. Westhelle observes that crossing margins or boundaries can result in condemnation, the novel, or the eschatological.[24] Only the lowest can be the vessel of the highest, he continues, so these narratives could be seen as *small/low literature* that found its way from the margins to the center.[25]

The act of writers such as Walsalam and Kochukunju giving voice to the faith of their respective communities may have been viewed by some as an act of transgression, the very point on which Martin Luther disagreed with the Magisterium. As lay writers, and at times even heretical,[26] both men spoke from the margins and boundaries in their act of shaping the theological perspective of the laity.

The objectives of hegemonic colonial assertion of identities and cultures were primarily to effect subjugation and convenient governance. Although missionaries of the colonial period were often in the forefront crusading against abuses perpetrated by both the British Raj and high caste Hindus, their zeal did not stem wholly from social philanthropy or altruism. They were also mandated to establish and enlarge the power base of the Protestant Christian faith and impose the assumed superiority of its capacity to save and uplift the downtrodden. What actually unfolded, however, was the appropriation of colonial knowledge and techniques by the colonized, who then utilized it to create and assert a new identity and self-awareness. This new assertion and self-understanding on the part of the *shanar/nadar* Christians, as well as the reform movement of the St. Thomas Church tradition, can be traced to the emergence of something new from the liminal space where two culturally, socially, and theologically different entities came together. Rather than being syncretistic in character, this new consciousness and identity—the unexpected byproduct of colonial knowledge—defied and confronted the old establishment.

24. Westhelle, Class Lecture LSTC, 2001.

25. Westhelle, "Hybrid Identities."

26. The "heretical" label could especially apply to Kochukunju, who wrote a number of songs about the millennial reign of Christ.

## Conclusion

The use of Indian styles of music and *bhakti* spirituality to express the Christian faith, along with various "liberative" faith movements that offered dignity and self-respect to a formerly broken and exploited community, were typical expressions of this new consciousness. This movement of lower-caste communities away from their "polluting" traditional occupations to take on a collective new identity reflects the practical outcome of replacing dehumanizing old systems with new ones that assured the self-worth of all. In the same way, old mission-driven systems that stifled spiritual aspiration were supplanted by new worshiping communities that enabled freedom of religious expression. The resulting articulations of theological thought and vocabulary were noticeably fresh and dissimilar from that of their roots or their colonizers. A single example among many was the use of *avataaram* to refer to the Incarnation. In this context it did not convey the same meaning as in the original, nor did it mean in the original what it conveyed now; instead, as *avataaram* it mimicked its precursor and developed into something novel and new.

## In Summary ...

The challenge in this study has been to look at hymns and songs as theological statements that reflect a community's experience and expression of faith and to study in particular those written by Moshe Walsalam Sastriyar and Sadhu Kochukunju Upadeshi, which are still in circulation among the churches of Kerala, India. In a context of change and growth, both at their inception and today, these songs have served as accessible vehicles to affirm the Word, and reflect the spirituality and faith of the people. In his Foreword to Gladstone's biography of Moshe Walsalam, Bishop I. Jesudasan notes that his songs facilitate the church and the faithful to worship and praise God with awe and respect.[27]

After placing Walsalam and Kochukunju in their respective historic, social and religious contexts, this study explored how the hymns and songs of faith groups serve as *loci* for their theology. Malayalam is the most recent of the four South Indian or Dravidian languages and cultures of Kerala, but the religio-social development of Tamil continued through the nascent Malayalam language and culture. Hence the *alwar* tradition of Tamilakam exerted a profound influence on Malayalam-speaking areas, with at least two *alwar* saints coming from that region. Alwar influence in turn permeated

---

27. Gladstone, *Moshe Walsalam*, 3.

the *bhakti* tradition, in which sacred music and the tradition of *bhajans* were central to religious life and the expression of faith; these forces shaped the spiritual traditions of the land.

From the early years of the Common Era, Eastern Christianity was also a formative presence in the area. Protestant missions were the most recent religious influence and through their parallel association with colonialism had the most profound and lasting impact, not only on local religion, but also in social, educational, political and other areas. Protestant missions set in motion several social justice movements among the lower castes.

The principle of *lex orandi, lex credendi* was also examined in detail, and in that light the relationships among liturgy, songs and theology were explored, as was the place of *bhakti* tradition in understanding Indian Christian music. In *bhakti* practice, poetry and music were distinguished as sacred media for the communication and recording of the scriptures.

In Walsalam and Kochukunju, along with other Christian writers, we see a coming together of local traditions and the Christian message, transforming social structures and relationships, as well as the spiritual dimensions of both personal and community faith experiences. It is important to recognize in this outcome the relationship between theological reflection, which speaks of the God that doxology praises, and doxology itself.

For the Indian context in particular, with its strong *bhakti* tradition, it could be argued that song is a language of the heart and therefore the truest language of religion. This also raises the question of the nature of religion itself. Is it a function of the intellect alone, or does it involve the entire person? And if it involves the entire person, what most comprehensively describes this experience?

## Songs of Walsalam and Kochukunju—*Locus Theologicus*

This exploration of songs by Moshe Walsalam and Sadhu Kochukunju has revealed a number of shared common features, as well as areas in which their emphasis and approach are markedly different. Walsalam's formal training stands out in the breadth of his musical and stylistic repertoire, as well as a more theologically varied range of themes. Kochukunju's compositions dealt mostly with Christian life and hope.

For both, their compositions typify the Carnatic style most closely. As the more accomplished practical and theoretical musician, however,

## Conclusion

Walsalam periodically branched out into composing in the Hindustani style.[28] One could legitimately question here why songs meant for worship and devotion would be associated with "high" styles of Indian music, rather than common folk traditions. Neither seems to have taken up that challenge, with the exception of a few folksy songs written for children.

As we have seen, both men reflected in their compositions the experiences of their communities and the social realities of their times. Even with their different musical techniques, one senses how deeply the character of their songs is rooted in local culture, while at the same time remaining faithful to scripture and the revelation of God in Jesus Christ. While local terms are used to give ordinary people relevant expressions of their faith and experience of God, these familiar words, titles and phrases take on newness of context and meaning.

The respective theological stances adopted by Walsalam and Kochukunju exerted considerable significance and impacted both their church traditions and society. Through their songs they imparted strong theological dimensions to various societal issues faced by their communities; this in turn widened the theological awareness and perspective of the folks who sang and remembered them. Where the pietistic and *bhakti* traditions had emphasized the personal dimensions of faith, theology now embraced a more activist stance, taking in social and corporate issues. The linking of activist and liberative movements to the action of the Spirit gave poor and marginalized believers added courage and strength to face a rapidly changing environment, as well as the comfort of identifying Christ's suffering with the suffering of the world.

Walsalam and Kochukunju's influence on evangelism, along with the church's growth and consolidation were noticeable. Their instrumental role in affirming the faith of the "weary and weak" continues to this day. Both were convinced that the church's role was to be the agent of transformation that would bring about the kingdom of God on earth, establishing a realm of justice and love. By affirming the universal domain and sustenance of God and reflecting this through the medium of Indian song, they freed their local culture from Western hegemony and gave legitimacy to the faith experiences and expressions of the East.

The understanding of God, as reflected in their songs, is of a deity who is simultaneously sovereign and creator. Both Walsalam and Kochukunju

---

28. Jose, *dakshinendhyan sangeethaswadheenam*, 55.

also picture God as the ultimate source of love, the transformer of creation, and liberator of oppressed society.

For both writers, God's redemptive act in Jesus Christ is understood primarily in sacrificial and substitutionary terms; thus Christ took on "my" curse—*ente shaapam*—and was sacrificed in "my" stead. Both portray Christ as judge, but also stress the incarnational Christ who identifies with the lowly and marginalized. Walsalam in particular takes on a very personal tone in describing how the Incarnate One became a slave, a servant "like me"—*ennepole*. It is this characterization of the incarnate Christ as the refuge of the meek and lowly that so convincingly calls the believing community to identify with Him and stand alongside the weak and marginalized of the earth. Both express the relationship between Jesus and the believer in terms of *bhakta* and *deva*. Additionally, the role of the Spirit is that which enlightens and empowers.

Other thematic aspects that stand out in my foregoing discussion of both writers include love, sin, salvation, Christian life, trust, church, social concerns, liberation, etc.[29] What stands out most powerfully about the songs of Moshe Walsalam Sastriar and Sadhu Kochukunju Upadeshi, is that they continue to be used among the communities for which they were composed; in so doing, they also maintain a life and meaning of their own while strengthening and facilitating the worship and praise of the people.

> *ithranaalum ninkrupaye vyarthamaakithiirthupoye*
> *athallellaam niiki nii kaithaanguga*
> *ninte sathya bodham njangalil nii nalkuka.*[30]
>
> For so long we wasted your grace;
> remove our pain and support us.
> Give unto us the awareness of your truth.

---

29. See chapters 3 and 4.
30. Kochukunju, *aashwaasagiithangal*, 42. No. 51, verse 2.

# Appendix I
## *Ancient Tamilakam Region with the Three Main Kingdoms*

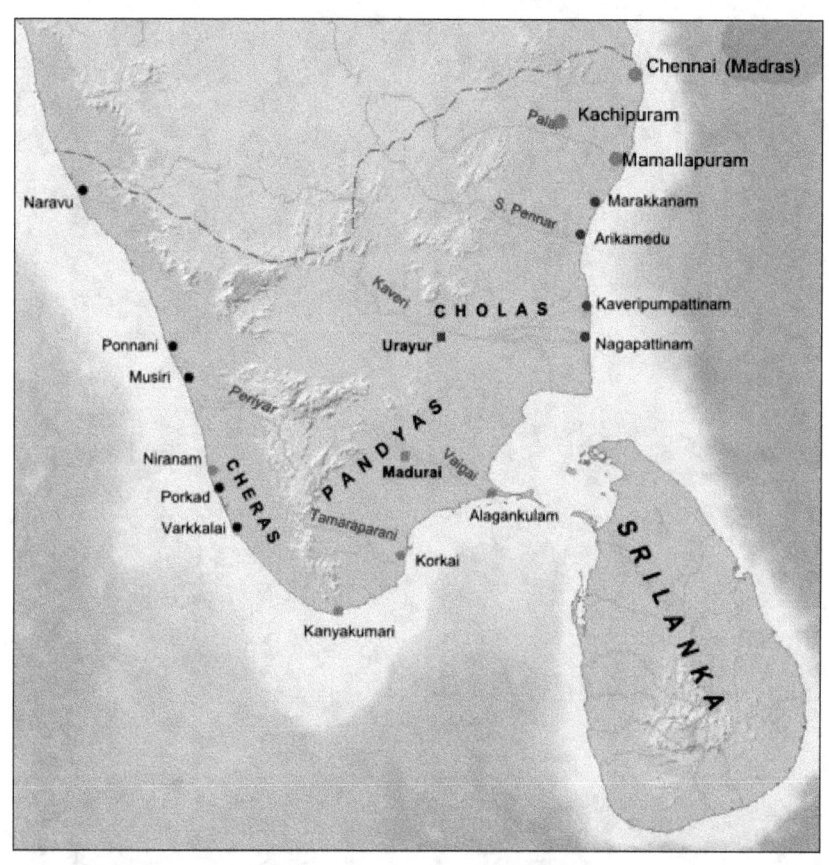

# Appendix II
## *Map of Cochin and Travancore Kingdoms*

# Appendix III

## Ninte hitham pole enne

Malayalam                                    Mosha Valsalam

**Nin-te hi-tham, po-le en-nne, Ni-thyam na-da- thi-de-na-me.**
En-te hi-tha-m, po-le al-le, En pi-tha-ve, en ya-ho-ve.
                                                    - Ninte hitham ...
Im-ba-mu-lla jee-vi-tha-vum, Ee-re dha-na ma-na-nga-lum,
Thum-ba-ma-ta- sow-kya-nga-lum, Cho-dhi-khu-nnil-le-aa-di-yar.
                                                    - Ninte hitham ...
An-dha-ka-ra bhi-dhi-ka-lo, A-ppa-ne- pra-ka- sha-nga-lo,
En-dhu ni kal-ppi-chi-dun-no, Ell-llam E-ni- kkar-shi-va-dham.
                                                    - Ninte hitham ...

# Appendix IV

# Halleluyah, Amen!

Malayalam  Mosha Valsalam

*Ch:* Halleluyah, halleluyah, halleluyah, Amen.
1. Anpu thingidum nal ananda pithaave, - Halleluyah ...
2. Krupa niranjiidum nal, kristu karthaave, - Halleluyah ...
3. Vishuddhi nalkiidum nal, parishudhathmaave, - Halleluyah ...
4. Thaathasutaathmavaam, daiva thriyeeka, - Halleluyah ...

# Appendix V

## Dhukkathinte Panapathram

Malayalam  Sadhu Kochukunju

1. Dhukkathinte panaa pathram, karthavente kaiyyil thannaal
   Sandhoshatthodathu vaangi, halleluyah paadiidum njan.  (2)
2. Doshamayittonnum enno-dente thathan cheyikayilla
   Enne avan adicchaalum, avan enne snehikkunnu.  (2)
3. Kashtta nashtta meri vannal, bhagyavanai thiiruunnu njan,
   Kashttameetta karthaavodu, kuuttaliyai thiiruunnu njan.  (2)
4. Lokasukhamendhu tharum, aathmakleeshamathin phalam
   Sowbhagyamullathma jeevan, kashtathayil varddhikkunnu. (2)
5. Lokatthe njan oorkkunnilla, kashtta nashttamorkkunnilla
   Eppol ente karthavine, onnu kaanam enneeyullu.  (2)

# Appendix VI

# Krushinmel Krushinmel

Malayalam　　　　　　　　　　　　　　　　　　　Sadhu Kochukunju

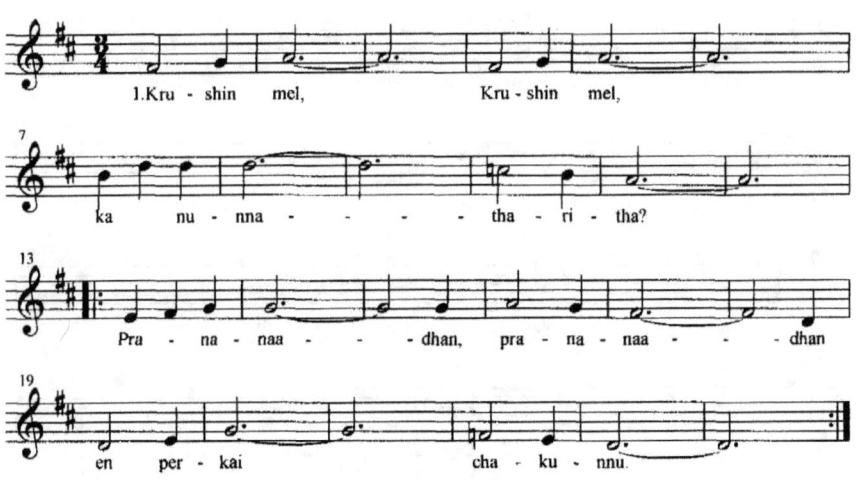

1. Kru-shin-mel, kru-shin-mel, kaa-nu-nna-tha-ri-dha
   Praa-na-naa-dhan, praa-na-naa-dhan, en per-kai chaa-ku-nnu. (2)
2. Aa-th-ma-vee paa-pa-thin kaa-zh-cha nee kaa-nu-ka,
   Dai-va-thin pu-thran ii shaa-pa-thil aa-ya-loo. (2)
3. Ith-ra-maam snee-ha-thee eth-ra-naal tha-lli njan,
   Ii ma-haa paa-pa-the dai-va-me oor-kka-lle.
4. Paa-pa-the sne-hi-ppan nja-nini poo-ku-mo?
   Dai-va-thin pai-tha-lai jee-vi-kkum njaa-ni-ni.

# Bibliography

Anderson, E. Byron. *Worship and Christian Identity: Practical Ourselves*. Collegeville, MN: Liturgical, 2003.
Appasamy, A. J. *Christianity as Bhakti Marga*. Madras: Christian Literature Society, 1930.
———. *The Gospel and India's Heritage*. London: SPCK, 1942.
———. *The Theology of Hindu Bhakti*. Bangalore: Christian Literature Society, 1970.
———. *What Is Moksa?* Madras: Christian Literature Society, 1931.
Appasamy, Grace Parimala. *Vedanayaga Sastriar: A Biography of the Suviseda Kavirayar of Thanjavur*. Dasarpuram: Thangai Vedanayaga Sastriar Peravai, 1995.
Augustine. *Confessions*. Translated by R. S. Pine-Coffin. New York: Viking, 1984.
Ayyar, R. B. L. K. A. *Anthropology of the Syrian Christians*. Ernakulam: Cochin Government, 1926.
Bakhtin, M. M. *The Dialogic Imagination: Four Essays*. Edited by Michael Holquist. Translated by Caryl Emerson and Michael Holquist. Austin: University of Texas Press, 1981.
Balakrishnan, V. *History of the Syrian Christians of Kerala: A Critical Study*. Thrissur: Kerala, 1999.
Balisky, Lila W. "Theology in Song: Ethiopia's Tesfaye Gabbiso." *Missiolory: An International Review* 25 (1997) 447–56.
Bangert, Mark. "A Brook Runs Through It: Fresh Water from the Bach for Today's Thirsty Church." *Institute of Liturgical Studies Occasional Papers* 111. 2003. http://scholar.valpo.edu/ils_papers/111.
———. "The Last Word? Dynamics of World Musics Twenty Years Later." In *Worship and Culture: Foreign Country or Homeland?*, edited by Glaucia Vasconcelos Wilkey, 124–36. Grand Rapids: Eerdmans, 2014.
Berger, Teresa. *Theology in Hymns? A Study of the Relationship of Doxology and Theology According to a Collection of Hymns for the Use of the People called Methodists (1780)*. Translated by Timothy E. Kimbrough. Nashville: Kingswood, 1995.
Best, Harold. M. *Music through the Eyes of Faith*. New York: Harper, 1993.
Bhabha, Homi K. *The Location of Culture*. New York: Routledge, 2004.
Bharathi, Shuddhananda. *Alvar Saints and Acharyas*. Madras: Shuddhananda, 1942.
Boehmer, Elleke. *Colonial and Postcolonial Literature: Migrant Metaphors*. New York: Oxford University Press, 2005.
Boyd, Robin. *An Introduction to Indian Christian Theology*. Madras: Christian Literature Society, 1975.
Brock, Sebastian, trans. *Hymns on Paradise*. Crestwood, NY: St. Vladimir Seminary, 1990.

# Bibliography

———. *The Luminous Eye: The Spiritual World Vision of Saint Ephrem*. Kalamazoo, MI: Cistercian, 1992.

Brown, Christopher Boyd. *Singing the Gospel: Lutheran Hymns and the Success of the Reformation*. Cambridge, MA: Harvard University Press, 2005.

Brown, Leslie. *The Indian Christians of St. Thomas*. Cambridge: Cambridge University Press, 1956.

Chendharassery, T. H. P. *Kerala Charitradhara* [Kerala History]. Thiruvanandapuram: Charithram, 1978.

Chrisman, Laura, and Patrick Williams. "Colonial Discourse and Post-Colonial Theory: An Introduction." In *Colonial Discourse and Post-Colonial Theory: A Reader*, edited by Laura Chrisman and Patrick Williams, 23–26. New York: Columbia University Press, 1994.

Clendenin, Daniel B. *Eastern Orthodox Theology: A Contemporary Reader*. Grand Rapids: Baker, 1995.

Cone, James H. *The Spirituals and the Blues*. New York: Seabury, 1972.

Connor, Kimberly R. "'Everybody Talking About Heaven Ain't Going There': The Biblical Call for Justice and the Postcolonial Response of the Spirituals." *Semeia* 75 (1996) 107–8.

Corbitt, J. Nathan. *The Sound of the Harvest*. Grand Rapids: Baker, 1998.

Crews, C. Daniel. "Zinzendorf: Theology in Song." 2011. http://zinzendorf.com/pages/index.php?id=zinzendorf-theology-in-song.

Cross, George. *The Theology of Schleiermacher: A Condensed Presentation of His Chief Work, "The Christian Faith."* Chicago: University of Chicago Press, 1911.

Cunningham, David S. *Ecumenical Theology in Worship, Doctrine and Life: Essays Presented to Geoffrey Wainwright on His Sixtieth Birthday*. New York: Oxford University Press, 1999.

Daniel, Mathew, ed. *Mokshayathrikante Rekha Mozhikal: Evangelist Sadhu Kochukunju* [Sayings of a Sojourner to Heaven]. Mumbai: GLS, 2001.

———. *Sadhu Kochukunju: A Biography*. Madras: Christian Literature Society, 1996.

———. *Sadhu Kochukunju Upadeshi*. Tiruvalla: CSS, 1994.

De Bary, Theodore, et al. *Sources of Indian Tradition*. New York: Columbia University Press, 1958.

Desai, Mahadev. *The Epic of Travancore*. Ahmedabad: Navajivan Karyalaya, 1937.

Devasahayam, V. "Pollution, Poverty and Powerlessness." In *A Reader in Dalit Theology*, edited by A. P. Nirmal, 1–22. Madras: Gurukul Lutheran Theological College, 1992.

Douglas, Mary. *Other Beings, Post-Colonially Correct*. Chicago: CCGM, 2002.

*The Elizabethan Prayer Book and Ornaments*. London: Macmillan, 1902.

Ephream, Syrus. *Hymns on Paradise*. Translated by Sebastian Brock. Crestwood, New York: St. Vladimir Seminary, 1990.

Eskew, Harry, and Hugh T. McElrath. *Sing With Understanding: An Introduction to Christian Hymnology*. Nashville: Broadman, 1980.

Farquhar, J. N. *An Outline of the Religious Literature in India*. Oxford: Oxford University Press, 1920.

Felde, Marcus Paul Bach. *Faith Aloud: Doing Theology from the Hymns in Papua New Guinea*. Goroka: Melanesian Institute, 1999.

Fillingim, David. *Redneck Liberation: Country Music as Theology*. Macon, GA: Mercer University Press, 2003.

# Bibliography

Foley, Edward. *Music in Ritual: A Pre-Theological Investigation.* American Essays in Liturgy 1. Washington, DC: Pastoral, 1984.

George, K. M. *Sadhu Kochoonju.* Kottayam: CMS, 1947.

Ghurye, G. S. *Caste and Class in India.* Bombay: Popular, 1950.

Gladstone, J. W. *Moshe Walsalam Sastrigal.* Trivandrum: Moshe Walsalam Sastriyar Memorial Committee, 1986.

———. *Protestant Christianity and People's Movements in Kerala.* Trivandrum: Seminary Publications, 1984.

Goodall, Norman. *A History of the London Missionary Society, 1895-1945.* London: Oxford University Press, 1954.

Govindacharya, Alkondavilli. *The Holy Lives of the Azhvars or the Dravida Saints.* Bombay: Ananthacharya Indological Research Institute, 1982.

Grafe, Hugald. *History of Christianity in India.* Tamilnadu in the Nineteenth and Twentieth Centuries 4. Bangalore: Church History Association, 1990.

Greeley, Andrew. *God in Popular Culture.* Chicago: Thomas More, 1988.

Gupta, A. R. *Caste Hierarchy and Social Change: A Study of Myth and Reality.* Delhi: Sangeetha, 1984.

Guha, Ranajit, and Gayatri Chakravorty Spivak, eds. *Selected Subaltern Studies.* New York: Oxford University Press, 1988.

Hacker, I. H. *A Hundred Years in Travancore, 1806-1906.* London: Allenson, 1908.

Hambye, E. R. *The Eighteenth Century.* History of Christianity in India 3. Bangalore: CHAI, 1997.

Hay, Stephen, et al., eds. *Sources of Indian Tradition.* New York: Columbia University Press, 1958.

Herzel, Catherine. *To Thee We Sing.* Philadelphia: Muhlenberg, 1946.

Human Rights Watch. *Broken People: Caste Violence against India's "Untouchables."* New York: Human Rights Watch, 1999.

Irwin, Joyce. *Sacred Sound: Music in Religious Thought and Practice.* Journal of the American Academy of Religion Studies 50/1. Chico, CA: Scholars, 1983.

John, J., ed. *The Collected Works of Walsala Sastriar.* Trivandrum: Popular, 1958.

Jose, Justin. "Dakshinendhyan sangeethaswadheenam moshewalsalam sastrigalude gaanangalil: oru padanam." [The Influence of South Indian Music in the Songs of Moshe Walsalam Sastrigal: A Study.] BD diss., Serampore University, India, 2002.

Jose, N. K. *Ayyankali.* Vaikom: Hobby, 1989.

Joy, C. I. David. "Mark 5:1-20: A Postcolonial Subaltern Reading." *Bangalore Theological Forum* 37 (2005) 26-39.

Kavanagh, A. *On Liturgical Theology.* New York: Pueblo, 1985.

Kay, James F. "Lex Orandi in Recent Protestant Theology." In *Ecumenical Theology in Worship, Doctrine, and Life: Essays Presented to Geoffrey Wainwright on His Sixtieth Birthday*, edited by David S. Cunningham, 11-23. New York: Oxford University Press, 1999.

Keller, Catherine, et al., eds. *Postcolonial Theologies: Divinity and Empire.* St. Louis: Chalice, 2004.

Kent, Eliza F. *Converting Women: Gender and Protestant Christianity in Colonial South India.* New York: Oxford University Press, 2004.

Kochukunju, Sadhu. *bhaktirasam* [Noble/Excellent Way of the Christian Faith]. Kozhencherry: CPMM, n.d.

———. *leelachittidoosham* [Evils of Subscription Lottery]. Kozhencherry: CPMM, 1929.

# Bibliography

———. *malankara sabhayum athmiya unarvum* [Malankara Church and Spiritual Revival]. Edayaranmula: n.p., 1924.

———. *paramaananda christhiiyajiivitham* [Joyful Christian Life]. Kunnankulam: KVP, 1925.

———. *paramaartha christhyaani* [Sincere Christian]. Mavelikara: Union Christian, 1930.

———. *paramachristhyaanithwam* [Essence of Devotion]. Kottayam: CMS, 1923.

———. *sthreedhanathyagam* [Sacrifice of Dowry]. Chengannur: John Memorial, 1927.

———. *vyapaaradharmam* [The Way of Trade]. Kozhencherry: CPMM, 1929.

———. *yahova bhakthanmaarkulla aashwaasagiithangal* [Songs of Comfort for the Devotees of Jehovah]. Chengannur: Bodhini, 1985.

———. *yahova bhakthanmaarkulla aashwaasagiithangal* [Songs of Comfort for Worshippers of Jehovah]. Edited by Mathew Daniel. Tiruvalla: CSS, 2002.

Kooiman, Dick. *Conversion and Social Equality in India: The London Missionary Society in South Travancore in the 19th Century*. New Delhi: Manohar, 1989.

*kristhiya aaradhanakkulla paattugalum aaradhanakramangalum* [Hymns and Lyrics and Orders of Service for Worship]. Trivandrum: CSI, 2005.

*kristhiya kiirthanangal* [Christian Hymns]. Tiruvalla: Mar Thoma Sabha, 1997.

Kumar, Suresh. *Political Evolution in Kerala: Travancore, 1859–1938*. New Delhi: Phoenix, 1994.

Kunju, A. P. Ibrahim. *Rise of Travancore: A Study of the Life and Times of Marthanda Varma*. Trivandrum: Kerala Historical Society, 1976.

Kuriakose, M. K., ed. *History of Christianity in India: Source Materials*. Madras: Christian Literature Society, 1982.

Kuruvilla, K. K. *A History of the Marthoma Church and Its Doctrines*. Madras: Christian Literature Society, 1950.

Kwok, Pui-lan. *Postcolonial Imagination and Feminist Theology*. Louisville: Westminster, 2005.

Lala, Chhaganlal. *Bhakti in Religions of the World*. New Delhi: BR Corp, 1986.

Leith, John H. *Basic Christian Doctrine*. Louisville: Westminster, 1993.

Loomba, Ania. *Colonialism–Postcolonialism*. New York: Routledge, 1998.

Luther, Martin. *Luther's Works*. Vol. 49. Edited by Gottfried G. Krodel. Philadelphia: Fortress, 1983.

Macquarrie, John. *Principles of Christian Theology*. New York: Scribner, 1966.

Majumdar, A. K. *Bhakti Renaissance*. Bombay: Bharatiya Vidya Bhavan, 1979.

Mar Thoma, Juhanon. *Christianity in India and a Brief History of the Mar Thoma Church*. Madras: Cherian, 1968.

Marthoma, Alexander. *The Marthoma Church: Heritage and Mission*. Manganam: Ashram, 1985.

Mateer, Samuel. *Native Life in Travancore*. London: Allen, 1883.

Mathai, Karimpanamannil P. "Indian Interpretations of the Work of Christ: Notable Contributions Made on this Subject by Indian Christian Theologians of the 20th Century." PhD diss., Drew University, 1984.

McVey, Kathleen E. *Ephrem the Syrian: Hymns*. New York: Paulist, 1989.

Menon, A. Sreedhara. *Social and Cultural History of Kerala*. New Delhi: Sterling, 1979.

———. *A Survey of Kerala History*. Kottayam: Sahitya Pravarthaka, 1967.

Menon, K. P. Padmanabha. *History of Kerala: Written in the Form of Notes on Visscher's Letters from Malabar*. Vol 2. New Delhi: Asian Educational Services, 1983.

# Bibliography

Menon, P. Shungoonny. *A History of Travancore from the Earliest Times*. Vol. 1. New Delhi: Cosmo, 1984.

Meyer, Donald. *Theology and Music: Meyer, Marty, Halter*. River Forest, IL: Concordia Teachers College, 1954.

Mongia, Padmini, ed. *Contemporary Postcolonial Theory: A Reader*. New York: Arnold, 1996.

Mundadan, A. M. *From the Beginning up to the Middle of the Sixteenth Century*. History of Christianity in India 1. Bangalore: Theological Publications, 1984.

———. *Traditions of St. Thomas Christians*. Bangalore: Dharmaram College, 1970.

Music, David W. *Hymnology: A Collection of Source Readings*. Lanham, MD: Scarecrow, 1996.

Naude, Piet J. "Regaining Our Ritual Coherence: The Question of Textuality and Worship in Ecumenical Reception." *JES* 35 (1998) 235–56.

Nayar, K. Shivashankaran. *venadinte parinamam* [The Evolution of Kerala]. Trivandrum: Government of Kerala, 1993.

Nayar, Nancy Ann. *Poetry as Theology: The Strivaisisnava Stotra in the Age of Ramanuja*. Wiesbaden: Otto Harrassowitz, 1992.

Neil, Stephen. *Bhakti: Hindu and Christian*. Madras: Christian Literature Society, 1974.

———. *A History of Christianity in India, 1708–1858*. New York: Cambridge University Press, 1985.

Oettinger, Rebecca Wagner. *Music as Propaganda in the German Reformation*. Burlington, VT: Ashgate, 2001.

O'Malley, L. S. S. *Indian Caste Customs*. London: Curzon, 1932.

Parker, Mrs. Arthur. *bharathiya christu bhakthar* [Indian Christian Saints]. Trivandrum: Kamalalaya, 1925.

Philip, Mammen. *sadhu kochu kunju: viswasathinte agnijwala* [Sachu Kochukunju: The Flame of Faith]. Tiruvankulam: Krupa Bible Center, 2007.

Pothan, S. G. *The Syrian Christians of Kerala*. Bombay: Asia, 1963.

Raimon, S., ed. *thiranjedutha rajakeeya vilambarangal* [Selected Royal Declarations]. Trivandrum: Kerala State Archives, 2005.

Ramshaw, Gail. *Words That Sing*. Chicago: Liturgy Training, 1992.

Rao, S. K. Ramachandra. "Foreword." In *Philosophy and Theistic Mysticism of the Alvars*, by S. M. Srinivasachari, ix–xi. New Delhi: Motilal Banarsidass, 1997.

Rao, R. R. Sundara. *Bhakti Theology in the Telugu Hymnal*. Madras: Christian Literature Society, 1983.

Robertson, S. *Bhakti Tradition of Vaishnava Alvars and Theology of Religions*. Kolkata: Punthi Pustak, 2006.

Routley, Erik. *Christian Hymns Observed: When in Our Music God is Glorified*. Princeton, NJ: Prestige, 1982.

———. *Hymns and Human Life*. London: Murray, 1959.

Sahayadas, R. "Can We Enter into Dialogue with Postcolonial Theory in Our Continuing Theological Discourses?" *Bangalore Theological Forum* 37 (2005) 79–128.

Said, Edward W. *Culture and Imperialism*. New York: Random House, 1993.

———. *Orientalism*. New York: Vintage, 1978.

Saliers, Don, and Emily Saliers. *A Song to Sing, a Life to Live: Reflections on Music as Spiritual Practice*. San Francisco: Jossey-Bass, 2005.

Schememann, Alexander. *Historical Road of Eastern Orthodoxy*. New York: St. Vladimir's Seminary Press, 1992.

# BIBLIOGRAPHY

Schleiermacher, Friedrich. *On Religion: Speeches to Its Culture's Despisers.* Translated by John Oman. New York: Harper, 1958.

Sedgwick, L. J. "Bhakti." *JRAS* 23 (1891) 109–34.

Segovia, Fernando F. "Interpreting Beyond Borders: Postcolonial Studies and Diasporic Studies in Biblical Criticism." In *Interpreting Beyond Borders,* edited by Fernando F. Segovia, 11–34. The Bible and Postcolonialism 3. Sheffield: Academic, 2000.

Shobanan, B. *Dewan Velu tampi and the British.* Trivandrum: Kerala Historical Society, 1978.

———. *Rama Varma of Travancore.* Calicut: Sandhya, 1978.

Simon, Robert Leopold. *Spiritual Aspects of Indian Music.* Delhi: Sundeep Prakashan, 1984.

Sirota, Victoria R. "An Exploration of Music as Theology." *Theological Education* 31 (1994) 165–73.

Soehngen, Oskar. "Fundamental Considerations for a Theology of Music." In *The Musical Heritage of the Church,* edited by Theodore Hoelty-Nickel, 7–16. St. Louis: Concordia, 1963.

———. "Music and Theology: A Systematic Approach, in Sacred Sound." In *Music in Religious Thought and Practice,* edited by Joyce Irwin, 1–20. Chico, CA: Scholars, 1983.

Spivak, Gayatri Chakravorty. *A Critique of Postcolonial Reason: Toward a History of the Vanishing Present.* Cambridge, MA: Harvard University Press, 1999.

Sugirtharajah, R. S. *Asian Biblical Hermeneutics and Postcolonialism: Contesting the Interpretations.* Maryknoll, NY: Orbis, 1998.

———. "A Brief Memorandum on Postcolonialism and Biblical Studies." *JSNT* 73 (1999) 3–5.

———. *Postcolonial Reconfigurations: An Alternative Way of Reading the Bible and Doing Theology.* St Louis: Chalice, 2003.

———, ed. *Voices from the Margin: Interpreting the Bible in the Third World.* Maryknoll, NY: Orbis, 2006.

Sylvan, Robin. *Traces of the Spirit: the Religious Dimensions of Popular Music.* New York: New York University Press, 2002.

Tapasvananda, Swami. *Bhakti Schools of Vedanta: Lives and Philosophies of Ramanuja, Nimbarka, Madhva, Vallabha, and Caitanya.* Madras: Sri Ramakrishna Math, 1990.

Thekkedath, Joseph. *From the Middle of the Sixteenth to the End of the Seventeenth Century.* History of Christianity in India 2. Bangalore: Theological Publications, 1982.

Thirugnanasambandham, P. *The Concept of Bhakti.* Madras: University of Madras, 1973.

Thistlethwaite, Susan Brooks, ed. *Lift Every Voice: Constructing Christian Theology from the Underside.* Maryknoll, NY: Orbis, 1998.

Tripathi, Govardhanram M. *The Classical Poets of Gujarat and Their Influence on Society and Morals.* Bombay: Forbes, 1958.

Trivedi, Harish, ed. *Interrogating Post-colonialism: Theory, Text and Context.* Shimla: Indian Institute of Advanced Study, 1996.

Tyrrell, G. *Through Scylla and Charybdis, or the Old Theology and the New.* London: Longmans, 1907.

Varadachari, K. C. *Alvars of South India.* Bombay: Bhavan, 1966.

———. *Aspects of Bhakti.* Mysore: University of Mysore, 1956.

Varghese, K. V. "marthoma christhyanigal." *sabhataraka* (Journal of the Marthoma Church), publication details unavailable.

# Bibliography

Vishvambharan, Kilimanoor. *kerala samskara darshanam* [An Overview of Kerala Culture]. Kilimanoor: Kanchanagiri, 1990.

Visvanathan, Susan. *The Christians of Kerala*. Madras: Oxford University Press, 1993.

Wainwright, Geoffrey. *Doxology: The Praise of God in Worship, Doctrine and Life*. London: Epworth, 1980.

Walsalam, Moshe. *The Collected Works of Walsala Sastriar*. Trivandrum: Nanthencode, 1958.

———. *dhyanamalika* [Meditation songs]. Kottayam: Church Mission, 1916.

———. *geetamanjari* [Garland of Songs]. Kerala: Keralodayam, 1903.

———. *sathyanadakaahalam* [Trumpet of Truth]. Thrissur: Kerala, nd.

———. *varsharamba keerthanangal* [New Year Songs]. Trivandrum: Mateer Memorial Church, 1915.

Ware, Timothy. *The Orthodox Church*. London: Penguin, 1997.

Warrier, M. I., et al., eds. *Malayalam–English Nighandu* [Malayalam–English Dictionary]. Kottayam: DC, 1999.

Westermeyer, Paul. *The Heart of the Matter: Church Music as Praise, Prayer, Proclamation, Story, and Gift*. Chicago: GIA, 2001.

———. *Let Justice Sing: Hymnody and Justice*. Collegeville, MN: Liturgical, 1998.

———. *Te Deum: the Church and Music*. Minneapolis: Fortress, 1998.

Westhelle, Vítor. "Creation Motifs in the Search for a Vital Space." In *Lift Every Voice: Constructing Christian Theologies from the Underside*, edited by Susan B. Thistlethwaite and Mary P. Engel, 146–58. Maryknoll, NY: Orbis, 1998.

———. "Displacing Identities: Hybrid Distinctiveness in Theology and Literature." In *Out of Place: Doing Theology on the Crosscultural Brink*, edited by Jione Havea and Clive Pearson, 42–64. London: Routledge, 2016.

———. "'Hybrid Identities': A Lutheran Reading of Chalcedon." Lecture given at the Society of Anglican and Lutheran Theologians, Philadelphia. 2005.

———. "Is There a Universal Theology of the Oppressed?" *Gurukul Journal of Theological Studies* 16 (2005) 92–108.

———. "Multiculturalism, Postcolonialism and the Apocalyptic." In *Theology and the Religions: A Dialogue*, edited by Viggo Mortensen, 3–13. Grand Rapids: Eerdmans, 2003.

Williams, Monier. *A Sanskrit–English Dictionary*. Delhi: Motilal Banarasidas, 1976.

Williams, Patrick, ed. *Colonial Discourse and Post-Colonial Theory: A Reader*. New York: Columbia University Press, 1994.

Yesudas, R. N. *British Policy in Travancore: 1805–1859*. Trivandrum: Kerala Historical Society, 1977.

———. *A People's Revolt in Travancore: A Backward Class Movement for Social Freedom*. Trivandrum: Kerala Historical Society, 1975.

Young, Robert J. C. *Postcolonialism: An Historical Introduction*. Oxford: Blackwell, 2001.

Zaehner, R.C. *Hinduism*. New York: Oxford University Press, 1966.

Zizioulas, John D. *Being as Communion*. New York: St. Vladimir Seminary Press, 1985.

# Index

aashwaasagiithangal, 8, 127, 129–31, 180
Abelard, Peter, 62
Abraham Malpan, 34–35, 121
Alwars, 4, 6–7, 19, 69, 71–76, 81–82
Ambrose, 54–55, 60, 63
Appasamy, 6, 71–82, 104, 106, 110, 151n97, 177
Aryan, 11, 13–14, 17, 29, 69, 70n76
Attingal outbreak, 26, 39
Augustine, 52, 54, 61, 105–6, 177
*avarna*, 29, 30–32, 38
*avataaram*, 167. *See also* incarnation
*ayitham/theendal*, 3
Ayyan Kali, 43, 179

Bakhtin, M. M., 163, 177
Bhabha, Homi, 163–65, 177
*bhajans*, 4, 6, 19–20, 82, 168
*bhakta*, 6, 69, 73, 78–81, 92, 102, 104, 113, 119, 127, 136, 139, 141, 144–46, 148, 150–52, 156, 164, 170
*bhakti*, x–xi, 4–9, 18–20, 22–23, 51, 69–72, 74–82, 93, 106, 110, 119, 125, 146, 148, 150, 164, 167–69
*bhakti* tradition, x, xi, 6–7, 9, 69, 72, 73n93, 73n95, 74n105, 82, 93, 106, 110, 119, 168–69,
bliss, 6, 70–72, 74, 77, 80–81, 92–93, 107, 119, 124, 127, 147–48, 156. *See also* moksha
Buddhism, 13–14, 18, 20, 72, 75

Carnatic, 7, 87, 96, 168
Caste system, ix, 3, 8, 12, 14, 15n28, 17, 20, 37, 38–39, 42,
  *brahmins*, 3, 7, 10n3, 12, 14–15, 17, 20, 29–31, 38–39, 41–42, 72–75,
  *ezhavas*, 3, 29, 42–44
  *kshatriya*, 15–17, 38n106, 39, 73,
  *nadars/shanars*, 3–4, 29, 44–45, 48–49;
  *nairs*, 3, 29, 38–39, 41, 44
  *parayas*, 3, 12, 29–30, 50; *pulayas*, 3, 29–30, 43, 50
  *shudras*, 15–17, 29, 73
  *vaisyas*, 15–17
Christian life, 128, 143, 145, 168, 170. *See also* christhiiyajiivitham
*christhiiyajiivitham*, 128, 180
Church Missionary Society (CMS), 3–4, 27–28, 33–34, 179–80
Church of South India, 2n5, 8, 31n90, 50, 77, 89, 97, 116n126
colonialism, 11, 41, 159–62, 168, 180
  British, 26–28, 33–34, 39–41, 44–49, 124, 166, 182, 183
  Dutch, 23–25
  Portuguese, 21–25, 27, 33

devotion, 4, 8, 23, 54–55, 57, 61–62, 64–65, 70–72, 75, 77, 81, 128, 145–46, 148–49, 169, 180,
devotional, 4, 6, 18–19, 23, 65, 69, 75, 88, 96n51
doxology, 5–6, 51, 53n9, 54n12, 56–57, 66, 68, 165, 168, 177, 183
Dravidian, 11, 12n14, 13–14, 17–18, 167

ecclesiology, 152
Ephraim, 61

# Index

George, K.M., 5, 65, 121, 122n6, 123, 124n13, 126–27, 129, 140, 143, 146, 179
God as Father and Mother, 133
God the Creator, 92
grace, 8, 35, 70, 73, 76–77, 91, 99, 103, 113, 117, 119, 137, 148, 151, 154

Hindustani, 87, 169
Holy Spirit, 35–36, 54, 90, 91–92, 101–4, 107
hope, 104, 109, 143–44, 148–49, 158, 168

incarnation, 97–98, 104–5, 111, 117, 132, 139–40, 167, 170

Jainism, 13–14, 18, 20, 72, 75
Jesus Christ, 35, 68, 88, 91, 94, 96, 98, 101, 103, 117, 128, 134, 137, 139, 143, 155, 169

*karma*, 70–71, 79–80, 106–7
*karuna*, 97. *See also* mercy
Kavanagh, Aidan, 56, 179
Keach, Benjamin, 63
Kulashekara, 17, 20

*lex orandi lex credendi*, 5, 7, 52–57, 58n27, 59, 78, 168, 179
liberation, 31, 104, 108, 114–15, 117, 165, 170, 178
London Missionary Society/LMS, 3–4, 7, 28, 44, 46–47, 49, 83–85, 126, 158, 179
love, 6, 8, 69–71, 73–74, 77–81, 91, 93, 100, 109–11, 113, 116–20, 128, 136–39, 141, 146, 148–50, 152–53, 155, 164, 169–70. *See also* vatsalyam, premam
Lutheran/ism, 2, 47, 57–59, 63, 178, 183
Luther, Martin, 51, 59, 62–63, 87, 106, 166, 180

Mar Thoma, Juhanon, 34, 126
Marthoma, Abraham, 130
Marthoma, Alexander, 34, 38,
Marthoma Church, 4, 8–9, 31n90, 34, 36, 38, 97, 116n126, 124, 127, 154, 156, 180, 182

mercy, 76, 97. *See also* karuna
Mission of Church, 38n107, 117
*moksha*, 70, 76, 80–81, 93, 105n87, 107, 127, 148
Moshe Walsalam, x, 1–2, 7, 9, 68, 83–120, 126–27, 129n29, 130, 159, 167–68, 170, 179

*naradevan, naraparan*, 98
Narayana Guru, 42
*nayanars*, 6, 19, 69, 71–72, 75–76
*nishkamyakarama*, 80, 113

*ooliyam*, 44–45, 48

Pazhassi Rajah, 39–40
Pazhassi revolt/upheaval, 40
postcolonialism/postcoloniality, xi, 161–63, 180, 182–83
prayer, 35, 52, 54–56, 59, 66–67, 78, 81, 103–4, 117, 123, 154, 183
*premam*, 136n59, 146, 149
Prosper, 52, 54–55

Ramanuja, 6, 69, 75–82, 90, 113, 151, 181–82
Ringeltaube, William Tobias, 46–48
righteousness/unrighteousness, 98, 100, 103, 113, 136

Sadhu Kochukunju, x, xiv, 1–2, 5, 7, 9, 36, 65, 68, 121–59, 163–70, 178–79
salvation, 77, 93, 99, 101, 103, 105, 107–9, 111, 141, 143, 151, 154–55, 170
Sangam age, 11–12, 14, 17–19
Sankara, 18–19, 41, 106
*savarna*, 29, 30–31, 38
Schleiermacher, Friedrich, 145–46, 178, 182
Scripture/s, ix, 16, 34, 41, 56, 67, 71, 78, 94, 157, 168–69
  Hindu, 16, 70, 72
  sacred, 14, 16
  use of, 130–32, 143n79
Simon, K.V., 124, 126
sin/sinful/sinner, 54, 93, 97, 99–101, 103–11, 113, 116, 135, 139–42, 148, 152, 154–55, 170

## Index

*sneham*, 111, 146
St. Thomas, 10, 32, 36–37
   Christians/Community, ix, 3–4, 7, 9–11, 22, 25, 27, 31n90, 32–33, 37–39, 44, 45n138, 84, 116n126, 122n2, 123, 181
   tradition, 7, 10, 98, 166
Suffering, 125, 137, 141, 151, 155–56, 169
   Christ's, 100–101, 139, 154, 169
Sugirtharajah, R.S., 9, 159, 162, 182
Swamigal, Chattambi, 41–43

Tertullian, 55
*thriyeekane*, 90–91
Travancore, ix, 1, 3–4, 7, 10, 21, 24–29, 32–33, 39–50, 84, 87, 121, 126–27, 130, 158, 172, 178–83
Trinity, 53–54, 90–92, 96–97. *See also* thriyeekane

trust, 6, 70, 80, 87, 89, 111, 113, 151, 154, 158, 170

*Upanishads*, 18, 70–71, 79
upper cloth revolt/ controversy, 43

*varna-sankara*, 16
*vatsalyam*, 111
*Veda/s*, 16, 70–72
   *Rig*, 16, 71
*vedanta*, 18, 74, 76–77
Vedanayagam Sastriyar, 85, 87, 177
Velu Thampi, 27, 40–41, 47, 182

Wainwirght, Geoffry, 51, 53–59, 178–79, 183
Watts, Isaac, 63–65
Westermeyer, Paul, 59, 61n37, 62–64, 183
Westhelle, Vítor, xiv, 134, 156, 163–66, 183

www.ingramcontent.com/pod-product-compliance
Lightning Source LLC
Chambersburg PA
CBHW051742230426
43670CB00012B/2121